DRESSAGE

A Guideline for Riders and Judges

DRESSAGE

A Guideline for Riders and Judges

WOLFGANG M. NIGGLI

J.A. ALLEN · LONDON

© Wolfgang M. Niggli
First published in Great Britain 2003

ISBN 0 85131 862 2

J.A. Allen
Clerkenwell House
Clerkenwell Green
London EC1R OHT

J.A. Allen is an imprint of Robert Hale Ltd

British Library Cataloguing in Publication Data
A catalogue record for this book is available from the British Library

Edited by Alison King
Line illustrations by Gisela Holstein

Colour separation by Tenon & Polert Colour Scanning Limited, Hong Kong
Printed by Kyodo Printing Co (S'pore) Pte Ltd, Singapore

Dedication

I would like to dedicate this book jointly to my mother and my wife.

Without my mother's support in the early days of my equestrian career, I would never have been able to achieve the success that I did. Throughout my whole life I have remained grateful for her help and understanding in many difficult situations.

And it would have been impossible to have done all that I have throughout my long and busy life without the uncomplaining support of my wife, Madeleine. She has willingly tolerated the long absences that my 'hobby' and working life imposed on our family life. As my voluntary secretary, she has spent years helping me with the paperwork that necessarily comes with dressage judging.

CONTENTS

About the Author xi
Foreword xiii
Preface xiv
Acknowledgements xvii

PART 1 A Guideline for Riders and Judges

Introduction   1

A Brief History of the Sport of Dressage 3
The Federation Équestre Internationale (FEI) 7

CHAPTER 1 · The Dressage Test   10

The Principles of Judging 11
The Way of Going of the Horse 14
  Basic Faults; Main Faults; Minor Faults
The Collective Marks 15
  The Paces – Freedom and Regularity; Impulsion; Cadence; Submission;
  Rider's Position and Seat – Correctness and Effect of the Aids

CHAPTER 2 · Straightness and Bend   26

CHAPTER 3 · Collection   30

The Principles of Collection 31
The Position of the Horse's Head 33

CHAPTER 4 · The Paces   39

The Walk 39
  Judging the Walk – General Principles; Medium Walk; Collected Walk;
  Extended Walk; Free Walk
The Trot 46
  Working Trot; Collected Trot; Medium Trot; Extended Trot;
  Judging the Trot

The Canter 54
> *Working Canter; Collected Canter; Medium Canter; Extended Canter;*
> *Judging the Canter*

CHAPTER 5 · Basic Work   59

Starting Work 60
Transitions 60
> *The Transitions from Walk to Halt, and Halt to Walk;*
> *Riding Transitions in General; Transitions to Canter*
Transitions within Paces 64
> *Collecting and Extending the Walk; Collecting and Extending the Trot;*
> *Collecting and Extending the Canter; Judging Transitions*
Changes of Direction – Turns, Circles, Serpentines and Voltes 69
> *Riding Turns, Circles, Serpentines and Voltes; Judging Turns and Circles*

CHAPTER 6 · Movements and Exercises   73

The Halt 73
> *Judging the Halt*
The Rein-back 76
> *Riding the Rein-back; Judging the Rein-back*
The Schaukel 79
Judging the Schaukel
Counter-canter 79
> *Judging the Counter-canter*
The Simple Change 80
> *Judging the Simple Change*
The Flying Change 81
> *Judging the Flying Changes*

CHAPTER 7 · Lateral Movements and Exercises   84

Leg-yielding 84
> *Riding a Correct Leg-yield*
Principles of Other Lateral Movements 86
Shoulder-in 87
> *Riding a Correct Shoulder-in; Judging the Shoulder-in*
Travers, Renvers and Half-pass – Relationship and Requirements 89
> *Travers; Renvers*
Half-pass 91
> *Riding a Correct Half-pass; Judging the Half-pass*

The Counter-change of Hand 95
Riding a Correct Counter-change of Hand; Judging the
Counter-change of Hand

CHAPTER 8 · The Pirouettes in Walk and Canter   97

The Half-pirouette in Walk 97
Riding the Half-pirouette in Walk; Judging the Half-pirouette in Walk
The Half-pirouette and Full Pirouette in Canter 100
Riding the Half-pirouette and Full Pirouette in Canter; Judging the
Half-pirouette in Canter; Judging the Full Pirouette in Canter

CHAPTER 9 · Haute École: the Passage and the Piaffe   106

The Passage 106
Riding the Passage; Judging the Passage
The Piaffe 109
How to Ride the Piaffe; Proceeding forward from Piaffe into Passage;
Judging the Piaffe
The Transitions Passage/Piaffe/Passage 115

CHAPTER 10 · Summary of Key Principles   116

CHAPTER 11 · Freestyle Competitions   119

Development of the Freestyle Tests 119
Assessment of the Performance 120
Guidelines for Judging the Artistic Element 126
Rhythm, Energy and Elasticity; Harmony between Rider and Horse;
The Choreography; The Degree of Difficulty; The Music; Specific Examples
to Aid Assessment of Artistic Marks

PART II Dressage and the Olympic Games

Equestrian Sport and the Olympic Games   132

The Origins of the Modern Olympic Games 132
Olympic Equestrian Sport 135
Dressage at the Olympic Games 136

An Olympic Games Archive   141

About the Author

WOLFGANG M. NIGGLI was born in Zurich, Switzerland in 1922 and began his riding career at the age of 12. Although keen to jump he first had to learn the basics and he won his first junior dressage competition in 1937. His first success in cross-country came just a year later. As a teenager he competed in dressage, showjumping and three-day eventing.

He studied to become an engineer at the Zurich Technological Institute and, at the same time, became an officer in the Swiss Cavalry. Thus, whilst training as an engineer, he was also acting as a part-time riding officer and afterwards, as a riding instructor at the Swiss Army Officer Schools.

In 1947 Niggli was seconded to the French Military Riding School in Fontaine-bleau where he was given a wonderful opportunity to improve his riding skills: a '*cours de perfectionnement équestre*'! (Fontainebleau had replaced Saumur as the main cavalry school at that time.) From here, he competed in many jumping and dressage competitions and rode in international steeplechases.

In 1949 he left with his family to work in the USA for almost three years as an engineer and there had only the opportunity to compete in a few local competitions. On his return to Switzerland in 1952 he became an engineer with the North-Eastern Swiss Power Company and was later appointed Vice-President (Construction). He continued to compete in all riding disciplines at a high level, and participated in cross-country steeplechases in Switzerland, Italy and France. He also remained a part-time riding instructor at the Swiss Army Officer Schools.

In 1957 Niggli became a Swiss National Dressage Judge and he was a member of the Dressage Committee of the Swiss National Equestrian Federation from 1961–1986, being Chairman from 1964–1973. During this time he acted as the Swiss Team's Chef d'Équipe at many international events, including the 1972 Olympic Games in Munich.

In 1964, he was promoted to FEI International Dressage Judge and he served on the Dressage Committee of the FEI from 1973–1976 and from 1979–1981. From 1981–1993 he was Chairman of this committee and as such, became a member of the FEI Bureau. He remains an honorary member of the Bureau to this day. Between 1964 and his retirement from the FEI Dressage Committee in 1993, he judged at numerous international competitions and at three Olympic Games: Los Angeles, Seoul and Barcelona.

Niggli has conducted courses and seminars for training international dressage judges since 1974 and still continues to do so, travelling all over the world. Nowadays he spends more time helping riders, and gives riders' clinics in numerous European, Far Eastern, North and South American and African countries. He is still in great demand and, despite his advancing years, may still be seen darting swiftly around a dressage arena encouraging his students. This is all the more remarkable since, in 1998, he suffered a catastrophic accident with his beloved horse Happy Star from which all thought he could never recover! But he did, and it has not restricted his activities on behalf of equestrian sport.

Wolfgang Niggli and his wife Madeleine still live in the beautiful lakeside suburb of Zurich where they brought up their four sons.

FOREWORD

IT IS A GREAT HONOUR for me to write the foreword to this book and I am proud to have the opportunity to collaborate with Wolfgang M. Niggli, who deserves my deepest gratitude for all that he has done and is still doing for our sport.

After my election as President of the FEI, now nearly nine years ago, I wanted to improve my knowledge of dressage and all its technical aspects and I could have no better adviser than Wolfgang M. Niggli, who at that time had just left the FEI Dressage Committee. He always gave me, with great enthusiasm, all the explanations I was asking for.

Later, when I thought that introducing a Kür test for the Olympic Games could be very important for the popularity of this wonderful discipline, Wolfgang was the first to bravely support this idea – now a consolidated reality with huge success.

I am sure that, within this book, both judges and riders will find very important clarifications by which clear and fair assessments can be achieved, which should satisfy both parties.

HRH The Infanta Doña Pilar de Borbon

President of the Federation Équestre Internationale

PREFACE

I T IS WITH SOME RELUCTANCE AND AFTER much coercion that I have finally taken the decision to write this book. I have been teaching riders for most of my adult life and I have been giving courses and seminars for dressage judges for more than 35 years. On many occasions I have been encouraged to publish my thoughts. However, it seemed to me that there were far too many books already on the subject of dressage and there did not seem to be a niche that needed to be filled. What could I add to the wealth of knowledge that is already available? In addition, with my hectic schedule, there never seemed to be time. However, in recent years I have become concerned over some of the things that I have observed in the modern sport of dressage and so I resolved that perhaps now was the time to set my thoughts down on paper.

I have written this book for both riders and judges. To be successful in the sport, the rider must have a clear understanding of what it is that the judge is looking for in a particular movement. In principle, where I have laid down ideals to be seen in each of the paces, movements or exercises that I discuss, a rider who can reproduce these criteria can expect to achieve a high mark. At the same time, I have offered some explanations about how the rider could go about producing a correctly ridden movement that should satisfy a judge.

Dressage judges must have a thorough understanding of the process of training a horse to the highest level and should be well versed in the criteria for awarding specific marks. As long as all judges keep to the same set of criteria, there should be no big differences between their final marks.

I realize that this book might cause some controversy amongst the dressage judging fraternity as I am well aware that, in many situations, I am perceived to be rather dogmatic about delineating what effect a particular occurrence during a movement should have on a judge's mark. Although we live in a time where we are encouraged to believe that everyone's opinion must be considered to have some validity, there have to be clear guidelines set down for the sport. Too many times nowadays, we see judges at wide variance with their colleagues in a single competition. This quite rightly upsets the riders and, because there is much media interest in the sport, there are frequent attacks on judges in the press. This situation has occurred before and was addressed by Colonel Gustav Nyblaeus. During his governance of the sport there was an unwritten rule – if two judges were more than 6 per cent apart in their total marks, there had to be a discussion following the competition. One of them had to be wrong!

As a young man I was extremely privileged to have been taught riding by a number of famous master trainers who could trace their methods back to earlier times; the times when the horse was a part of normal life. Military training was compulsory and a strong personal discipline was considered to be a necessary characteristic of an accomplished rider. The care and training of a horse was part of our everyday existence. Because of the military discipline, we were never allowed to go to the next step before perfecting the first. I was not interested in dressage as a young boy. I sought the thrill of the cross-country or showjumping competitions! However, we were not allowed to jump unless we also practised dressage! So with the remarkable teachers that I had, I received an excellent education in all aspects of riding and I am grateful to them all for the knowledge that they have imparted to me. I came to specialize in dressage a little later.

In 1957 I became a National Dressage Judge. That was a time when there was no formal training for dressage judges. Instead, International Dressage Judges' training was conducted more along the lines of a discussion group, or was based on a consensus between representatives from different countries. In 1962 I assisted at one such meeting held in Switzerland and the first formal course that I attended was in 1963, when the FEI introduced a training system. After that I was promoted to International Dressage Judge. Colonel Gustav Nyblaeus of Sweden was the first Chairman of the FEI Dressage Committee and he took over the formal training of international judges himself to ensure that everyone received the same level of education. In 1981 I took over from him and it became my responsibility to pass on this knowledge.

Since my appointment as Chairman of the FEI Dressage Committee in 1981, dressage as a sport has become increasingly popular. More and more people have begun participating in the sport. At the same time – indeed for some years now – riding has become less and less a way of life and more of a leisure pastime. Today, few people work with horses on the land and there is a lack of instinctive knowledge of horsemanship.

It is the dressage judge's responsibility to assess and inform the rider of the correctness of the horse's training at that point in time. Therefore, in my opinion, it is even more important in the current times that judges hold fast to the established criteria of the discipline, in order that competitors do not become diverted from the correct path of training their horses. As I point out in this book, there are extreme pressures put upon trainers, riders and judges in modern day competitions and we should all be aware that there must be no compromise in the requirements of training a horse to Grand Prix level. Training to Grand Prix is a little like building a tower: if the foundations are not sound, the tower will be unstable. The process does not work if the trainer cuts corners. Although the best trainers know this, there are many people who aspire to compete at the highest level and try to do so with a lack of knowledge and patience. The losers are the horses and, ultimately, the sport.

The first part of this book is a presentation of what the dressage judges would like to see from horses and riders. I have endeavoured to explain the process of training the dressage horse to the highest level and the importance of the various stages along the way. I explain my principles of judging and provide what I hope are straightforward descriptions of how the rider's desires might be communicated to the horse. If both judges and riders adhere to these principles, the standards within the sport should remain correct. We are seeing better and better horses being bred specifically for the discipline of dressage. It would be a pity if this effort in selective breeding were to go to waste because of the lack of skill, patience and knowledge of the correct requirements of the discipline. Many of the correct principles and criteria have already been outlined elsewhere, but not necessarily in a format aimed specifically at riders and judges in a competition environment. I have tried to be clear and concise and to address both riders and judges. For the sake of dressage, I hope I have succeeded.

I have judged at three Olympic Games during my career as an International Judge. The Olympic movement has always interested me and I already had a considerable number of records dating from early times. In the second part of this book I have presented this archive of Olympic dressage data for those who are interested in the history of our sport. The data comprises details of the dressage tests used, the arenas, the judges and the special rules that applied as well as the detailed results for all of the Olympic Dressage Competitions since the introduction of the discipline into the Olympic Games. As such I hope it will provide interesting reading and a valuable source of information.

WOLFGANG M. NIGGLI

Throughout this book I have used the term 'his' or 'him' when referring to riders, judges and horses of either gender. This decision was taken in order to make the book easier to read, being less cumbersome than the format of 'his/hers' etc.

ACKNOWLEDGEMENTS

GISELA HOLSTEIN

Much of the material presented here is based on courses and seminars that I have conducted for dressage judges. Many years ago, Gisela offered to create some drawings to illustrate my text as I gradually put together my teaching material. I am indebted to her, as these wonderfully simple illustrations always seem to manage to get exactly to the point. Being an International Dressage Judge herself, she has an excellent eye for what is right and what is wrong in the riding of a movement and she is able to show this in her perfect and artistic drawings. Recently, she has produced many more of these to help me elaborate on various issues. I would like to thank Gisela for her support over many years. Her generosity in producing illustrations for me has made my job so much easier.

ALISON KING

Over the years that I have been training judges and riders, many people have asked me to publish my material but I have never had the time or felt that it was appropriate. Three years ago, Alison said that she would help me if I agreed to do it. So I did, and this is the result. Alison collated all of my seminar notes and others that I have accumulated over the years, and we sat down together and filled in the gaps. Without her enthusiasm, commitment and endless energy I could never have contemplated such a project. She has been the guardian angel behind it all. Alison, also an International Dressage Judge, has participated in many of my judging seminars and is very conversant with my methods of judging and teaching. This, combined with her editorial experience, has enabled us to produce what we feel is a valuable contribution to equestrian sport.

International Olympic Committee

I am indebted to the personnel of the IOC Library in Lausanne who made it possible to obtain most of the data from the protocols of the Olympic Games and the meetings of the various committees, used in compiling Part II of this book.

The Horse

We should be happy to have such a colleague as the horse. He accepts our requirements of him so long as we treat him in a friendly, understanding way. We should always treat him with fairness, even if there are moments when he and we disagree. If you follow this principle, your horse will always be your best friend.

PART I

A Guideline for Riders and Judges

INTRODUCTION

Although there are still a few adherents to dressage as practised in earlier times it has, over the centuries, largely evolved from an art practised by those with the opportunity, time and academic interest, into a modern Olympic sport using specialist horses bred for the quality of their paces and their trainability. With the advent of modern competition have come the inevitable pressures of time and money resulting, in some cases, in riders and trainers resorting to so-called 'quick' methods in an attempt to save time and to bring the horse more quickly to the required level.

I should like to state at this juncture that there is absolutely no quick way, or short cut, to the correct training of a dressage horse. The speed at which a horse learns is largely dependent upon the skill of his trainer. If the trainer makes no mistakes, the training progresses smoothly. If the trainer does something wrong, it takes a long time to undo that wrongly learned process. It follows, then, that to train a horse to the highest level (which currently, in competition, means Grand Prix), the rider must have the requisite ability, skill, knowledge and experience to communicate his intentions to the horse. Likewise, the horse must demonstrate a certain talent and willingness to cooperate and be trained. While it is possible for most horses to be trained to perform the movements of the Prix St Georges test, not all horses have the ability to go on to execute the demanding exercises of piaffe and passage that are required at Grand Prix.

A fundamental requirement for training a horse is that the rider should possess a strong personal discipline and an ability to control his body and actions so that he may educate the horse in the same, correct, way all of the time. This is true for any level. The rider should always ask for a similar movement from the horse in a similar manner. This creates confidence in the horse and prevents misunderstandings. For example, when executing a halt the rider should ensure that a correct halt is achieved at every opportunity – no matter whether the halt is during the training period or outside the school at the end of a period of relaxation.

In an attempt to compensate for their own lack of ability, discipline and patience as trainers, many riders are tempted to resort to so-called 'short cuts' motivated largely by their desire to succeed quickly in competition. It is here that the responsibility of the dressage judge lies in that it is the judge's job to comment on the correctness of the training of the horse at that time. The judge's remarks on the rider's performance of tests of increasing difficulty should give the rider clear guidance as to the success or otherwise of his training process. It is, therefore, an obvious requirement that the judge should possess credibility in his knowledge and experience of the process of training dressage horses. However, it should be mentioned at this juncture that the judge should only comment on what is right or wrong in a movement and why the mark is given. He should never try to tell the rider what to do. The judge is not the trainer!

I hope that in this book I can clearly and simply describe the criteria that dressage judges should be looking for in the performance of tests at various levels, along with an indication of why high or low marks might be awarded for a specific movement. The book is intended as a guideline for both judges and riders, so that each may gain a deeper understanding of the requirements of the sport of dressage. In addition, I will explain how the rider might produce that which the judge is looking for. My explanations to the rider are founded on training methods passed down from centuries of experience, based on kindness and sympathetic handling of the horse as opposed to brutality and force. A little later I will elaborate more on these foundations as I discuss the history of the sport.

Both the rider and the judge should know something about the psychology of the horse, that is, how the horse is likely to react in certain circumstances. My explanations on training the horse are based on an assumed knowledge of this aspect. The system that I use has stood the test of time and is simple and easy to understand for both rider and horse. With these explanations you will appreciate how easy it becomes for the horse to understand the language of the rider as communicated through the aids. So long as the rider can ask for a similar action using exactly the same aids, he will have no problem in getting the horse to understand him immediately. Therein lies the skill! The world's best trainers of horses have spent many years developing this skill. It comes from a strong personal discipline so that, when they use a specific aid to ask a horse for a particular response, they are fully in control of their bodies and no involuntary movement occurs that might confuse the horse. This is the main difference between a novice rider and a master. The novice has limited control of his body, limbs and balance and has little appreciation of the horse's sensitivity to minute involuntary actions.

Another great asset to the training of the horse is the rider's sense of timing. The application of the aid at just the right moment will enhance the horse's understanding and ability to comply. The skill comes in applying the aid the instant before the horse was going to perform the movement anyway. This makes it even easier for the horse to associate the aid with the movement. This is particularly true in the basic training of the young horse and is developed as the horse progresses to more difficult movements. The rider's ability to feel when the appropriate aid will be most effective in producing the required movement is a skill that allows the master trainer to make progress faster than the novice. This skill is acquired only after years of training both himself and a large number of horses.

A horse is highly conscious of everything that his body experiences. He is aware of all that happens to him. In contrast, humans are much less aware of their bodies. They are more aware of what they are thinking and their thought processes can be distracted by day-to-day problems so that, when we humans ride a horse, we are not always aware of what we are doing with all the parts of our bodies. However, since the horse can feel everything, he has to try to make sense of what it is that we are 'asking' him, whether or not this 'asking' is a conscious act. This is why it is so important to develop a good seat on a horse; a seat or position that does not interfere with the movement of the horse. In such a position, the rider is less likely to produce involuntary movements that the horse might misinterpret.

Many authors of books on dressage over-complicate the subject, making it difficult for riders to understand what is required. By combining clear descriptions of what judges want to see with simple explanations as to how the rider might achieve this, I hope to make dressage easy for everyone. By this I mean not only that it should be easy to understand, but also that it should be done without force in a light, easy way because, in the end, we would like to see the horse performing willingly and in complete harmony with the rider.

A Brief History of the Sport of Dressage

Earlier, I alluded to the foundations of the sport of dressage and to the fact that these are based on kindness and sympathetic handling of the horse, the aim being for him to carry out what is required with cooperation and a degree of harmony with the rider. These methods work but they take time and, over the years, because of human failings, riders and trainers have resorted to less gentle – and sometimes extremely brutal and cruel – methods to subdue and control their horses. These 'fashions' in training methods have come and gone over the ages and there is a danger that, because of the extreme pressures placed on trainers and riders nowadays, there might again be a move towards the less gentle ways of training. Although the history of the art of dressage is well documented elsewhere, I think that it would be appropriate to provide a brief summary in order to put the modern-day situation into context.

I would like to start with a little Greek history. The Greek historian, economist, philosopher and military commander, Xenophon (430–354 BC), wrote extensively about the cavalry and in particular, on the art of riding. It is known that Xenophon was intensively occupied with the study of all aspects of equestrian matters throughout his life and he is more or less considered to be the founder of modern 'hippology' – the study and science of horses (and riding). His best-known work is *The Art of Horsemanship*, although he also wrote several treatises on the use of the horse in war. What we can learn from him is still valuable and relevant today and relates to the ethics of classical riding. He was remarkable for his time in that he advocated the training of horses through understanding their psychology and argued that this was much better and more successful than the use of force. He insisted that the horse could be handled in an agreeable way in every situation and that a horse was only useful if he was reliable and submissive. From his writings we can deduce that Xenophon performed certain dressage movements to a high level, including the piaffe and levade – which he describes in detail.

Unfortunately, these wonderful classical principles were forgotten or neglected during the time of the Romans and thereafter. The times were barbaric and unstable: there appears to have been no interest in the pursuit of riding as an art. About one thousand years would elapse before the principles and methods of Xenophon were rediscovered during the Italian Renaissance.

However, by the end of the tenth century, times had become somewhat calmer and there was some resurgence of interest in the arts. The European aristocracy became interested in riding to the extent that they began to concentrate on the basic training of their horses, in order that they could show off and impress people at tournaments. Simple exercises on straight lines in walk and canter were used and certain rules were introduced. Soon, trainers developed the techniques and exercises that enabled them to produce an agile horse that was useful in battle and obedient to his rider. Specific movements were developed for reasons of defence, an example being the capriole, wherein the horse performs a controlled leap off its hind legs and strikes out with these legs while still in the air.

These developments notwithstanding, the re-emergence of true classical riding began only in the sixteenth century, in Italy. In 1532 the Italian, Federico Grisone, opened the first 'modern' riding school in Naples. A good education in riding was soon considered to be a requirement of any young gentleman if he was to be successful in the courtly society of the time. This remained true for some three hundred years and was still the fashion when the young Duke of Wellington was sent to study the art of riding at the French school of Saumur because his parents did not like the way that he was taught in the well-known British schools.

What Grisone taught was based on the written principles of Xenophon. Grisone had a model student by the name of Giovanni Battista Pignatelli, who first continued the school in Naples and then moved to Rome. Pignatelli was, in effect, the inventor of the double bridle and his pupils spread his art of riding throughout the English, French, Austrian, Danish, German and Spanish courts. Although what they taught was based on Xenophon's principles, as time went by they adopted more forceful techniques.

However, one of the foremost riding masters of the seventeenth century helped to reverse this trend. Antoine de Pluvinel was riding instructor to the French King, Henry IV, and founded a riding academy in Paris where he also taught King Louis XIII. In 1623 Pluvinel's famous book *Le Maneige Royal* was published, with its wonderful illustrations. Pluvinel believed more in trying to make the horse submissive and obedient through kind treatment and reward and, by virtue of this stance, moved away from the more forceful disciples of the Neapolitan school and back towards the gentler, classical methods.

A similar style was also practised in England in the seventeenth century by William Cavendish, who later became Duke of Newcastle. An exile in Europe after the English Civil War, Cavendish ran a riding school in Antwerp before returning to his homeland. His book *A General System of Horsemanship* was originally published in a French translation in Antwerp in 1658, the first English edition being published nearly a century later, in 1743. William Cavendish was an excellent horseman, who lived for his horses and whose work influenced the great de la Guérinière. Unfortunately, however, he too started to introduce more forceful methods of training and it is said that he introduced the 'running rein'.

The Frenchman, François Robichon de la Guérinière, was the most celebrated riding master of the late renaissance period. In 1717 he opened his 'humane' dressage school in Paris where he employed once again the more gentle methods and ideas of Pluvinel. In 1729 he published his famous book *École de Cavalerie*. He refused to use any brutality or tricks from the earlier, more forceful schools. He devised and introduced the movement known as 'shoulder-in'. What we call 'classical dressage' today is based on that of the time of de la Guérinière. He brought about a dramatic change in the thinking of riders and trainers in Europe by precisely formulating his training system. The Spanish Riding School in Vienna used his work as a basis for their training programme, and it still carries great weight today.

During and for a while after de la Guérinière's era, classical equitation in France flourished, with royal patronage. In 1771, the cavalry school at Saumur was founded. However, there followed a great period of upheaval: the French Revolution and the Napoleonic era, during which there was little opportunity to practise classical equitation as an art form. Nevertheless, Saumur was revived in 1814 and from that period came a number of riding masters who were part of the *'Cadre Noir'*, who were responsible for educating many more well-known instructors and riders.

In the French school of the nineteenth century we should also consider the influence of Baucher and Fillis, if only because of the controversies surrounding them. Baucher was an intelligent instructor with a great deal of influence over his pupils, but unfortunately his methods took him along the wrong path, as even he acknowledged later. Fillis, a pupil of Baucher, was English, but he spent many years in France. At one time he was considered to be the best and best-known rider in the world! In principle, he followed the methods of de la Guérinière but finally he, too, strayed away from classical dressage. This was mainly the case when he started to ride for the circus. Fillis went to Russia with the circus and there he was offered the post of head of the cavalry school. He is acknowledged as playing a large part in building up the skills of the Russian cavalry and his influence on dressage in Russia is still noticeable today. He died in 1913 after his return to Paris. The methods of Baucher and Fillis caused great controversy amongst the various schools of training at the time, resulting in a split between the 'French' and 'German' schools that, to a certain extent, still exists even to this day.

As mentioned earlier, following the Italian Renaissance, the concept of riding as an art had been introduced to other countries besides France. These countries saw developments broadly parallel to those in France. In Spain, the instigator of this development was Charles I of Spain (1516–1556). It is said that the Duke of Newcastle referred to him as having been the best rider in the world. In keeping with the national complexities of the time, Charles was also Emperor Charles V of Austria. The Austrians (Habsburgs) exerted a great influence on the Spanish and the name of the Spanish Riding School in Vienna is derived from the style of riding and the type of horses in Spain. Many Spanish horses were imported into Austria, from which were developed the famous Lipizzaners. The first references to the Spanish Riding School date from 1572. It was finally completed in 1735.

In Germany as well, the art of riding began to be developed in the royal courts in the sixteenth century. In the nineteenth century, Germany saw the publication of Gustav Steinbrecht's famous treatise on the training of the dressage horse *Gymnasium des Pferdes* (*Gymnasium of the Horse*). First published in 1885, this is perhaps the best-known German work of its era, but there were many other books by authors such as Oyenhausen and Seeger. Steinbrecht was, himself, a pupil of Seeger and throughout his career as a trainer, he kept extensive notes. These were published after his death by his pupil, Paul Plinzner. Through Plinzner, and Plinzner's own pupil, Hans von Heydebreck, the work of Steinbrecht was to have a major influence on German equitation.

In the twentieth century the development of dressage as a sport has come mainly from the cavalry schools in Saumur (France), Germany, Sweden and Switzerland. One of the most useful treatises on the training of the horse and rider is Wilhelm Müseler's *Reitlehre* (translated as *Riding Logic*), first published in Germany in 1933.

The Federation Équestre Internationale (FEI)

Created in 1921, the FEI is the governing body of equestrian sport worldwide. It sets the rules by which the sport is governed and the codes of conduct for participants and officials in all equestrian disciplines. These include the supervision and maintenance of the health and welfare of the horse during competition. The FEI *Rules for Dressage Events* are, in principle, based on the ideas of de la Guérinière. A section of these rules is devoted to the description in detail of the requirements of all the paces and movements to be shown by a dressage horse in competition.

We can see that, throughout history, the use of force in training the horse comes and goes through a cycle and that the gentler methods do return because they work and because horses trained by these methods demonstrate a greater degree of harmony with their riders. It can be seen again and again throughout history that there has been a temptation to veer away from the gentle, classical training methods toward more forceful ones. This happens largely because humans are always trying to do things more quickly and easily for themselves. These forceful methods are rarely successful and have inherent in them more of the rider's ego than the horse's best interest. Indeed, so long as the horse carries an element of tension arising from fear or lack of harmony, he can never develop his paces fully because any tension in the back or neck will restrict his movements. The best trainers go slowly, without expectation or assumption, and achieve a greater harmony with their horses – which is the true reward of training. This also produces an equine athlete who moves with a powerful yet relaxed body and who can develop his paces to the utmost, which is the object of dressage training – to improve upon what Nature has provided.

We should take care in the present not to make the same mistakes that many have made before and resort to the more forceful methods of training. In the current climate, the sport of dressage has become driven largely by money, success and winning competitions – in other words, everything is done in a hurry, not always with the horse's interests as the first principle. Never before has there been so much pressure on the producers of competition horses. I want to emphasize that it *is* possible to train and compete at the highest levels employing techniques proven over the centuries, using kindness and sympathy. However, to do so requires a dedication from the rider to improve himself as well as his horse.

The dressage judge who has the necessary knowledge can have an enormous influence on the way that the sport is conducted. We in the FEI introduced the freestyle dressage test in the early 1980s with the hope that it might improve and encourage the light and elegant, harmonious style of riding so that once again dressage might become an art form.

It appears that nowadays there is a tendency for riders to aspire to compete at the highest level without paying attention to the basic principles of riding. We see better and better horses being bred for the sport but this is not going hand in hand with better and better riding. In fact, the opposite appears to be the case! I believe that there are several reasons behind this, the first of which I have already referred to in respect of the pressures on the trainer. However, I believe that other factors are perhaps even more relevant.

Naturally, the judging of competitions also has a huge influence and it is noticeable that with good judging, the level of riding and training goes up, or is at least maintained. However, if basic mistakes are neglected by the judges, the eventual result is that the standard deteriorates. If, on the other hand, the judging community notices that certain movements or exercises are generally not performed well, they have the opportunity to create new dressage tests which incorporate such movements in ways that encourage their correct riding, thereby maintaining the standard.

It is important that the people creating the dressage tests have an especially deep and sound knowledge of the requirements of training to the highest level. All dressage tests should have a focus. For example, in the current Grand Prix Special test, it is the sequence of movements: passage to extended trot to passage, which produces impulsion and suspension in the passage. Another example was the use of the counter-canter loops in the 1995 Prix St Georges test. This required control of the hindquarters to prevent them from swinging to the outside and ensured that the rider maintained a correct seat. In general, the objective is to see the horse improving as he progresses through the test.

In times gone by, riding was taught by masters to their pupils using a type of apprenticeship system, in that the pupil learned by example and there was little of a formal nature written down to which he might refer. Students were taught on trained or well-schooled horses. They established a balanced, supple seat by constant practice on the lunge without recourse to reins. They learned discipline and control of their bodies, so that action by one part did not interfere with the whole. Over the centuries, people have attempted to explain in writing what they do and how they do it. There is no lack of information about what is required of the horse in the movements and exercises. In my opinion, what have been lacking are clear and simple explanations of what is required of the rider. Many have tried to explain; however, in their desire to clarify they have often over-complicated matters and even confused the reader. There have been some slight misunderstandings that have crept in, that have been perpetuated thereafter.

In addition, as stated earlier, the recent era has seen a general loss of contact with horses as a way of life, and this has reduced the base of knowledge available to most modern riders. Nowadays, we have to start by explaining things that were once natural instincts in riders and trainers.

I believe that reality is simple. When you are attempting to explain something to a horse it is important that you, the rider, can find a way of enabling the horse to understand what you want. To produce similar movements and actions, you should use similar aids. Otherwise the horse becomes confused. This confusion leads to a lack of confidence in the rider and, consequently, to a lack of harmony between the two.

I quote here from the current FEI *Rules for Dressage Events*:

> The object of Dressage is the harmonious development of the physique and ability of the horse. As a result it makes the horse calm, supple, loose and flexible, but also confident, attentive and keen, thus achieving perfect understanding with his rider.
>
> Art 401.1 (2003)

I will now try to explain, simply, how it might be possible to attain this end.

CHAPTER ONE

THE DRESSAGE TEST

THE DRESSAGE TEST, when well constructed, serves as an opportunity for the rider to present his horse to the judge for comment as to his degree of success or otherwise in training his horse to the requisite level. Dressage tests are written for every level of training from Preliminary through to Grand Prix. Individual national equestrian federations are free to choose which tests they will use at any level, but at international competitions, the tests are drawn up and specified by the FEI.

I have noticed in my travels that there are many dressage tests in use at the lower levels in many countries that contain unreasonable requirements, especially for horses working at Preliminary and Novice levels. The elements of a dressage test should be put together in such a way that the horse can demonstrate his ability to bend, or go straight; his obedience and suppleness in transitions and his desire to move forward in three clear paces. The rider should show that he understands the requirements of that level of training and that the horse is well prepared for the level of the test. As already stated, the training of a Grand Prix horse must be done carefully and thoroughly and it must be built on solid foundations. Sadly, many lower level dressage tests do not support a progressive training system and include elements that are counter-productive in terms of progressive training towards the higher levels. It is essential, in my opinion, for these tests to be designed and written by people with a deep understanding of the training process and what is required for each level.

It is important that any rider planning to perform a dressage test understands exactly what the judge is looking for, and how what the judge sees will affect the mark received. In addition to the correctness or otherwise of the specific movement required by the test protocol, there are other factors, such as mistakes in the 'way of going' of the horse, that may affect the judge's marks. These can be divided into sections depending upon their relative importance with respect to the progression of training. (Remember, the dressage judge is there to give the rider an indication of his success in training his horse at that point in time.)

A dressage test consists of many elements, most of which lay down what movement the horse is required to perform and where. The process of judging a dressage test requires the judge to form an opinion of first, the 'way of going' of the horse and rider according to certain criteria and, second, the correctness or otherwise of the performance of the individual movements that comprise the test.

The dressage horse should demonstrate three clear paces: walk, trot and canter. In the following chapters I set out in detail what the judges will want to see with respect to the variations within each pace. However, there are certain aspects of the general demeanour of the horse which will influence the judge's assessment of the 'way of going'. These can be classified primarily into 'basic faults', 'main faults' and 'minor faults'. Whenever and wherever the judge notices any of these faults occurring, he will modify the mark that he allocates to that particular movement.

The Principles of Judging

While this section is addressed primarily to dressage judges, it will also be of interest to riders as it will help to explain the thought processes that go on during the judging of a competition. It might help to dispel preconceived ideas held by some riders that a judge 'likes' or 'dislikes' a particular horse and rider combination. There is no place in correct judging for personal likes or dislikes. The judge must be independent, unbiased and fair in conducting his responsibility. He must give the last person into the arena as much attention and concentration as he does to the first in that class. He must have great powers of concentration because to lose concentration means to lose consistency of marking. The judge must also have the necessary knowledge and must have gone through the requisite training process. Individual national federations are free to organize their own national training programmes but, at international level, these judges are trained by a very small number of people authorized by the FEI. A thorough training of judges to a universal system teaches them to see what is correct and what is not correct; what is good and what is not good. It provides clear guidelines about how the movements should be assessed. In a judges' course it is essential to include both good and mediocre horses. In this way, the international judges form a body with a consistent training background. This helps to maintain the consistency of judging in the sport worldwide.

Whilst judging each movement as it occurs, the judge must be thinking about what the 'ideal' would be and must mark the horse in front of him against that standard. It is obvious, then, that the judge has to know what the ideal should look like. Judges have an obligation to maintain their standards by continually refreshing their 'eye'. They should do this, whenever they have an opportunity, by watching horses perform and work at the highest levels of quality possible. *On no account, except in the artistic marks in the freestyle, should the judge ever compare the performance of one horse against another.* Once the rider has left the arena, the judge should erase the mental tape he has been running and start again with the next competitor.

The FEI rules lay down the marks to be awarded (from 10–0) according to the judge's interpretation of how well the horse has performed the required movement. The range of marks is defined as follows:

10	Excellent		
9	Very good	4	Insufficient
8	Good	3	Fairly bad
7	Fairly good	2	Bad
6	Satisfactory	1	Very bad
5	Sufficient	0	Not executed*

* This means that practically nothing of the required movements has been performed.

(It must be remembered that, in the text of this book, wherever I have indicated in the judge's assessment a comment referring to the marking procedure, that comment is only a guideline. Each mark allocated by each judge is still open to their personal interpretation, based upon what they see from their judging position.)

The more completely the criteria of the relevant movements or paces are fulfilled, the higher the mark will be. It can go from 'sufficient' to 'excellent'. By this I mean that, depending on the way that each judge sees a movement it can be judged as 'sufficient', 'satisfactory', 'fairly good', 'good', 'very good' or 'excellent'. The judge is free to choose what he thinks. I have always advocated that the judge should try to follow a per-formance by giving comments to *himself* and thus be thinking in *words*. From the words, he automatically derives the appropriate corresponding mark. In my opinion, it can be dangerous to think in figures (marks) because the judge may hesitate a good deal before giving the mark. Thinking in words produces a much more consistent marking process that avoids comparisons of one horse with another. The judge is then judging against his own perception of the 'ideal' and will keep on line.

Whenever assessing a movement, a dressage judge should always bear in mind the classical ideal. The description of the ideal is laid down in the FEI *Rules for Dressage Events* and from this ideal (a comment of 'excellent' and a mark of 10) he adjusts the mark downward in comparison to it. The ideal is the very best perform-ance of that movement that the judge can imagine being achieved. As the judge moves down the scale he might describe something as 'fairly good', or maybe some-thing happens and it becomes, therefore, only 'sufficient' – or it might be basically wrong. Knowing whether something is the best possible, 'fairly good', only 'sufficient' or wrong is the basic requirement of every judge. This allows the judge to immediately set his marks in the following ranges:

9/10   7/8   5/6   less than 5

(When I spoke earlier about a judge's 'freedom' to give a mark, I mean that this freedom is within each of these ranges.)

In principle, all of the horses who are entered in a competition should be capable of performing the movements required at least to the level of 'sufficient'. Indeed, there is very little point in entering a competition if the horse is not at least able to fulfil the basic requirements of the test. The judge is free to go up or down a little from this level and may have to go up or down a lot, depending upon the performance of each movement. What the judge must *not* do is be influenced by what the horse or rider has shown before, whether outside the arena or in a previous test. Also, the judge should not be influenced by 'names'.

Over the years, the marks awarded to horses in competition have gone higher and higher. In my opinion this has not always been correct. I do not believe that the horses and riders are always performing significantly better. It is perhaps more because someone has said 'you have to give higher marks'. In addition, the media and sponsors want to see something that is 'better than ever', 'record scores', etc. This attracts interest, sells magazines and brings more spectators to the sport, and it also puts a lot of pressure on judges.

However, giving unjustifiably high marks is, in fact, cheating the riders and horses. The judge must not give high marks if they are not merited. In many such cases the judges are hiding behind their lack of knowledge as they succumb to the pressures of the media. The consequence of such behaviour is inevitable; there is no doubt that the standard of dressage will go down.

With every horse and rider in a competition the judge should start afresh and should not compare one combination with another. The only time comparison is allowed is in the artistic marks in a freestyle competition. This is the main reason why there is a limit to the numbers of competitors in these competitions. Too many competitors make it impossible for the judges to assess all of them correctly and fairly.

There is no place in correct dressage judging for being a 'book-keeper'. By this I mean that no judge should keep records of marks. This has nothing to do with dressage judging and it will not produce a fair or correct result. I have observed that some judges keep a running total of the marks they have awarded so that they know immediately the test has ended what percentage score they have given. *There is no place for such concern whilst judging a competition!* Any distraction of this kind can interfere with the correct awarding of individual marks for each movement as there could be a temptation to compensate if the judge feels that he has given a mark that is too high or too low. This has nothing to do with correct judging. The judge should not concern himself with such details. If the judge considers that he has made a mistake, he should ask the scorekeepers to check the score and acknowledge that a mistake has been made.

The judge should be completely impartial and not care who is the winner, only that all competitors and riders have been equally judged to the same standard.

Applying the principles of judging that I describe might not be the only way to judge, but I am convinced that it is a correct way and, if the judges adhere to it, they will produce the correct result at the end of a competition. Based on my experience over more than twenty years of training judges, I have found this system to be reliable and reproducible.

The Way of Going of the Horse

As mentioned earlier, mistakes in the way of going of the horse can be divided into three categories: Basic Faults, Main Faults and Minor Faults.

Basic Faults

Wherever these occur, the movement is unlikely to receive a mark of 'sufficient'. These are fundamental problems that reveal basic errors in the progression of training. In addition, if these faults are sustained throughout the test, they will also have an effect on the collective marks at the end. The comments in brackets relate to the relative fundamentals, which I shall discuss further in due course.

- Uneven movements (see 'Paces – freedom and regularity').

- Sustained irregular movements (see 'Paces – freedom and regularity').

- Lack of submissiveness (see 'Submission').

- A disobedient horse (see 'Submission').

- The horse not remaining straight (see 'Straightness and Bend').

- The horse not bending correctly (see 'Straightness and Bend').

- A lack of impulsion (except in working paces).

- The faulty seat of the rider (see 'Rider's Position and Seat').

Main Faults

Incorrect training of the horse will result in many problems, some of which are less fundamental than others. Nevertheless, they will have an effect on the judge's mark whenever they are seen. Movements in which these are manifested may still score marks of 'sufficient', but they will never score high marks. The judge will comment on them where they are seen and these comments should give the rider an indication of what is wrong with the horse's performance as well as an indication of where he is at that point in the progressive training of his horse. If many of these problems have occurred in the test, or if one problem has occurred repeatedly, the rider should reassess his methods of training.

- An unsteady position of the horse's head (too high or too low).

- A faulty position of the head (tilted).

- The horse not steady on the bit.

- Irregular transitions.

- Transient irregular movements.

- The horse changing canter lead when not asked to do so.

- A lack of harmony between rider and horse.

- Incorrect figures.

Minor Faults

Whenever these problems occur, if the judge sees them, they will have an effect on the mark. These problems are transient in nature and will have no bearing on the rest of the test. However, if they happen again and again, the judge will take note of them and they may end up influencing the overall picture of the test, as a main fault then becomes apparent. In summary, minor faults are those things which may happen to any rider at any time, such as a careless mistake caused by momentary inattention, the horse shying, etc.

The Collective Marks

At the end of every FEI dressage test there are four marks, known as the 'collective marks'. It is these that reflect the overall way of going of the horse throughout the test. These marks are for:

- Paces (freedom and regularity).

- Impulsion (desire to move forwards, elasticity of the steps, suppleness of the back and engagement of the hindquarters).

- Submission (attention and confidence, harmony, lightness and ease of the movements, acceptance of the bridle and lightness of the forehand).

- Rider's position and seat; correctness and effect of the aids.

I will discuss these marks individually.

The Paces – Freedom and Regularity

A dressage horse should have three clearly defined, regular paces – walk, trot and canter. The dressage judge must assess each of these paces for its intrinsic quality on straight or curved lines, uninfluenced by lateral movements. The mark for paces in a dressage test is given for all the paces together so it is theoretically possible for a horse who displays one faulty pace to win a competition, but such a horse would not get a high mark for his overall paces. For example, a horse with a completely incorrect walk might still have an absolutely correct trot and canter. That horse could still be considered 'satisfactory' but could never be 'fairly good'. High marks are given in this section for horses with three regular, expansive, elastic, expressive paces. We see many young horses bred for dressage who can show paces worth a '9' at the age of three years. Sadly, many of these fail to maintain the quality of their paces as their training continues. They lose their freedom and sometimes their regularity. This is largely a consequence of incorrect training and riding. Correct training will enhance what Nature provides, while incorrect training will detract from it.

The evenness and regularity of the paces does not only include even and regular footfalls. The horse's legs can be placed in a rhythmic sequence and still not be called regular when the back is not supple and the hindquarters are not engaged enough, for example, a trot which is not *diagonally* regular. This means that the horse may be trotting with diagonal pairs of legs as normal but that the hind and fore feet of the diagonal pair are not set to the ground at quite the same time.

The judge has to distinguish between *uneven* and *irregular* movements of the horse. A horse is described as 'uneven' when, at walk, trot, passage or piaffe he is more or less limping. Whenever the judge sees a horse clearly uneven throughout a movement, he is obliged to penalise this by giving a mark that is less than 'sufficient'. Indeed, in most cases of obvious unevenness the mark will be even lower and a clearly unsound horse should be eliminated by the President of the Ground Jury (the judge at C).

A horse is described as being 'irregular' when, for example, at walk, trot, passage or piaffe he is not keeping the same rhythm throughout the movement. An example is 'stealing steps' in extended trot. This occurs when a horse, for any reason, loses the rhythm in extended trot and takes one or two short steps, thereafter regaining his balance and rhythm. Other examples are 'double steps' behind in passage or piaffe, a canter which occasionally becomes 'four-beat', or a horse showing a 'jogging' walk.

With errors of a transient nature within a movement, the judge will deduct marks accordingly from the mark that would have been awarded had the irregularity not been shown. In such cases the judge may make a comment as to the degree of irregularity, but still award a mark of 'sufficient', or maybe even in some cases, 'satisfactory'.

In summary:

Uneven movements

- Wrong footfalls or incorrect sequence of footfalls (for example, in walk there are sustained irregular steps or even ambling, which is a regular two-beat, lateral walk; a canter which is regularly four-beat).

- More or less limping.

Irregular movements

- Steps of different length within a movement.

- One or more legs lifting more or less than the others.

- Transient irregular steps in medium or extended trot.

Impulsion

This is expanded upon in the collective marks as the 'desire to move forwards, elasticity of the steps, suppleness of the back and engagement of the hindquarters'.
The FEI rules define impulsion as follows:

> Impulsion is the term used to describe the transmission of an eager and energetic, yet controlled, propulsive energy generated from the hindquarters into the athletic movement of the horse. Its ultimate expression can be shown only through the horse's soft and swinging back to be guided by a gentle contact with the rider's hand.
>
> Art 417.3 (2003)

An even and regular pace still cannot be good unless the horse's back is free from tension. The horse develops his forward motion from his hindquarters. Only a well-balanced horse, whose hindquarters are trained to develop pushing and lifting power at the same time, can show lightness and ease of movement.

> Schwung ist die Folge des schwingenden Rückens in Verbindung mit dem energischen Abfedern der Hinterbeine.
> (Impulsion is the result of a swinging back in combination with an energetic, elastic lifting of the hind legs.)
>
> (citation by Horst Niemack) Reiten und Fahren 1960

During his assessment of the performance, the judge will be looking for the degree of impulsion appropriate for the stage of training of the horse. The pushing from behind is more obvious in medium and extended trot and is easier to see than in the collected trot. When deriving the mark for impulsion it is useful to review what was seen in the medium and extended paces. The judge has to ask himself 'was that impulsion?' This helps to create the correct mark. Another way is to look at the collected canter. If it appears to be 'uphill' and shows round strides, this is an indication of more impulsion.

Elastic, energetic steps are an indication of a high degree of impulsion. However, there are some horses who produce a trot that resembles a passage but in which the forelegs remain unnaturally straight. It is sometimes termed 'trot balancé'. This type of trot is not normally a sign of impulsion but is a clear sign of tension in the horse. It can often be an evasion or sign of resistance on the part of the horse to the rider's forward driving aids. The judge must ask 'is this really going forward?'

A supple back is a prerequisite for transmission of power from the hindquarters into an athletic stride. There should be no apparent tension in the back. There should be longitudinal suppleness shown by the horse's willingness to shorten and lengthen his frame according to the rider's requests and the requirements of the differing paces.

Engagement of the hindquarters means that the hind legs are willingly stepping forwards underneath the horse and taking his weight. They are not left out behind the horse's body. There should be a clear difference (increase) in engagement visible during transitions, showing that the horse has the necessary strength to perform the movements. All transitions, even those in working paces, should demonstrate an increase in engagement of the hindquarters. If this is not apparent, the training of the horse is incorrect.

As the horse moves towards collection at the higher levels of training, the hind legs remain more and more engaged during the paces themselves. This provides the horse with a degree of lightness in the forehand as he takes more weight all of the time on his hind legs. This taking of weight on the hind legs can be noted by the horse's willingness to remain longer on a leg as his weight travels over it. A horse who takes the weight correctly on the hind legs has, as a result, a degree of self-carriage. That is, the horse does not bear down on the rider's hand but supports his own head and neck. Horses unwilling to take weight on a leg place the foot down, move over it rapidly and then snatch it off the ground again.

If a horse has been correctly trained and can keep the engagement of the hind legs and maintain a supple back, it follows that he can now produce true medium and extended paces because the self-carriage that has been established provides him with a freedom and lightness of the forehand. All he then needs is the strength and power from the hind legs to develop the stride to the utmost without losing his balance.

Signs of a lack of impulsion are often manifested in the following ways.

- The horse not showing enough engagement of the hindquarters.

- The horse not taking weight on his hindquarters.

- Little collection observable (see Chapter 3).

- Lack of elasticity of the steps.

- A lack of self-carriage.

Cadence

I mention the term 'cadence' here because, in my experience, it is a poorly under-stood concept and over the years, its use has been confusing. The word has a Latin root (cado = fall) and comes to us through Italian as a musical term. It has nothing to do with horses! It did not appear in the FEI rules before 1983 but after this it was defined in these rules as follows:

> …the result of the proper harmony that a horse shows when it moves with well marked regularity, impulsion and balance…

The term 'cadence' had been widely used in equestrian circles before this but had never been clearly defined. The definition remains to this day (Art 401.7). In judging terms, the word is used to describe the quality of a pace. For example, a 'cadenced trot' implies a trot that demonstrates regularity, a slightly elevated movement and a degree of suspension along with impulsion, rhythm and balance.

Submission

This is expanded upon in the collective marks as 'attention and confidence, harmony, lightness and ease of the movements, acceptance of the bridle and lightness of the forehand'.

The FEI rules define submission in part as follows:

> Submission does not mean subordination, but an obedience revealing its presence by a constant attention, willingness and confidence in the whole behaviour of the horse as well as by the harmony, lightness and ease he is displaying in the execution of the various movements…
>
> Art 417.1 (2003)

The submission of the horse is based on the suppleness of his joints, his education and repeated training. When assessing the degree of submission shown by a horse during the dressage test, the judge will take into account a range of factors such as the absence of any resistance, especially during transitions. The judge will be looking for a lightness of the forehand and to see the sensitivity with which the horse reacts to the rider's aids.

The horse must accept the bridle quietly and confidently, submitting willingly and obediently to the guidance of the rider. The horse must *look* for guidance from the rider and not be forced by the rider. There should be a clear, soft contact with the bit. The contact can be just the weight of the rein, or it may be considerably more.

The contact is a reflection of the amount of power and the manner in which it is being transmitted through the horse from the hindquarters and, as such, it may vary throughout the test. For example, in a piaffe or passage, the contact may be very light as the horse is very engaged and taking weight on his hind legs and not covering much ground. However, in an extension, there may be quite a strong contact result-ing from the energy being transmitted from the hind legs through the horse's body as he thrusts himself forwards over the ground. A strong contact should not be con-fused with a horse who is hanging on the rider's hand. Likewise, a light contact with a soft rein should be clearly distinguishable from a horse who is 'dropping' the contact.

In all cases, the appearance of the horse's mouth provides a clue as to the degree to which the bit is accepted. A horse accepting the bit well is likely to have a moist, supple mouth, perhaps showing foamy saliva, with the jaw relaxed and very softly champing the bit. The lips should not be distorted by the action of the bit and there should be no tension observable in the horse's jaw and the muscles under the neck. There should be the feeling that, if the rider were to advance his hands a little, the horse would follow and stretch out his neck. The tongue should be inside the mouth and should be still, not trying to get above the bit or push the bit out of the mouth. The mouth should be closed.

Transitions should be fluent and smooth but clear. The more advanced the horse is, the quicker it is possible to produce a transition. There should be no resistance. The judge will be checking to see that the degree of collection corresponds to the requirements of the test and that the rider is not merely forcing the horse into a cer-tain head and neck position. This results in an incorrect form of collection express-ing itself in a lack of freedom of the paces (see 'The Position of the Horse's Head' in Chapter 3).

The horse should demonstrate a willingness and ability to bend evenly to both sides. This suppleness must not only be in the neck but also in the back. This is demonstrated as a willingness to 'track true' on circles and turns, which means that the horse's inside hind leg steps clearly towards the footprint of its inside foreleg without deviating across towards the direction of its outside foreleg.

In medium and extended paces the frame should lengthen as the stride length-ens. This should not result in the horse becoming longer and flatter but it should look more as if he is travelling uphill. This shows a longitudinal suppleness and a willingness to open and close his frame in the medium and extended paces which will also be seen in the transitions back to the collected paces.

Obedience, which is one of the main requirements of a dressage horse, is the result of fulfilment of the other demands and can therefore be considered last, but this does not reflect its importance.

In summary, submission entails:

- A light acceptance of the bridle, showing a clear soft contact.

- Soft but clear transitions.

- A suppleness and flexibility, demonstrating correct bend.

- A possibility of lengthening the frame in medium and extended paces.

- Suppleness in the neck.

- Lightness of the forehand.

- Obedience.

Rider's Position and Seat — Correctness and Effect of the Aids

Some of the errors or faults exhibited by the horse arise from the rider's faults in his seat or his aids. These, too, have to be considered in the mark for the rider.

The skill of a rider cannot only be recognized by his seat but also by the movements of the horse. Only the rider sitting smoothly and freely in harmony with the movements of the horse, being able to engage the horse's hind legs as well as bringing his own centre of gravity into accordance with that of the horse when travelling on turns and in lateral movements, is able to use his aids unobtrusively. We would like to see a rider sitting still while using his aids (which means his loins, his legs and his hands) so discreetly that the judge can hardly notice them move.

The rider should be sitting straight and upright in the saddle in a well-balanced position. In a normal situation there should be a more or less vertical line from the middle of the shoulder to the rider's heel. The arms, from the shoulders to the elbow, hang down without being tense. From the elbow to the bit, a straight line is appropriate (Figure 1). Hands held too high might be unsteady and they have the tendency to bring the front line of the horse's head behind the vertical. The rider's knees and thighs should not be fixed or gripping the saddle. They should be relaxed so that they can move appropriately for each pace or movement. The knees should be as low as possible. If they are raised, then the rider assumes what is known as a 'chair seat'. It is not correct simply to bend the knee to bring the lower leg back. If the lower leg is required to be back, the whole leg should move back from the hip.

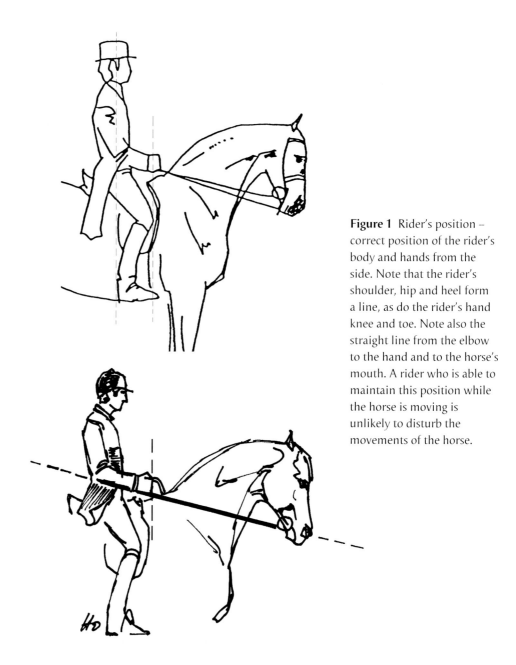

Figure 1 Rider's position – correct position of the rider's body and hands from the side. Note that the rider's shoulder, hip and heel form a line, as do the rider's hand knee and toe. Note also the straight line from the elbow to the hand and to the horse's mouth. A rider who is able to maintain this position while the horse is moving is unlikely to disturb the movements of the horse.

Some riders can be seen sitting with an artificially hollowed back. This is not correct as it tends to lead to stiffness in the shoulders, which inevitably leads to stiffness in the arms and hands.

The riders' hands

Riders can frequently be seen holding their hands in an incorrect position, that is, flat – steering the horse as if they were riding a bicycle How many judges deduct marks if it is a well-known rider?

The position and steadiness of the rider's hands are of great importance (see Figures 1 and 2). A rider needs to develop the skill of using his hands voluntarily and independently both of his own body movements and of each other. Of great importance is the ability to maintain a steady contact with the outside hand whilst making the soft 'suppling' movements with the inside hand that are necessary to ask the horse to flex in the jaw. Riders are frequently exhorted to 'keep both hands the same' but, while they should aim to keep both hands in a similar position to that shown in the illustration, one hand should always be quiet and steady (and may be deliberately strong on occasion), while the other one should be constantly suppling the horse with soft, eventually vibrating, movements of the wrists or just the fingers. I am talking here of very delicate movements. In general, hands that move too much disturb the horse. This usually happens because the rider shows stiffness in the upper body, which can come from stiff wrists or stiff shoulders. Other faults are that the rider may move his hands up and down, or forwards and backwards for extensions or in piaffe and passage; or the rider's hands are carried in an unnaturally high position. In these cases the rider does not deserve a high mark – it is no longer 'fairly good'.

The rider's legs

Involuntarily flapping, unsteady legs will rarely produce consistent, regular work. They disturb the horse and make it impossible for the rider to hold the horse forward in medium and extended paces – this is particularly noticeable in trot. Such legs usually arise from stiffness in the hips or thighs. However, sometimes riders can be seen to be deliberately kicking or flapping with both legs, usually in an attempt to extend the pace. This is not the correct aid and it will serve only to upset or irritate the horse.

Precision and presentation

Perhaps 80 per cent of corners are not ridden correctly. To a certain extent, judges are as much to blame as the riders for this state of affairs for not marking the rider down because of this fault. Every corner is an opportunity to collect, engage or rebalance the horse. Although there are no separate marks for corners, the correct riding of corners shows the judge that the rider is educated and understands the process of progressive training.

The rider must execute each movement at the designated markers. In most cases this means when the rider's body is level with the marker. However, there are exceptions, such as transitions that occur at the end of a diagonal. These should always be executed when the horse's head arrives at the track.

Precision is a question of discipline and it should be addressed and rewarded, especially at the lower levels. Unfortunately, however, the requirement for precision has been removed from many lower level dressage tests, especially where transitions

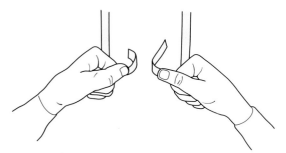

a. Correct (hands more or less vertical).

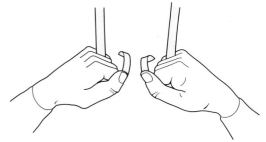

b. Incorrect (flat hands).

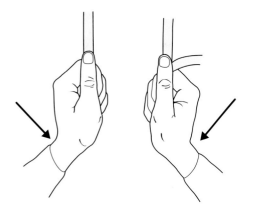

c. Incorrect (stiffness in the wrists).

Figure 2 Rider's position – correct and incorrect positions of the rider's hands. When held correctly as shown in (a) the rider can maintain the contact with the horse's mouth with supple wrists and relaxed arms. The two other positions which are commonly seen create tension and stiffness in the rider's arms, which causes discomfort in the horse's mouth. (Photos: H. Max-Theurer)

a. Correct (hands more or less vertical).

b. Incorrect (flat hands).

c. Incorrect (stiffness in the wrists).

are concerned. Many lower level tests require horses to make transitions between markers rather than at a marker. I believe this results from a misplaced concern that too much 'pressure' will be put upon a young horse. In my opinion, this is not helping the horse and rider to progress at all. Of course, the young horse might make the transition one or two metres from the marker and still receive a mark of 'satisfactory', but the young horse who can make a good transition when the rider asks for it at the marker should receive a much higher mark. Thus, correct training can be rewarded by the judge.

To a certain extent, the rider's mark will reflect the general level of marking of the whole test. If the test has many high marks, the rider's mark should reflect this because it would have been impossible for the horse to perform so well unless the rider was very competent. Conversely, if the test has many low marks, the judge will ask himself how much effect the rider had on the horse producing poor movements. Rough riding should always be punished by the judge, as this has no place in the sport of dressage. The judge should not be influenced by 'names' but must make an assessment based on what has been seen and on his knowledge of riding.

The rider in summary

To achieve high marks in this section, the rider should demonstrate the following characteristics:

- Movements are performed without apparent effort of the rider.

- The rider is in a well-balanced position.

- The rider's loins and hips are supple.

- The rider's legs and hands are steady.

- The rider moves smoothly and freely in harmony with his horse, without exaggeration.

- The rider should show an understanding of the correct application of the aids.

- The rider should ride with precision.

CHAPTER TWO

STRAIGHTNESS AND BEND

…ride your horse forward and set it straight!

When I say riding forward I do not mean driving the horse forward in the fastest and most extended gaits, but rather for the rider to take care to maintain an active thrust of the hindquarters in all exercises such that, not only in the movements in place, but even when moving backwards, the forward motion, namely the desire to move the load forward, remains in effect.

Gustav Steinbrecht

A HORSE IS STRAIGHT WHEN his hind legs step straight, and with impulsion, in the direction of the movement.

The horse's body is narrower at the front than at the back. Whenever a horse is travelling along the side of a school or an arena there may be a tendency for him to 'stick' to the wall with his shoulder. This produces a horse that moves with his inside hind foot always a little further to the inside of the line taken by the inside forefoot (see Figure 3). The rider must be aware of this tendency and, particularly with a young horse, he must endeavour to ride the horse on straight lines in the correct way. It is a good idea to ride frequently on the inside track of an arena to check that the horse is indeed travelling straight. It is easier to prevent the error occurring in the first place than it is to correct it once it has become a habit.

The horse must travel straight on straight lines and bend accordingly on curved lines. This means that on all occasions (except when performing lateral work) the hind feet must step on the same line as the forefeet. This is termed 'tracking true'. On circles and turns the horse is inclined to fall out with his hindquarters or his shoulders. The horse is then not bending correctly. This should be penalized heavily by the judge whenever it is seen because it is a sign of incorrect basic training. Figure 4 shows a horse bending correctly on a circle and Figure 5 shows a horse spiralling in from a large to a small circle correctly.

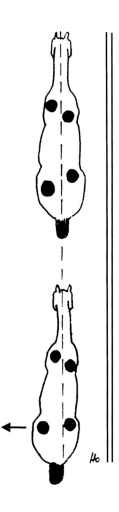

Figure 3 In the lower picture it can be seen that the horse falls out on his right shoulder and brings his quarters a little to the inside. The process of training the horse correctly will produce a horse that travels straight, as shown in the upper picture.

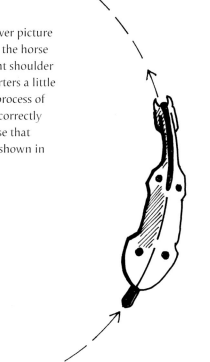

Figure 4 A horse bending correctly on a circle. Note that the horse's body conforms to the line of travel from his head to his tail. His feet will 'track true' and his body will remain vertical.

Figure 5 The illustration shows a horse bending correctly as he spirals inward from a large circle. As the rider reduces the size of the figure, it becomes more difficult for the horse to stay correctly bent. The rider must pay attention to what is happening underneath him so that the horse does not escape through his shoulders or hindquarters. The experienced rider will not spend too long on a small circle with a young horse in case the horse learns how to avoid bending.

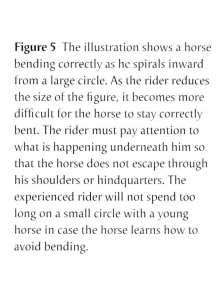

In the training of a young horse, the horse should not be asked to bend on very small circles and turns until he is well balanced and displaying a degree of suppleness. Once the horse is more advanced, he will be able to make small circles correctly with the hind feet following the forefeet. The experienced rider/trainer should be aware of how much or how little each individual horse can handle. A horse will always tend to take the path of least resistance and if the circle is too tight, he will try to avoid bending in some way because bending is harder work and he may be weak or stiff. In extreme cases, the horse will fall out with his hindquarters completely. If this issue is addressed correctly by the rider, the young horse will never learn to cross an inside hind foot out or fall out with his hindquarters because of a loss of balance.

While it would appear obvious that, in order to bend correctly, the hind feet have to step towards the footprints of the forefeet, I have observed that this is rarely considered to be of importance by riders and trainers. It is *essential* that this is addressed early in a horse's training in order to establish a correct procedure for riding circles and turns so that, later on, collection is made easier for the horse. The horse must learn to bring his inside hind leg willingly forward towards his inside front hoofprint without dropping his inside hip. There are misconceptions abounding about what this means. It is quite simple: the horse must 'track true' on any curved line. Any deviation of the horse's inside hind foot from the line of the inside forefoot means that he is not taking the weight on that leg and is, therefore, not bending. Many times we see horses travelling on circles – even quite large circles – and crossing their inside hind leg towards the direction of the outside foreleg. This is not tracking true, it is the beginning of the horse learning to avoid carrying weight and a demonstration that the horse does not bend correctly because of the use of incorrect aids by the rider.

Frequently, this lack of bend is the fault of the rider. An educated rider knows that, in order to bend a horse, he does not pull with his inside hand. The inside hand should merely be used to supple the horse's jaw with tiny half-halts on the rein, that come from just the use of a soft wrist. The rider's outside hand is still and low and maintains a steady, soft contact with the horse's mouth. This hand may, if necessary, become quite strong, whereas the inside hand must always be soft and light. Once the horse has submitted to this suppling action of the inside hand, it is easy for the rider to ask for bend with his inside leg at the girth and his outside leg behind the girth. Because the rider is not pulling with his inside hand, he does not restrict the movement of the horse's inside hind leg and the horse will be able to step correctly towards the path of the inside foreleg. The continuous riding of curved lines in this way will teach the horse to move correctly. With time and patient, correct riding, the horse will develop the ability to bend to a greater and greater extent.

When travelling on a straight line, the horse's body is vertical and it must remain so whilst travelling on a curved line. He should not lean inwards. A correctly ridden circle with correct bend is demonstrated by the horse remaining upright as he travels around the circle. The process of training the young horse both strengthens and straightens him so that he is able to travel straight. Correctly ridden circles strengthen the horse's back muscles and make him more supple. The opportunity to engage the inside hind leg more on every circle or turn is appreciated by the best trainers and riders, but rarely by many others. Without this ability to bend correctly, the horse cannot progress to perform the exercises of shoulder-in, travers and half-pass correctly.

A horse should be straight and moving forward with impulsion. The horse shows impulsion when he develops his forward motion from his hindquarters. The horse's back has to be free from tension. Only a well-balanced horse, whose hindquarters are trained to develop pushing and lifting power at the same time, can show lightness and ease of movement. Whilst travelling on a circle, the horse should remain in balance and the pace should be regular.

Performed correctly and with impulsion, circles develop strength and engagement of the hindquarters. Educated riders will take every opportunity to create more engagement by riding the corners of a dressage test correctly (at FEI levels, the equivalent of riding one quarter of a 6 m diameter volte or small circle). Although corners in dressage tests do not have a specific mark allocated to them, the judge will be looking to see whether the rider is riding them correctly and the horse is executing them correctly. This gives the judge an indication of the suppleness, obedience and balance of the horse and will be taken into consideration in his overall assessment of the 'submission' mark in the collectives and the mark for the rider's use of the aids.

CHAPTER THREE

COLLECTION

COLLECTION IS NEEDED FOR ALL WORK at the higher levels of dressage. The process of collection makes it possible for the horse to perform advanced movements, such as those required in lateral work, and to develop better quality paces. In respect of the latter, it is collection that makes it possible for the horse to produce powerful extended paces. The consequences of collection are a lightening of the forehand and freedom of the shoulders. A horse does not require collection to move in the basic paces used early in its training, which are termed 'working' paces.

Since I believe it is essential that both riders and judges understand the concept of collection, I have chosen to devote a chapter to this subject. The specific requirements of the individual collected paces and movements are discussed in later chapters. It should be noted that these principles apply only to the trot and canter; walk being an exception.

Collection is literally 'gathering together'. It is so termed because this is exactly the process. The rider generates energy and impulsion from the hindquarters and collects this energy, with a soft, supple hand, into a higher and shorter frame as the horse steps more and more underneath himself, taking more and more weight on the hind legs. The ultimate form of collection would be the levade, a classical movement that is performed, for example, by the horses of the Spanish Riding School. In the levade, all forward movement ceases and the horse takes all of his weight on his hind legs, which are placed well forward underneath his body, with highly flexed hocks and a lowered croup. He raises his forehand completely off the ground and remains there, with bent forelegs, softly and without tension, accepting the bit. This movement demands great power and strength in the horse's back and a high degree of muscular control. This degree of collection is not required in competition dressage. However, the next degree of collection down from this is required in Grand Prix competitions in the form of the piaffe, in which the horse effectively trots on the spot with elastic steps while still maintaining a degree of suspension.

In my experience, very few people really understand the meaning of the term 'collection'. This is demonstrated in competitions when we see horses more or less 'pulled together' by their riders in a misguided attempt to produce collected paces. This has the effect of restricting the horse's freedom of movement, the quality of the paces deteriorates and they become dull. This is in total contrast to true collection, which is a lightening of the forehand and a shortening of the frame, arising from the correct development of the power of the hindquarters controlled by a light hand, which creates freedom of movement and expression in the paces. The development of correct medium and extended paces follows only from the correct development of the hindquarters and the creation of collection.

The Principles of Collection

In order to explain the principles of collection to both judges and riders, I have devised the illustrations accompanying this chapter. These diagrams formed part of an earlier publication and I have incorporated them here because of their continued relevance. In them I have endeavoured to explain the relationships between collected and working, medium and extended paces.

Through correct training, the horse develops in his hindquarters the power to carry his body and the weight of his rider (vertical lifting power), as well as the power to move forward (horizontal pushing). These actions are represented on vector diagrams which show the resultant force.

In collected trot and collected canter (Figure 6(a)), the pushing (horizontal) and lifting (vertical) components are approximately the same, so that the resultant force appears at an angle of about 45 degrees. This leads to a movement of the foot corresponding to an arc as shown in the drawing and it can be called collected trot (or collected canter). The horse shows self-carriage; he takes the weight on his hindquarters and so the forehand becomes lighter and more mobile.

If the horizontal (pushing) component is increased, while the vertical (lifting) component is slightly reduced, the movement will become longer (Figure 6(b)). The resultant force will appear at an angle of slightly less than 45 degrees. The corresponding arc of movement of the foot is not as high as, but longer than, that in collection. The movement thus becomes a medium trot (or medium canter).

If the horizontal (pushing) component is increased to the maximum (utmost lengthening) whereas the vertical (lifting) component is about the same, or slightly less than in Figure 6(b), the lengthening of the steps or strides increases to the maximum and it becomes extended trot (or extended canter), see Figure 6(c).

If the ends of the arcs of foot movement of the collected, medium and extended

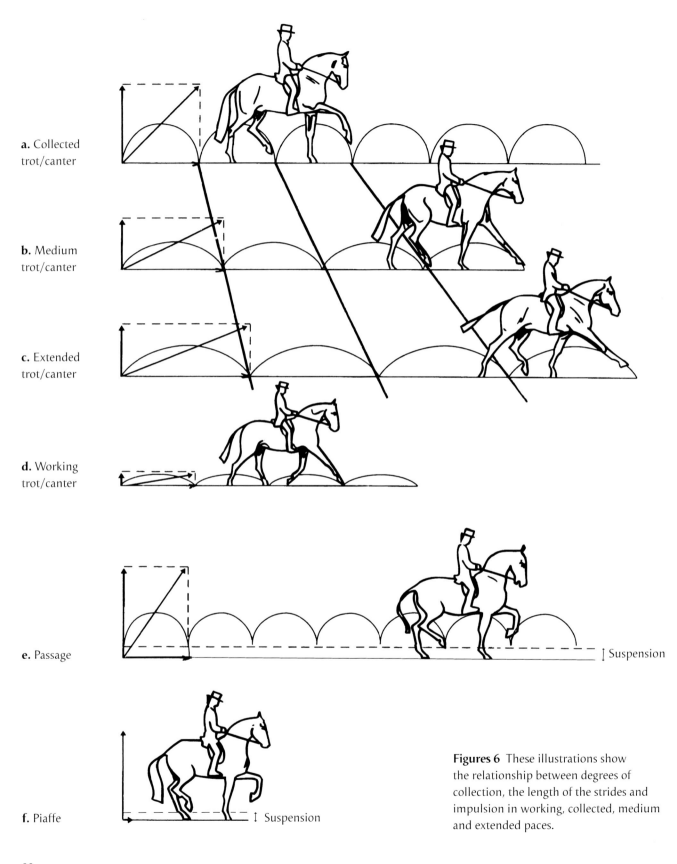

a. Collected
trot/canter

b. Medium
trot/canter

c. Extended
trot/canter

d. Working
trot/canter

e. Passage

⌶ Suspension

f. Piaffe

⌶ Suspension

Figures 6 These illustrations show
the relationship between degrees of
collection, the length of the strides and
impulsion in working, collected, medium
and extended paces.

paces (when represented on a mathematically accurate diagram) can be connected by a straight line, this indicates that, while the steps or strides become longer, the rhythm in all three movements is the same.

In working trot (or canter) (Figure 6(d)), the horizontal (pushing) component is similar to that of collection but the vertical (lifting) component is much less (the horse is less 'engaged'). Therefore a rather flat movement, with a resultant force appearing at an angle of much less than 45 degrees, will occur.

If the vertical (lifting) component in trot is increased and the horizontal (pushing) component is slightly reduced, the horse's body can be seen clearly in a moment of suspension and the pace becomes passage (Figure 6(e)). The resultant force in this case will appear at an angle of considerably more than 45 degrees. The horse thus carries much more weight on his hindquarters.

If the vertical (lifting) component in trot is increased to a maximum and the horizontal (pushing) component is reduced to a minimum, the horse will lift his body on the spot, with a clear suspension. In this movement, which is called piaffe (Figure 6(f)), the horse is effectively trotting on the spot ('dancing').

The resultant combined power of the pushing and lifting components is – in trot, canter, passage and piaffe – called 'impulsion'. It can be seen that the steeper the angle of the resultant force, the greater the degree of impulsion that is required. In working trot and canter the horse moves forward in his natural balance without producing clear impulsion. In these paces, required at the beginning of the horse's training, we talk not of impulsion, more of 'activity'.

Walk is the exception with respect to impulsion. In walk, where the horse's body does not leave the ground (that is, there is always at least one foot on the ground) and no suspension is shown, impulsion is not the appropriate term to use in respect of any variants of the pace. Instead the description is, again, the 'activity' of the steps. (In collected walk, however, there should be a very active, energetic movement, with the horse flexing his joints and raising his feet clearly higher than in other types of walk.)

The Position of the Horse's Head

In all dressage movements the horse has to accept the bit. Depending upon the level of collection, the neck should be raised to an appropriate degree (the poll being the highest point), with the nose a little in front of the vertical. The degree of elevation of the head and neck depends upon the level of training of the horse. Generally, the more collected the horse is, the higher and shorter will be the outline. There should be a light contact with the bit.

Great care must be taken on the part of the rider not to over-shorten (and as a result, compress) the horse's neck in a desire to create a collected outline. If the neck is compressed, or restricted by the rider's hand, the horse's back will become stiff and the quality of his paces will consequently deteriorate. Figure 7 shows the relative positions of the head and neck with respect to the level of training.

The position of the horse's head during a dressage test, and what he does with it during transitions, are very good indications to the judge as to the way of going and the correctness of training. Faults in the head carriage will have an adverse effect on the mark given for the movement in which they occurred and the judge will also take this into account when assessing the collective marks. I will now discuss some examples of faulty head position and consider their effects on the judge's marks.

a.

Figures 7 (a) Correct head position for a young horse and, (b) Correct head position for an advanced horse.

b.

• There has been a trend in recent years for trainers and riders to advocate the bringing of the horse's head behind the vertical. The argument is that this stretches the back. Whether or not this is appropriate in training, if it is seen in a dressage test it must be penalized. The FEI *Rules for Dressage Events* state clearly that the poll should be the highest point and the nose should be always a little in front of the vertical. Whether it is the horse or the rider who creates the problem is not the judge's place to decide; his job is only to comment on what he sees. If the poll is not the highest point and the front line of the nose is almost constantly behind the vertical (Figure 8), the movement itself cannot be described as 'sufficient' and the overall submission mark cannot be more than 'sufficient'.

• However, if the poll is (more or less) the highest point but the front line of the nose is behind the vertical and this happens in a movement for a short moment, the movement can still be described as 'satisfactory', but never 'fairly good'. However, the overall submission mark for the horse in a test can still be 'fairly good'.

• A horse who is 'leaning' on the bit, or leaning on the rider's hands, is not in self-carriage. Even at the lower levels of training it is possible and desirable for the horse to distribute his weight so that he does not hang in the rider's hands. This requirement to balance and carry himself is a prerequisite of a dressage horse right from the beginning. If the horse is leaning on the bit and, with this, is heavy on the forehand (Figure 9), the movements can no longer be described as 'satisfactory'. This has also to be taken into account for the overall submission mark, which cannot be more than 'sufficient'.

Figure 9 Horse leaning on the rider's hands. The horse is heavy on the forehand and the poll is no longer the highest point.

Figure 8 Head position of the horse slightly behind the vertical, and stiff in the back.

• In order for the horse to be 'on the bit' there should be a continuous stream of energy coming from the lively impulsion of the hindquarters that is received in the rider's hands via the reins. The horse should not be merely 'holding' himself in a particular frame or shape. This stream of energy is felt by the rider as a tendency for his hands to be drawn forward and is an indication to him of the horse's willingness to go forward in response to his aids. If the horse wants to evade the rider's driving aids, one way of doing so is to break the contact with the bit. This can be done by the horse in many ways, but the most obvious and common method is for him to drop the contact by bringing his chin closer to his chest, either momentarily or for protracted periods. This can be seen clearly by the judge, who must mark it appropriately. How it might appear is illustrated in Figure 10. The horse is evading by 'dropping the bit', leaving the rider with no contact. If there is no contact with the mouth, the horse does not go to the bit and, in extreme cases, the horse may be constantly 'behind the bit'. The movement can then no longer be described as 'sufficient' and the overall submission mark cannot be 'sufficient'.

• In cases when the horse has dropped the contact, it is often also not willing to go freely forward and the movements shown are generally 'insufficient'. There is an overall lack of submission and impulsion and the collective marks for both of these categories would be unlikely to be more than 'sufficient'.

Figure 10 Head position showing a horse who has dropped or broken the contact. Notice that the rein is loose and the poll is no longer the highest point. Also, the horse's neck appears over-shortened and it lacks the correct muscle tone and outline.

• The musculature of the horse's neck and back are intimately connected. Thus, unless the whole of the spinal column is free to move evenly, the horse cannot increase the length of the step that he takes and ultimately, his paces will not improve. When the horse's neck is too short because the rider has too much contact with the horse's mouth, this is indicative of the rider 'pulling the horse together' with his hands (Figure 11). Shortening the neck by using the reins too strongly in order to create a particular frame only serves to restrict the action of the horse's lower back and loins. The movement of the horse's hindquarters is then blocked and the horse cannot develop the activity needed. This applies especially to the trot and canter. In addition, the shoulder is restricted. The net result is that, when asked to lengthen his strides, the horse will just quicken his steps. In medium or extended paces the steps or strides become more hurried (faster) instead of longer. In walk the forelegs cannot reach forward enough. These movements can then no longer be considered 'satisfactory'.

Figure 11 This shows a horse who is 'pulled together'. The rider has over-shortened the horse's neck and as a consequence, the horse is unable to move his hind legs freely. He is being blocked behind. This is manifested by a lack of activity of the hind legs in comparison with that of the forelegs. This is often seen when riders try to collect the horse by shortening the front half rather than by riding the horse up to the hand from behind.

• A tilted head carriage is created by the rider (Figure 12). If the horse does not want to bend and the rider pulls on the inside rein he will create a tilted head position. A horse who has a tilted head is resisting and not bending. This can be corrected by riding circles in the proper way and by the rider 'suppling' the horse to the inside with a soft wrist, rather than by pulling. If head tilting occurs throughout the test the submission mark is unlikely to be greater than 'sufficient'.

Figure 12 The horse is showing a tilting of the head to the right. This problem is most usually the result of the rider trying to bend the horse on a circle or turn by pulling on the inside rein. This will have no influence on the bend, rather it will encourage to horse to avoid using his inside hind leg because he will feel restricted on that side. The impulsion is lost, as is the engagement of the hindquarters, with the result that the horse avoids working correctly on the curved line.

CHAPTER FOUR

THE PACES

WITHIN THE THREE BASIC PACES OF WALK, trot and canter there are variations that are required to be shown during a test. The degree of training of the horse dictates the degree of collection and extension that is possible at any time and the FEI rules lay down the specific requirements for each of the variations within the paces. I will summarize here the most important requirements for each of them. In presenting a horse in a dressage test, it is most important that the rider pays particular attention to the requirements of that test. The judge will award his marks according to how closely he believes that what he sees relates to the ideal picture.

It should be remembered that the process of training a horse is gradual and therefore, the degree of collection required in tests at different levels varies. The judge must be knowledgeable and take care not to demand too high a level of collection at the earlier stages of training compared with that required at Grand Prix. Conversely, the judge will penalise those horses competing at an advanced level of training if they do not show the requisite degree of collection.

The Walk

The walk is a marching pace with four beats, well marked, equal and regular. The horse travels in walk from support on three legs (2 hind + 1 fore), to support on two legs (diagonal pair), to support on three legs (1 hind + 2 fore) to support on two legs (lateral pair), and so on. The footfalls are as follows (starting with the left hind leg):

left hind, left fore, right hind, right fore.

Figure 13 A correct walk showing the phase of the stride where a 'V' can be seen created by the lateral pair of legs. (Photo: Y. Doornmalen)

Any deviation from the regularity of this sequence must be heavily penalized by the judge. A reliable guide to the correctness of a walk (for both judges and riders) is to be able to see a 'V' formed for an instant by the fore and hind legs on each side as the horse grounds the hind foot just as he is preparing to lift the corresponding forefoot (Figure 13). In addition, it is easy to count the beats of the footfalls to check their regularity.

The worst deviation from the correct walk can be seen when a horse walks in what is termed a 'lateral walk' or 'ambling'. This occurs when the horse loses the four-beat rhythm of the walk completely and swings both legs on the same side of his body forward at the same time, producing an almost clear two-beat walk, somewhat like the walk of a camel (Figure 14). If the rhythm of the walk is neither clearly four-beat nor clearly two-beat, it can be described as an 'irregular' walk.

The walk should appear relaxed and should not be pushed out of rhythm by the rider. This creates a hurried walk and in this case the strides of the horse will not develop to a maximum, so it will have a particular effect upon the extended walk.

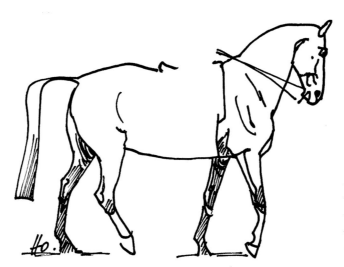

Figure 14 A lateral walk. The regular rhythm of the footfalls of the walk has been lost. This is a typical example of what happens when the horse is 'pulled together' by the rider, which produces stiffness in the horse's back.

Judging the Walk – General Principles

Between the two extremes described above there are variations which are commented on by the judge according to the severity of the error. I list below some examples and include the likely comment (mark) that would be awarded by the judge:

- Jogging is often a result of tension in the horse, or in the rider, or possibly occurs because the rider is pushing too much. If it is repeated it will not achieve a mark higher than 'insufficient'.

- Short jogging steps – may be just 'sufficient'.

- Sustained irregular steps – 'insufficient', towards 'bad'.

- Clear ambling is always penalized heavily whenever it is seen, especially when it is sustained. A horse with a clear amble would almost certainly be awarded a mark of 'bad'. It is uncommon for horses to demonstrate this sort of walk naturally but degrees of ambling are frequently seen. It nearly always occurs as a result of bad training or extreme tension in the horse.

Even if the walk is clear and regular, there are other problems that can occur which will be noted and marked by the judge according to the effect that they have on the particular movement.

- Not remaining on the bit – can be between 'sufficient' and 'bad'.

- Not accepting the bit – 'insufficient' to 'very bad'.

- Stiffness in the neck – not more than 'sufficient'; exceptionally it may be 'satisfactory'.

- Steps too hurried – not more than 'satisfactory'.

- Any clear resistance – not more than 'insufficient'.

Within the FEI rules there are four types of walk recognized. These are the 'medium walk' (which is, effectively, the working equivalent in this pace), 'collected walk', 'extended walk' and 'free walk'.

Medium Walk

In addition to a clear rhythm, the following characteristics should be present in the medium walk (see Figure 15):

- The walk should be free, regular and unconstrained.

- The horse should be well balanced, willingly accepting the bit with a light contact.

- There should be a moderate extension of the stride, that is to say, the hind feet should touch the ground in front of the imprints of the forefeet (this is termed 'overtracking').

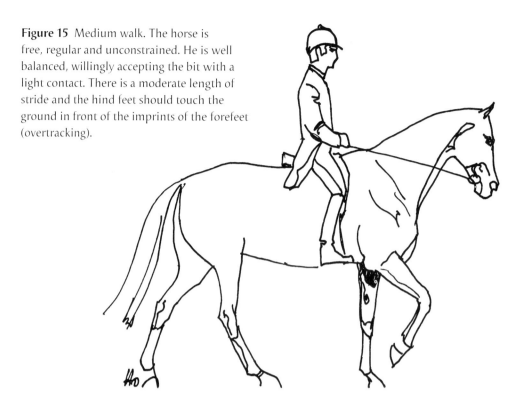

Figure 15 Medium walk. The horse is free, regular and unconstrained. He is well balanced, willingly accepting the bit with a light contact. There is a moderate length of stride and the hind feet should touch the ground in front of the imprints of the forefeet (overtracking).

Collected Walk

In addition to a clear rhythm, the following characteristics should be present in the collected walk (see Figure 16):

- The horse should move resolutely forward.

- The steps should be active and regular, not hurried but shorter and higher than those of the medium walk.

- The neck should be raised and arched, with the head approaching the vertical position.

- The frame of the horse is shorter overall than in medium walk.

- There should be a light contact with the mouth.

- The horse should be 'on the bit'.

When a collected walk is just slow and there is a lack of activity, the judge may still consider it to be 'sufficient' or even 'satisfactory'. However, when the horse fails to demonstrate any collection, this means that the walk cannot be considered to be worth more than a mark of 'insufficient'. Frequently, riders do not collect the walk because they are afraid that their horse will become irregular.

Figure 16 Collected walk. The horse should be moving resolutely forward. The steps should be active and regular, not hurried. The steps are higher and shorter than those of medium walk. The neck is raised and arched, with the head approaching the vertical position. The frame of the horse is shortened. The horse is 'on the bit' and there is a light contact with the mouth.

There are some horses who overtrack a little even in the collected walk. This is not necessarily a sign that the horse is not collected, it might be a product of the horse's conformation, and/or this might be a horse with an enormous overtrack in the extension.

Extended Walk

In an extended walk the reins should not be loose, but on the other hand the rider should lengthen the reins in order to lengthen the frame of the horse. The horse's nose must stay in front of the vertical. The head and neck can be clearly lowered. The horse should overtrack clearly. A good extended walk looks rather slow because the horse has to reach forward out of the shoulders. Frequently, riders push their horses forward too much, with the result that the steps become faster (more hurried) but, at the same time, they become shorter. Because there is no moment of suspension in the walk, there can be no mention of the word impulsion. The term that judges should use to describe the walk is 'activity'.

In addition to a clear rhythm, the following characteristics should be present in the extended walk (see Figures 17 and 18):

- The horse covers as much ground as possible.

- He takes long, regular steps, reaching forward out of the shoulder.

Figure 17 Extended walk. The rider has allowed the horse to lengthen his neck whilst keeping only a light contact on the rein. The horse should cover as much ground as possible and clearly overtrack. He should take long, regular steps reaching forward out of the shoulder. There is a clear lengthening of the frame with the horse lengthening and lowering his head and neck. The horse's head is in front of the vertical.

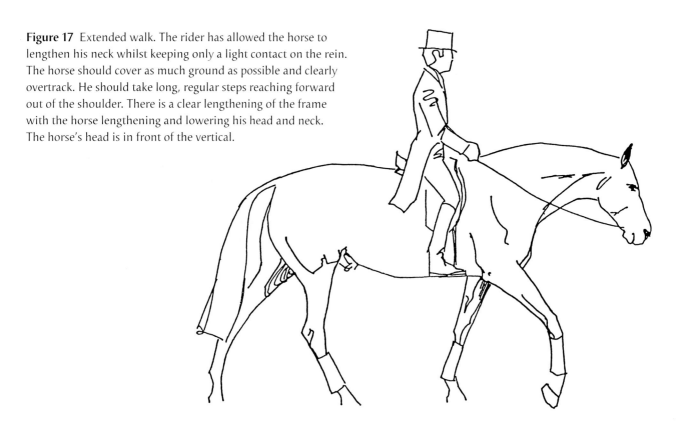

Figure 18 Extended walk showing a *really* lowered head and neck. This is still correct as the horse is keeping his nose out in front of the vertical.

- The hind feet must touch the ground clearly in front of the imprints of the forefeet.

- There should be a clear extension of the frame with the horse lengthening and lowering his neck and head.

- There should only be a light contact with the bit.

Free Walk

This movement (Figure 19) is sometimes asked for in lower level tests.

In a free walk the horse should just be allowed to show his own natural walk. The horse should be completely relaxed and the rider should allow the horse complete freedom to lower and stretch his head and neck. There is no requirement for a contact with the bit. The horse should demonstrate a clear walk rhythm. For a high mark, the judge would be expecting to see a clear overtracking with the hind feet and considerable lowering and lengthening of the head and neck. There should be no tightness or restriction in the shoulders. The free walk should appear slow, but not inactive.

Figure 19 Free walk. The rider has surrendered all contact with the rein.

The Trot

Trot is a pace of two-time separated by a short moment of suspension. The horse steps from one diagonal pair of legs to the other. The most important requirement is that the steps remain regular. Except in the working trot (where the horse should move just normally and actively forward), the horse should be going forward with impulsion originating from the hindquarters. The rhythm of the pace must always be maintained.

The FEI rules recognize the following four types of trot: 'working trot', 'collected trot', 'medium trot' and 'extended trot'.

Working Trot

A working trot is a natural pace in which the horse moves forward actively but not hurriedly in a well-balanced position. The horse should remain steady on the bit with a light contact (see Figure 20). This is the trot that is asked of a young horse early in its training before it is ready for collection. Although the hocks should be active, the word 'impulsion' is not really appropriate when describing this pace. Activity, regularity and rhythm are the requirements.

Figure 20 Working trot. This is a natural pace in which the horse moves forward actively but not hurriedly in a well-balanced position. This is the trot asked of a young horse early in his training. The outline is somewhat flat.

Collected Trot

I refer here back to Chapter 3. In addition to a clear rhythm, the following characteristics should be present in the collected trot (see Figure 21):

- The horse's neck should be raised and arched.

- The hocks should be well engaged and the horse should be light in the forehand.

- The steps should be shorter but more accentuated than the working pace, demonstrating a greater flexibility of the joints.

- There should be an energetic impulsion.

Medium Trot

In addition to a clear rhythm, the following characteristics should be present in the medium trot (see Figure 22):

- The horse should move with free, moderately extended steps.

- There should be engagement of the hindquarters (impulsion). This is also shown by an increase in the degree of impulsion.

A good example of a medium trot as shown by a young horse (5 years old). Christine Stückelberger on *Bernstein*. (Photo: E. Weiland)

- The horse should be well on the bit and there should be no stiffness in the neck.

- The horse's head should be a little in front of the vertical.

- The steps should be as even as possible.

- The whole movement should be balanced and unconstrained.

- The overall impression should be that of the horse travelling uphill. In other words, the horse should appear to grow in front during the medium trot.

Figure 21 Collected trot. The horse's neck is raised and arched. The hocks are well engaged and the horse is light on the forehand. The steps are shorter but higher than in the other forms of the pace demonstrating a greater flexibility of the joints. There should be energetic impulsion.

Figure 22 Medium trot. The horse is moving with free and moderately extended steps. There is engagement of the hindquarters. The horse is well on the bit and there is no stiffness in the neck. The horse's head is a little in front of the vertical. The steps should be as even as possible and the whole movement should be balanced and unconstrained.

Extended Trot

In the extended trot the judge wants to see the horse covering as much ground as possible. In addition to a clear rhythm, the following characteristics should be present (see Figure 23):

- The horse covers as much ground as possible, maintaining the same rhythm.

- He lengthens his steps; his neck and frame are extended.

- There should be powerful engagement of the hindquarters.

- There should be good suspension (the horse should appear to be 'flying', not running).

- The forefeet should touch the ground on the spot to which they are pointing when at maximum extension.

- The horse should remain steady on the bit.

Figure 23 ABOVE Extended trot. The horse should cover as much ground as possible whilst retaining the same rhythm. The steps are lengthened as are the frame and neck. The horse is on the bit. The forefeet should touch the ground on the spot to which they are pointing at maximum extension. There should be good suspension.

Extended trot. The horse is well engaged and the rider is in a perfect position. This shows harmony between the rider and the horse. Henri Chammartin riding *Wolfdietrich* at the World Championships, Berne 1966. (Photo: HorseSource/ Col. Pondret)

Extended trot. This is a horse with a very impressive high movement. Nadine Capellman riding *Farbenfroh* at the Olympic Games, Sydney 2000. (Photo: HorseSource/ P. Llewellyn)

BELOW A very nice extended trot. Beatriz Ferrer-Salat on *Vital Robert Beauvais* at the Olympic Games, Sydney 2000. (Photo: HorseSource/ P. Llewellyn)

ABOVE A good extended trot. Reiner
Klimke on *Ahlerich*. (Photo: W. Ernst)

A beautiful extended trot. Ann Grethe
Tornblad on *Marzog*. (Photo: E. Olsen)

Judging the Trot

When assessing the trot, especially the medium or extended trot, the judge should take care not only to check the moderate extension, or the utmost lengthening of the steps respectively, but also to ascertain whether the relation between the forelegs and the hind legs is correct. In other words, whether the impulsion originates in the engagement of the hindquarters. This is also very important in judging collected trot and the lateral work.

One of the problems that occurs – especially in extensions – is seen in the horse who shows a flamboyant action of the forelegs without corresponding effort from the hind legs. This may look spectacular to the casual observer but it is not correct. An example of what I mean is shown in Figure 24.

There are other problems that may occur from time to time during the trot work. Whenever these are seen, the judge will reduce his mark accordingly. Some examples are as follows:

- When there is a permanent irregularity (lameness) – this can only be marked as 'fairly bad' to 'bad' and may eventually result in elimination.

- When there are irregularities of short duration – the judge will deduct one mark.

- If there is irregular hock action, such as snatching one hind leg – this cannot be more than 'sufficient'.

Figure 24 Extended trot showing stiffness in the back and neck. Also showing exaggerated movement of the forelegs and inactive hind legs.

- If there is a hurried movement in medium, or extended trot, in other words the horse is running, then it cannot be regarded as more than 'sufficient'.

- In collected, medium and extended trot, if there is no clear engagement of the hindquarters then the movement cannot be considered to be more than 'sufficient', because the horse is just pushing forwards without carrying the weight and therefore lacks self-carriage (Figure 25).

- If the horse shows stiffness in the neck or back, depending on the degree, the judge will not award a mark higher than 'satisfactory'. However, if the horse is also not pushing forward then it cannot be more than 'sufficient' (see Figure 24).

- If, as a result of incorrect training, the horse spreads his hind legs to each side as he makes the extension (Figure 26), the judge would note this and would not award a mark higher than 'satisfactory'. However, this would depend very much on where the judge was sitting because it is only really seen clearly from in front or from behind.

  This spreading of the hind legs happens with some horses when they are pushed to produce extensions too early, before they have enough strength to balance themselves. A horse only spreads his hind legs to control his balance and, once he has learned to perform an extension this way, it is very difficult for it to be corrected. Extensions should be introduced by degrees carefully over a long period, with great attention being paid to the horse's individual strength and ability.

Figure 25 Extended trot with no engagement of the hindquarters. The horse is too heavy on the forehand and the hindquarters are not pushing enough: the hind legs are out behind the horse.

Figure 26 Extended trot going 'wide behind'. The horse is spreading his hind legs to help himself balance as he makes the extension.

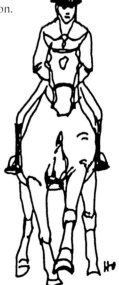

The Canter

Canter is a pace of three beats followed by a moment of suspension. The footfalls for canter are as follows:

(right lead) left hind, right hind and left fore together, right fore.
(left lead) right hind, left hind and right fore together, left fore.

This sequence is followed by a moment of suspension with all four feet off the ground.

At all times the canter should be light, cadenced and rhythmical. I will repeat what the FEI rules say about cadence:

'…the result of the proper harmony that a horse shows when it moves with well marked regularity, impulsion and balance….'

Art 401.7 (2003)

The FEI rules recognize four types of canter, which correspond to those of the trot: 'working canter', 'collected canter', 'medium canter' and 'extended canter'.

Working Canter

As in the working trot, this is a natural pace shown by the horse early in his training, before he is ready to show collection. The horse should demonstrate a natural, well-balanced movement with rounded strides and a clear rhythm (Figure 27). The strides should be even, light and cadenced and the horse should maintain a light acceptance of the bit. In working canter we can use the word 'cadence', which implies an element of impulsion, because the horse, in a good natural canter produces a degree of impulsion. In a young horse the balance would normally be towards the forehand and the appearance might be as shown in Figure 28.

Collected Canter

Depending upon the degree of training, and along with a clear rhythm, the following characteristics should be present in the collected canter (see Figure 29):

• The head should be raised and the neck well arched.

• The hindquarters should be well engaged, showing increased flexibility of the joints.

• The forehand should be light and mobile.

• The horse should demonstrate good forward movement with shorter strides than in the working pace.

Figure 27 Working canter. This is a good working canter. The horse is very well balanced in his natural pace.

Figure 28 Working canter a little on the forehand. This is a very common type of canter seen in young horses before they have developed any collection. It is the horse's natural canter. The rider's position is deliberately shown to be a little forward in the saddle. This is because the whole balance of the horse and rider is a little towards the front and the rider is mirroring the horse.

Medium Canter

In addition to a clear rhythm, the following characteristics should be present in the medium canter (see Figure 30):

- There should be moderate extension of the strides.

- The strides should be active, rounded and as even as possible.

- There should be a natural balance.

- The horse should remain steady on the bit.

Figure 29 Collected canter. The horse's head is raised and the neck is arched. The hindquarters are well engaged and there is increased flexibility in the hocks. The forehand is light and mobile. The horse should show good forward movement with shortened strides.

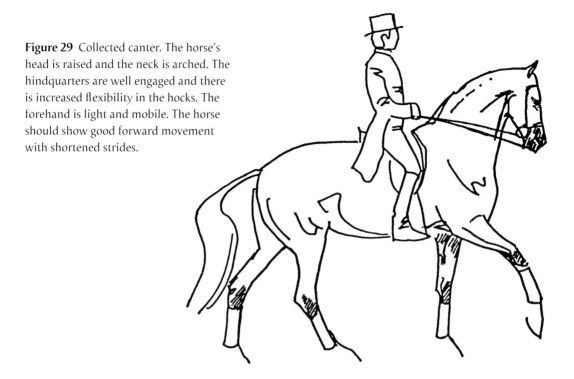

Figure 30 Medium canter. There is a moderate extension of the strides. The strides should remain rounded and active. There should be a natural balance and the horse should remain on the bit.

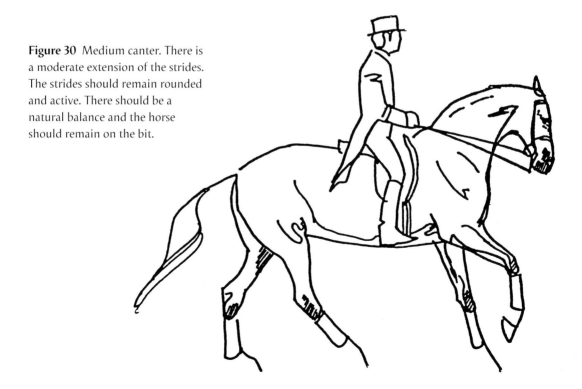

Extended Canter

In the extended canter, as in the extended trot, the horse must cover as much ground as possible. In addition to a clear rhythm, the following characteristics should be present in the extended canter (see Figure 31):

- There should be a clear lengthening of the strides and of the frame.

- The horse should push powerfully forward with his hindquarters well engaged and without losing calmness and lightness.

- The horse's neck should be slightly extended and he should accept the bit.

Figure 31 Extended canter. There is a clear lengthening of the stride and the frame. The hindquarters are well engaged. The horse should push powerfully forward without losing calmness and lightness. The horse's neck is slightly extended and he is accepting the bit.

Judging the Canter

In collected canter, the judge should check that the footfalls are correct, that is, that the pace is regular. Any deviation from a correct canter rhythm must be penalized. However, it should be noted that, in very collected movements such as pirouettes, the horse's forehand may become so light and mobile that it appears that the diagonal pair of legs is slightly separated. Thus it is possible in such cases that, when a judge sees a round, but not absolutely clear three-beat movement, he can still give a mark of 'satisfactory'. However, if this movement occurs frequently and is accompanied by

A good extended canter.
Pia Laus on *Renoir*.
(Photo: H. Czerny)

the horse being heavy on the forehand, or inactive in the hocks, it can only be 'insufficient' to 'bad'.

When assessing medium or extended canter, the judge has to be sure that the strides are lengthened, that the horse really does produce an extension and that there is not simply an increase in speed with shorter but more hurried strides. It is very common to see only an increase in speed instead of lengthening of the movement and the frame.

There are other problems that can occur during the canter that can affect the judge's marks. Some examples are:

• If the horse does not stay steady on the bit, the judge cannot give a mark that is more than 'sufficient'.

• If a horse is not straight in canter, the work can never achieve a mark that is more than 'satisfactory'.

CHAPTER FIVE

BASIC WORK

S O FAR, I HAVE TALKED ABOUT WHAT JUDGES are looking for within the
horse's basic paces in a dressage test. The correct performance of a specific
movement or exercise, such as a circle or a lateral movement, requires that the
prescribed pace is maintained – with all the qualities already mentioned – during the
execution of the movement or exercise. It is the judge's responsibility to be very clear
about what are the essential components of each movement. In judging a specific
movement, he must first ensure that these essential components are demonstrated
correctly and then take into account the more minor aspects.

These movements and exercises are used throughout the systematic training of
the horse to develop his strength, suppleness and balance. They should not be practised mindlessly in isolation, but used as an integral part of the gymnastic development of the novice horse into the athlete who is the Grand Prix horse.

A horse simply ridden forward in a novice frame will never develop the lifting
muscles in his back and hindquarters. The muscles over the loins, croup and
hindquarters are responsible for allowing the horse to increase the amount of weight
that he carries on his hind legs. In a young horse these muscles are weak and the only
way to strengthen them is by movements and exercises that momentarily increase the
weight carried on the hind legs. Over time, the movements can be sustained for
longer and longer and, as the horse becomes stronger, a greater degree of effort can
be requested. At all times the rider and trainer must be aware of the ability of each
individual horse because, if the exercise becomes too difficult, resistance, irregularities and a lack of confidence will ensue. The rider must not be in a hurry and must
allow the horse to develop his strength slowly and with confidence.

The accomplished rider or trainer will understand the relative importance and
usefulness of the exercises and will regard them as the tools of his trade. I intend here
to discuss these various exercises from the point of view of how they should be

performed and how the rider should go about training the horse. I have gone into considerable detail about what the judge wants to see so that he can award a high mark, and what mistakes will result in a loss of marks. If the rider is aware of all the aspects of the sport – the horse's point of view and the judge's as well as his own – this will indicate what he might do to avoid losing marks in a test.

Starting Work

A horse should always be considered as an athlete. Therefore, in training for suppleness, we have to encourage the horse to stretch to get his back rounder and more supple. The rider should not be putting all of his weight in the saddle, in other words, he should be rising to the trot. The muscles need to be warmed up before moving on to more difficult work in the same way that a human athlete would prepare for a performance. The more advanced horse has more muscle than the young horse and thus requires more care in warming up and cooling down.

Many riders are seen chasing the horse in a fast trot or canter at the start of their work. This does not supple the horse because pushing the horse too fast only leads to tension. The horse should be ridden in a natural, well-balanced position and at a moderate tempo.

Transitions

In its basic form, a transition is a change from one pace to another such as from walk to trot. Transitions can also take place within a pace, for example, from collected to medium trot, or vice versa.

If he is to remain light in the rider's hand, any change of pace, upwards or downwards, requires that the horse must momentarily take additional weight on his hind legs. Thus, even at the earliest stages of training a young horse, transitions can be used to start to develop strength in his hindquarters. However, it is essential that these transitions be performed correctly. If not, their value is totally wasted. At all times the rider must endeavour to keep the horse supple and light in the mouth and must, at no time, allow him to bear down onto the hand and become heavy on the forehand. In a transition that is performed correctly, the horse will step a little further underneath his body with one or other hind leg, thereby increasing the degree of engagement of the hindquarters. He should at no time lean on the bit.

Transitions within paces also help to improve the horse's balance. All transitions should be ridden in a similar manner so that the horse develops confidence in and harmony with his rider. There are many different transitions possible and each one has its associated difficulties. I will use the transitions from walk to halt and from halt to walk to illustrate the basic principles of riding correct transitions. The aids that the rider uses for the downward transition are the same for any downward transition. The aids for the upwards transition are characteristic of all upwards transitions.

The Transitions from Walk to Halt, and Halt to Walk

Before the horse can make any sort of downward transition from a faster to a slower pace, he must prepare to take a little more weight on his hindquarters. The rider helps in this respect by asking for more engagement of the hind legs. This is effected by the rider pressing with both legs firmly on the horse behind the girth. The rider should clearly move both legs back a little. The rider's outside hand should be firm, with a good contact. His inside hand gives half-halts which are quick 'give-and-takes' made using only the wrist. On no account should the rider lean his body backwards, or pull on the reins.

At the moment of the halt the rider should release the pressure of his legs and make both hands soft by relaxing his arms, easing the hands slightly forward. It helps if the rider relaxes internally immediately after releasing his legs. This helps the horse to remain relaxed and stand still.

In order to proceed forward out of halt into walk, the rider should attract the horse's attention to tell him that he is about to move forward. To do this, the rider makes a slight vibration with the inside hand and touches the horse lightly with both legs. The rider then gives the corresponding aids for the next required pace which, for walk, would be a quick nudge with both legs at the girth.

Riding Transitions in General

The rider's aids are used in the same way as described for going into and out of halt, but the intensity has to be adapted to the expected transition. In other words, a more energetic action of the rider's legs would be used to ask the horse to proceed into trot out of halt, than to proceed in walk. Likewise, proceeding from trot to halt would require a little stronger action of the rider's legs (to engage the horse more) than would be necessary if the transition were from trot to walk. This is because, in preparation for a balanced transition from trot to halt, the horse has to step more underneath himself. Nevertheless, the basic process remains the same. The horse will ultimately have no difficulty in understanding the rider.

In principle, immediately before every transition, whether upward or downward, the rider should slightly shorten the steps by use of half-halts. These half-halts will ensure that the maximum effect will be gained from the transition, as the horse is prevented from losing engagement. The half-halts must be used quickly and with the appropriate timing so that the rider can avoid pulling on the horse. If the half-halts are used correctly, the horse will not feel restricted by the rider's hand and will be prepared to step more underneath himself with his inside hind leg, thereby increasing the engagement.

Using the reins by pulling or resisting in the transition only encourages the horse to go against the reins and becoming heavier in the hand. If this happens, the hind legs cannot step forward to take the horse's weight. The horse is then induced to leave his hind legs out behind him and fall onto his forehand because this will be the only way that he can effect the transition. Transitions such as these will never lead to the development of strength in the loins and hindquarters.

Riders should be aware that, in the early stages of training a young horse, what appear to be simple transitions actually require a great deal of effort and coordination from the horse. Therefore, they should allow sufficient time for the young horse to make the transitions correctly. Particularly weak horses may take a considerable distance to effect a transition and there will be a temptation for the rider to pull on the reins to make the horse slow down or change pace. The rider must be sure that he is constantly riding forward, giving the half-halts throughout the transition, no matter how long it takes.

Transitions to Canter

A slight variation occurs in the rider's aids for proceeding in canter. This is because of the natural asymmetry of the pace. In a transition to canter from any pace the horse always advances his inside shoulder further than his outside shoulder. Throughout the canter, the horse keeps this inside shoulder always a little in advance of the outside one. If the rider is not to interfere with the movement of the horse, it will be necessary for him to sit in a position that corresponds with the horse, that is, the rider's hips and shoulders should mirror those of the horse.

During the course of my teaching I have observed that many riders have been incorrectly taught the process of the transition into canter. This incorrect teaching is being promulgated by well-established 'names' within the sport and they are doing so at both the lowest and the highest levels. Many times I have come across riders who have been taught to sit in canter, especially on circles, bringing their inside shoulder back and the outside shoulder forward. This is incorrect and this teaching must be stopped. I believe that this has resulted from a misunderstanding propagated over time because of the lack of appreciation that the movement of the horse in canter is different from that in trot. It just requires a few minutes thought about how the horse actually moves in canter and then it becomes perfectly clear. Then, when riding circles, voltes and especially pirouettes in canter, remember that the horse's inside shoulder is always further forward than his outside shoulder. The smaller the circle, the more pronounced is this difference. So the rider's inside shoulder should never turn to the inside of the movement.

If the rider does turn his inside shoulder to the inside, just consider what will happen. In the first instance, the rider will be sitting out of harmony with his horse and he will feel uncomfortable. By turning to the inside, he will tend to bring his inside hip back a little. This produces a tendency to come back with the inside leg and forward with the outside leg. In addition, the rider's inside hip coming back a little will be enough to interfere with the freedom of movement of the horse's inside hind leg. This will be blocked and if the horse is a little stiff, he may change behind, or swing his hindquarters to the outside. The rider will tend to pull the horse around on a turn with the inside rein because now the horse will be unwilling or unable to bend correctly. The ultimate consequence is that the horse will never canter straight, he will never carry weight and it will be impossible to perform movements of a high level such as voltes, canter pirouettes or canter half-passes. In addition, the rider will have extreme difficulty teaching his horse to do flying changes!

It is important that riders understand why things are done in the way that they are. If they understand the reasons behind the method, all becomes logical and clear. As I have said before, riding is simple. Virtually everywhere that I have travelled, this has caused the greatest controversy. I find that I have to teach people right from the beginning again because the wrong method has become so ingrained. Riders are often astonished at how easy the canter becomes to sit, when asked to sit in the correct manner. What I am saying is not new. Wilhelm Müseler made it quite clear in his book *Riding Logic*, which was first published in 1933. As Müseler states, in canter it is the horse's whole musculature that is bent to the leading leg. Thus, it is easy to feel from the horse what is the correct position to be in. Only a rider who has learned to sit in harmony with his horse will understand the significance of this.

So, in preparation for a transition to canter from walk, the rider should ask for a very slight bend of the horse to the inside with a soft, suppling inside hand, whilst maintaining a good contact on the outside rein. In asking for the bend the rider will put his inside hip a little forward and his outside hip and leg back. The walk steps should first be shortened, just before the transition.

In the moment of the transition, the rider's inside leg at the girth gives the signal for moving forward into canter. It should be applied, in a slightly forward manner, towards the shoulder. The rider's outside leg is back behind the girth, but not moving, and it then has the effect of holding the hind legs on the track. At the same time, the rider allows a little in a slightly forwards and upwards movement with his soft inside hand – in such a way as to give the feeling that he invites the horse to take up the canter.

If the rider follows this procedure he prevents the horse from falling out with his hind legs – or from falling in because of too much use of the rider's outside leg. Thus, the rider can keep the horse straight in the transition to canter.

When executing a transition from trot to canter the rider must be careful that the horse does not speed up the steps immediately before cantering. This happens more often than not because the horse finds it more difficult to balance in the trot as he prepares to canter. This is described as 'running into canter'. As in the transition from walk to canter, the rider should prevent the horse from producing longer or more hurried steps. The effect of allowing the horse to 'run' either from walk or trot into canter reduces the usefulness of the particular transition as an aid to increased engagement and collection, as the horse falls onto his forehand and flattens his frame.

The horse finds it relatively easy to make a transition from walk to canter – even at an early stage in his training – because he is more balanced than in trot. It is also easier to make a transition that is a little 'uphill', in that the horse's shoulders stay up and the hindquarters remain engaged. There is a misconception that this is a difficult movement – or at least it would appear so, because most early level dressage tests contain transitions from trot into canter and back to trot. It is only later on, at Elementary or Medium, that the direct transition from walk is required in a dressage test. This is unfortunate because, unless they are carefully controlled, transitions from trot to canter only encourage horses to run into canter and these running transitions, as I have pointed out, have no value in the progressive training of the horse. Once a horse and rider have got into a habit of not doing transitions correctly, of course they will find it difficult to perform a walk/canter/walk transition. If there has been no discipline in the transition from the beginning, then the rider has to change his techniques halfway through the training process. This does not engender confidence in the horse.

Transitions within Paces

Transitions within paces, such as collected to medium to collected, or collected to extended to collected are performed in a similar manner.

Collecting and Extending the Walk

To collect the walk the rider should endeavour to maintain the activity of the steps with his legs whilst shortening the frame. It is of great importance that the horse is supple and lacking tension as any resistance will result in an irregularity of the walk. This is why it is not recommended that the walk be collected too much too early in the horse's training programme.

All too often, horses can be seen who are not regular in their walk; this is especially true of collected walk. Most of the time this is because the rider is holding back the horse with the reins. If the rider does this, the horse is not free in his movement, so he becomes tense and irregular. Pushing the horse too much also creates an irregularity as the horse is hurried out of his natural rhythm. It is most important that the rider sits free from any tension and in a well-balanced position in the saddle.

To extend the walk out of collected walk, the rider should slowly lengthen the reins. He can activate the lengthening by touching the horse once or twice with his inside leg, used slightly towards the shoulder. As the horse starts to reach for the bit, the rider allows him to take the rein out and then relaxes his legs. Thereafter, he should sit in the walk without tension and he will feel that his legs make a slight inward movement left and right and left and right as the horse's ribcage swings from side to side. There is a possible way of increasing the length of step in extended walk by using this natural movement of the rider's legs. If the rider, still without tension, increases the contact of his legs on the horse but in a slow rhythm, the horse will react by making longer steps.

Collecting and Extending the Trot

To collect the trot the rider performs a series of half-halts. These are a short taking, followed by a clear giving of the rein out of the wrist. A half-halt starts as the preparation for a transition to halt and just before the transition is completed, the rider rides forward again. The preparation for the downward transition has the effect of momentarily engaging the hind legs more, and riding strongly forwards again keeps the horse's weight over them for a few strides. In the beginning, with a young horse, these transitions take a little time since the horse is learning to find his balance as he engages his hind legs more. As training progresses, the transitions can be performed more quickly and more frequently. It can be seen that successive half-halts produce the result of collecting the trot and keeping it collected. A skilled rider who knows the value of the half-halt can keep a horse well collected and light in the forehand. This will allow the trot to become light and expressive.

Errors that occur in the execution of the extensions in a dressage test are frequently the result of the rider training the horse to extend incorrectly. The principle behind an extension is the same, regardless of pace. A good medium or extended trot comes out of a good collected trot.

In order to engage the hindquarters (which is necessary if the horse is not to run onto his forehand), the rider should press on both sides of the horse with his legs behind the girth, whilst keeping a good contact with the reins and his hands in a low position. In the early stages of training, the horse will try to increase speed and the rider should hold him back. Once he feels that the horse is trying to push from behind he should put his hands slightly forward and down a little, keeping his legs pressing on the horse's sides. This will encourage and allow the horse to lengthen his frame slightly and, if properly done, will produce a movement that is correct from the judge's point of view. The nose will stay in front of the vertical and the horse will push from behind. During the extension, it is important that the rider's hands and legs do not move. Any movement of the rider's hands or legs may disturb the movement of the horse and produce an irregularity in the rhythm.

For the transition from extension to collection the rider should release the pressure from his legs and make the horse supple with little suppling movements on the inside rein. If the horse has been pushing from behind correctly, this will have the effect of making the horse light in front and produce the feeling that he is growing taller in the transition.

The better the transition, the higher the overall mark, because if a judge sees a good medium or extended trot, he will already be looking to award a high mark. However, the transition is an important part of the movement and, if executed well, the judge may give a significantly higher mark for the whole movement.

The ability of a horse to demonstrate good medium and extended trots is largely dependent upon his natural ability and his strength. A horse who is not talented can be trained to show good extensions, but this takes a great deal of time and patience on behalf of the rider. However, many try to force the horse before he is ready and this results in the problems that I have referred to earlier. The horse becoming wide behind is a consequence of forcing him before he is strong enough. In particular, I would like here to mention the use of so called 'running reins'. Running reins used incorrectly can produce a typical way of going as shown in Figure 32. The back is stiff, the hocks are not engaged, the neck is 'broken' at about the third vertebra and the nose is behind the vertical. If a judge saw this demonstrated in a dressage test he would be unlikely to award a mark higher than 'sufficient'.

Figure 32 Extended trot showing the result of using running reins. The horse's back and neck are stiff. The horse's head is behind the vertical, the neck is 'broken' at about the third vertebra and he is pulling on the rider's hands.

Collecting and Extending the Canter

Again, many mistakes in the canter movements are caused by the rider asking the horse for the movement incorrectly. Collecting the canter is particularly difficult as the horse must maintain the impulsion and roundness of the stride but shorten the forward step across the ground. This can only be achieved through systematic, gymnastic training of the horse so that he is strong enough to carry more weight on his hindquarters. The rider must not simply slow down the horse. If he does so, the quality of the pace will be destroyed. In the collected canter, the hocks must remain active.

Achieving the medium or extended canter is similar in principle to achieving medium or extended trot. However, there is one difference and this relates to the innate energy of the collected canter. If the collected canter has been achieved correctly, there will be a lot of energy contained in the horse. Consequently, to ask for a medium or extended canter, all the rider has to do is to put his hands down and allow the horse to go forward without especially pushing him. This will allow the horse to take longer strides. If the horse is pushed, he will tend to become tense and simply go faster.

For the return transition to collection, the rider should maintain a firm contact with the outside rein, make the horse supple on the inside rein and, with clear half-halts (short taking and clear giving of the rein), indicate to the horse that he wishes him to shorten his stride. The only other thing the rider needs to do is to keep the horse in canter with a strong inside leg at the girth (touching the horse for every stride).

Judging Transitions

Changes of pace should be clearly shown at the marker prescribed in the test, executed quickly but smoothly, not abruptly. In principle, 'at the marker' means at the point where the rider's body is level with the marker. However, when a transition is required at the end of a diagonal, it should be executed as the horse's head arrives at the prescribed point. In other words, the transition should be performed on a straight line.

The more advanced a horse is in his training, the more precise the transitions can be. For example, the current Grand Prix Special test requires the horse to perform the transition from passage to extended trot in just a few strides, and the return transition from extended trot to passage in a similar fashion. These are very demanding transitions that require great strength in the horse's loins and hindquarters.

However, in lower level tests, transitions are regularly asked for between markers, allowing for the fact that a young horse is not yet ready to make clear transitions on demand. In such tests, even if a transition were required at a given marker, it would be quite acceptable if the horse performed the transition one or two metres before or after the marker, so long as the transition was of good quality. However, a high mark can be given if the good transition occurs exactly at the marker.

Clearly increased engagement of the hindquarters should be shown during transitions (even in working paces) and the horse should remain light on the bit and calm in the hand.

Transitions within paces are frequently performed poorly and may even not be obvious to the judge. They are an important part of the whole movement. A good transition can earn the rider more marks. Unfortunately, there is a tendency in some of the modern tests to separate the transitions from their associated movements, especially in extensions. In my opinion, this is a retrograde step because the transitions at the start and end of an extension are integral parts of that movement and belong to the extension. The transitions increase the level of engagement momentarily and are, therefore, essential tools for the development of and increase in collection. Without good transitions, the extension cannot be good. Besides this, requiring the judge to consider the transitions separately adds an extra stress because there is no time for the judge to make the appropriate remarks (which are very often necessary).

Several things may happen during the execution of the transition that may affect the judge's marks. In lower level tests, transitions are allowed to be progressive. However at Prix St Georges and above it is required that the horse moves directly into the new pace at a given point. Some examples of what may happen to affect the transition adversely are as follows:

- *Walk/halt*
  The horse should shorten the last steps before coming to the halt. This shows that the hindquarters are engaging and taking the weight in a balanced way. Any irregularity in the walk prior to the halt will result in a mark of no more than 'sufficient' for the whole movement.

- *Halt/trot*
  If walk steps are shown the judge is unlikely to award a mark of more than 'satisfactory'.

- *Trot/halt*
  If any walk steps are shown the mark cannot be more than 'sufficient'.

- *Trot/canter and canter/trot*
  If accelerated steps are shown in trot in the upward and downward transitions, the judge cannot give a mark more than 'sufficient'.

- *Walk/canter*

  If several trot steps are shown the mark cannot be more than 'sufficient'. An unclear transition into canter (because the first stride should be a clear canter stride) can never be more than 'satisfactory'.

- *Canter/walk*

  This should be a clear transition, but not abrupt, without any trot steps. If any trot steps are shown the mark cannot be more than 'sufficient'.

- *Canter/halt and halt/canter*

  Trot steps should not be shown; however, one walk step is acceptable and the transition can still be rated as 'satisfactory'.

Changes of Direction – Turns, Circles, Serpentines and Voltes

When changes of direction are made, the horse should adjust the bend of his body to the curvature of the line he is following. This bending should be performed without any resistance or change of pace. The movement must appear fluent and supple and the horse must not fall out, either with his shoulders or his hindquarters.

As mentioned in Chapter 2, when the horse is moving on a circle, he should bend according to the line of the circle. The hind legs should step on the same lines as the forelegs. Depending upon the level of training, the basic position of the horse's head should remain as it was on the straight line, but with flexion corresponding to the curve of the circle or turn. In other words, the poll should remain the highest point and the horse should stay steady on the bit. The horse should remain in balance and should maintain the regularity, rhythm and cadence of the required pace (see Figure 33).

Serpentines are figures that involve multiple changes of direction, joined by parts of circles. At the early stages of training, the horse is asked to perform a 'three-loop serpentine' which, if performed in a 20 m x 60 m arena, amounts to three 20 m half-circles joined together. As the horse becomes more supple and stronger, these half-circles can be reduced to 10 m or less.

The overall impression of a well-performed serpentine is the fluency of the movement. If the horse is falling out with his hindquarters and not bending, the change of direction clearly is 'not sufficient' and the judge will award a mark that reflects this and will tell the rider through his remarks what has to be improved.

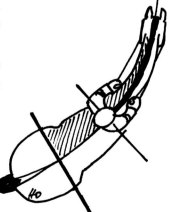

Figure 33 A horse travelling correctly through a corner.

Riding Turns, Circles, Serpentines and Voltes

There are some basic principles of riding these figures that need to be emphasized. I have mentioned before that, to execute a turn or circle correctly, the horse must stay upright and not lean inwards. In order to do this and to counteract the forces acting on his body, the horse transfers his weight a little towards the inside of the circle. The rider must sit correctly – that is, he must also adjust his weight towards the inside to remain in balance with his horse (Figure 34). At the same time, the rider should keep his shoulders parallel to the horse's shoulders and his hips parallel to the horse's hips (in canter, the rider's inside hip should be a little forwards). The rider should not collapse the inside hip as shown in Figure 35, neither should he turn his shoulders too much to the inside.

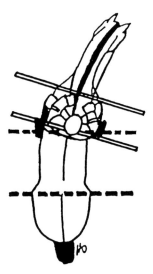

Figure 35 Showing a rider with collapsed inside hip on a circle or turn. The rider's inside stirrup leather can be seen to appear shorter because he has collapsed his hip. This illustration also shows the horse tilting his head – he is not bending correctly.

Figure 34 The correct seat of a rider going through a circle or a turn. The rider's shoulders are at the same angle as the horse's shoulders while the rider's hips match the horse's hips.

The rider's position is of great importance, as it is only by using his legs and hands correctly that he can bend his horse. The rider's outside leg should be behind the girth (to hold the horse's hind legs on the track), the inside leg should be at the girth (normal position) and is used to push the horse forward. The horse can then bend around the rider's inside leg. The rider's outside hand should be steady and low, not stiff but with a firm contact. The inside hand should be light, suppling the horse and producing the bend without pulling.

There is a great temptation to pull the horse onto the circle with the inside hand, especially if the horse is stiff and unwilling to bend. However, if the rider resists this temptation and, instead, supples the horse's mouth with his inside hand whilst maintaining contact with the outside rein, and uses his inside leg at the correct position on the girth with his outside leg behind the girth, the horse will eventually submit and bend his body. The horse must not be forced to bend. Too often, riders can be seen pulling on the inside rein and bending only the horse's neck. This has a twofold result. First, of course, it does not bend the horse's body, but only his neck. Second, it blocks the action of the horse's inside hind leg and prevents him from bringing it forward correctly, thus making it impossible for him to bend. The inevitable consequence is that the horse falls out with his hindquarters.

Incorrect riding of circles and turns can be seen at all levels of performance. Riders and trainers should be especially vigilant with young horses, because performing a correct circle might be difficult for the horse and he will look for ways to avoid engaging his inside hind leg. The rider easily falls into the trap of pulling on the inside rein because the horse appears stiff. Once this has started as a habit it is difficult to change.

I am most particular about the riding of circles and turns because these are the foundations upon which all advanced work is based. Only those riders who understand the importance and significance of correct bend will be able to develop the physique of their horse to enable him to collect. Without correct bend, progressing to the performance of high quality lateral movements is impossible.

Judging Turns and Circles

A horse who is not bent when going through a corner is either not submissive, or is not being ridden correctly. Although, during a test, a corner does not have a specific mark allocated to it, the way in which a horse goes through a corner gives the judge a very good indication of the degree of submission and straightness. The judge will therefore take this into account when assessing the horse's general way of going and also the ability of the rider, especially his use of the aids.

On a circle, the horse must maintain the same rhythm and tempo as on a straight line. Sometimes, however, it can be seen that a horse speeds up on a circle. Speeding up on a circle means either that the rider has ridden the horse too fast onto the circle, or else he has pulled the horse onto the circle with the inside rein and the horse has increased speed in order not to lose his balance. As a result, on most occasions, the horse will then lose his hindquarters to the outside or completely fall out of the circle.

Many things can happen during the execution of a circle or turn that will affect the mark that a judge gives. Some examples are:

- If the horse is not bending correctly and his quarters are falling out, this is a basic fault and the mark must be 'insufficient' (Figure 36).

- A horse 'crossing out' with the inside hind leg, which means that the inside hind leg is moving in the general direction of the outside foreleg or even further out, is showing that he is not bending correctly and the mark cannot be more than 'sufficient'.

- If the horse's head is a little too low and slightly behind the vertical throughout the whole movement, the mark cannot be more than 'satisfactory'.

- A horse accelerates on a circle if he loses his balance. Where there is a clear loss of balance, the mark cannot be more than 'sufficient'. However, if this is relatively minor, then the circle might still be considered to be 'satisfactory'.

- If, as is seen often, the horse's head is pulled to the inside and the neck shows more bend than necessary for the size of the circle, the mark cannot be more than 'sufficient' (Figure 37).

- A horse clearly tilting his head on a circle indicates that he does not bend (see Figure 35). This could be considered to be a resistance to bend and cannot be more than 'sufficient'. However, if the horse is only slightly tilting his head on the circle, the mark might just be 'satisfactory'.

- Where irregularities of pace occur on the circle, the judge will penalise these as mentioned before in Chapter 4.

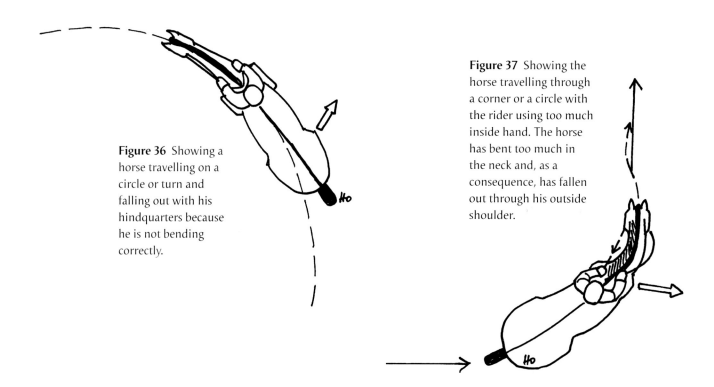

Figure 36 Showing a horse travelling on a circle or turn and falling out with his hindquarters because he is not bending correctly.

Figure 37 Showing the horse travelling through a corner or a circle with the rider using too much inside hand. The horse has bent too much in the neck and, as a consequence, has fallen out through his outside shoulder.

CHAPTER SIX

MOVEMENTS AND EXERCISES

The Halt

The halt can be considered to be a test of obedience and submission. In dressage tests there is a requirement for a period of immobility immediately following the halt. In halt the horse must stand motionless but attentive, with his weight distributed evenly on all four legs, standing square (Figure 38). To a degree commensurate with his level of training, his neck should be raised, with the poll being the highest point, and his face should be a little in front of the vertical. Throughout the halt the horse should remain lightly on the bit.

The transitions into and out of the halt are integral parts of the halting process and they should be smooth and balanced, with engagement of the hindquarters. The transition to halt should be well prepared and the rider should slightly shorten the steps of the pace just before the halt by an active engagement of the hindquarters. The procedures for riding the transitions into and out of the halt have already been described in the previous chapter. Whilst in halt the rider must endeavour to sit absolutely still and not disturb the horse. Immobility is one of the most important aspects of this exercise. There is no excuse for badly performed halts from the point of view of the horse's immobility. It is simply a matter of discipline and training. As part of the training process, the rider should regularly ask for correct halts and should sustain them for longer and longer periods.

Judging the Halt

Depending on what the judge sees during the execution of the halt he will mark it with respect to the FEI ideal. The closer the performance conforms to the description above, the higher will be the mark awarded. To attain a mark between 'fairly good' and

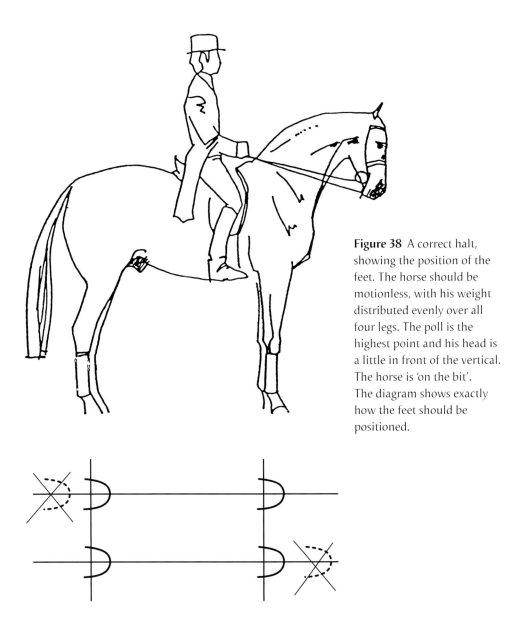

Figure 38 A correct halt, showing the position of the feet. The horse should be motionless, with his weight distributed evenly over all four legs. The poll is the highest point and his head is a little in front of the vertical. The horse is 'on the bit'. The diagram shows exactly how the feet should be positioned.

'excellent' the horse should always be straight, square, well engaged and on the bit. However, it is the quality of the transitions that will determine whether the mark is, in the end, 'excellent' or just 'fairly good'.

The way that a rider performs the halt will give the judge a very good indication of his ability. Here are some examples of what might go wrong and how the judge is likely to respond:

- If the horse is not absolutely square with all four legs, but has the hindquarters well engaged, then the judge may still award a mark of 'satisfactory'. An adjustment forward to achieve a squaring up would also be acceptable.

A very correct halt that also shows the rider's position at the moment of the salute Isabell Werth riding *Gigolo* at the Olympic Games, Sydney 2000. (Photo: HorseSource/P. Llewellyn)

- If the horse does not remain steady on the bit (a little below or above), the judge can still award a mark of 'satisfactory'.

- If the horse does not stand straight then the judge is unlikely to give a mark of more than 'satisfactory' and is more likely to give a mark of 'sufficient'.

- However, if the horse does not stand still or shows clear resistance, the judge will always mark the halt no higher than 'insufficient'.

- If a horse shows a step back in the halt then either he is not submissive or the rider is too hard or too rough with his hand. Another possibility is that the rider does not engage his horse's hindquarters enough. An example of the appearance of a rough, abrupt transition to halt is shown in Figure 39. Stepping back in the halt with one or more legs should always be marked as 'insufficient'.

Figure 39 A rough, abrupt transition to halt. The rider is leaning backwards and pulls on the reins!

The Rein-back

The rein-back is a retrograde movement in which the feet are raised and set down simultaneously by diagonal pairs. The horse remains 'on the bit', maintaining his desire to move forward (Figure 40). There should be no lowering or lifting of the horse's head. The poll remains the highest point and the horse's nose should remain a little in front of the vertical. There should be no resistance to the rider's request to step backwards. The horse should lift and put down his feet clearly and not drag them backwards. The horse should not rush backwards.

Riding the Rein-back

The principles of riding the rein-back are, as usual, simple and easy to explain to the horse. If applied correctly they will result in a rein-back that will satisfy the judge. In principle, the rein-back is a request from the rider to move forwards, immediately followed by a denial as the rider prevents this movement with his hands. If the horse is supple and obedient, this will immediately result in the intended forward movement being converted into a backward movement. The procedure is as follows.

In the halt the rider should move both legs back behind the girth. He should squeeze with both legs (to engage the horse's hind legs) and at the same time, with light hands, supple the horse in his mouth by giving tiny half-halts, using just his fingers or wrists. *The rider should not pull on the reins and should not lean back.*

The horse will start to move forwards but must not be allowed to do so. When

Figure 40 A correct rein-back. The horse is on the bit with the poll remaining the highest point. There is no apparent resistance to the rider's aids.

the horse feels this slight resistance of the rider's hands, he will immediately step backwards.

During the rein-back the rider should keep the horse light and supple on both reins and squeeze with his legs for as long as he wants to go backwards.

In order to move forwards, the rider should place both legs forward in a normal position at the girth and give both of the reins slightly forward.

At all times during rein-back, the rider must feel that if he allowed the horse to move forward he would immediately revert to a forward direction. The movement requires coordination of the rider's hands and legs. In the beginning, when the rider is training the horse to rein-back, he must reward the slightest tendency of the horse to move backwards with a relaxation of the rein. In this way the horse will learn to move back with confidence and with a rounded back.

The action of moving backwards automatically engages the horse's hindquarters and this exercise can be used to strengthen the hindquarters and encourage the horse to take weight on the hind legs. However, the rein-back must be used with caution with a young horse, as it is easy to damage underdeveloped or weak back muscles by overdoing this exercise.

Pulling on the reins in an attempt to get the horse to move backwards will only result in the horse performing the movement incorrectly and will create discomfort and resistance in the horse. Rushing backwards is an indication that the horse is trying to avoid the rider's aids. Many problems with the rein-back are caused by the rider asking incorrectly or being impatient with the horse.

Judging the Rein-back

In order for a high mark to be awarded for a rein-back, the movement should appear as described above and there should be no resistance to the rider's aids. The movement should be fluent and the horse should step back with confidence, without dragging his feet. There are many things that can go wrong in a rein-back, usually caused by the rider asking the horse in the wrong way. Some of these faults are discussed below:

- If the footfalls are not clearly diagonal the mark can still be 'satisfactory' so long as all other criteria are satisfied.

- Lowering the head or coming behind the vertical, sometimes termed 'diving' (Figure 41), cannot be more than 'satisfactory'.

- Inactive, spreading hind legs (losing the balance) can possibly still be considered to be 'satisfactory'.

- Anticipation or precipitation of the movement can never be more than 'sufficient'.

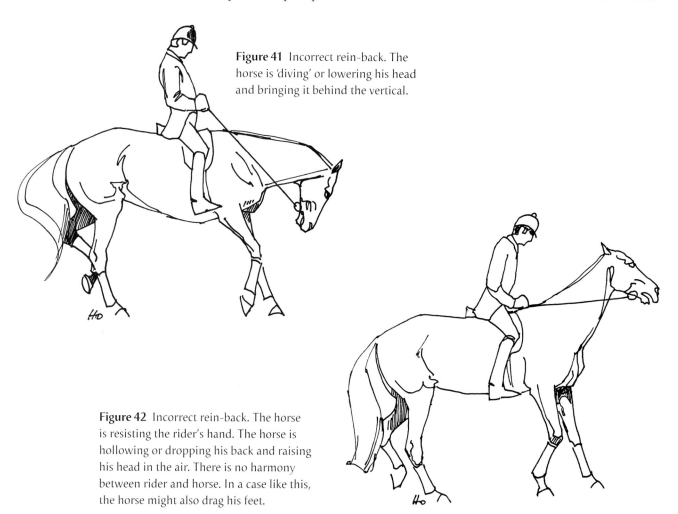

Figure 41 Incorrect rein-back. The horse is 'diving' or lowering his head and bringing it behind the vertical.

Figure 42 Incorrect rein-back. The horse is resisting the rider's hand. The horse is hollowing or dropping his back and raising his head in the air. There is no harmony between rider and horse. In a case like this, the horse might also drag his feet.

- Deviation from the straight line cannot be more than 'sufficient'.

- A horse dragging the forefeet cannot be more than 'sufficient'.

- Resistance to, or evasion of the hand is always 'insufficient' or less (Figure 42).

The Schaukel

The movement known as the schaukel comprises some steps in rein-back followed immediately by some forward steps, followed by more steps in rein-back and then again moving forward. It is a demonstration of submission and obedience. The rider should attempt this movement only after the rein-back has been well established and can be executed without resistance or other difficulties.

Judging the schaukel

To gain a high mark the horse should be very fluent in his changes of direction from forwards to backwards to forwards. This is the most important aspect of the movement beside the basic requirements of the rein-back.

- If the movement involves a 'half-step' before moving forwards or backwards at the change of direction, it can still be considered 'fairly good'.

- The same mark might be awarded if the number of steps was not exactly as prescribed but if everything else was correct.

Counter-canter

Counter-canter is a movement in which the horse is, for example, cantering on the right lead but is travelling on the left rein. It is a suppling movement. The horse should remain slightly flexed at the poll towards the inside (which means to the leading leg).

Counter-canter supples and strengthens the horse because he has to travel around the arena, at times on a curved line, in one direction whilst remaining flexed to the opposite direction. At all times the horse must remain upright (that is, he must not lean over). This results in him having to take more weight on the outside leg. The tendency always is for the horse to bring his hindquarters to the outside to avoid the effort. The rider must endeavour to prevent this by keeping his position very clear and by sitting correctly, as described earlier, in the direction of the canter lead. The rider's outside leg (of the canter) should be used a little more strongly to help the horse but care should be taken to keep the horse's shoulders properly in front of the hindquarters.

In principle, the quality of the canter should not change and the balance and the impulsion should be maintained.

Judging the Counter-canter

To award a high mark, the judge will be looking for suppleness, balance and ease in the movement. The rhythm and quality of the canter should be maintained. Examples of errors in the counter-canter that will influence the judge's mark are as follows:

- If the horse clearly pushes the hindquarters to the outside, the mark cannot be more than 'satisfactory'.

- An unsteady, bobbing head cannot be more than 'satisfactory'.

The Simple Change

A simple change is a change of lead in canter through walk. Depending upon the level of the test being performed, the horse should clearly show two to five steps in walk before he resumes the canter with the other leg leading. The most important components of this movement are the transitions from canter to walk and walk to canter. These must be submissive, clear, smooth and balanced and must show engagement of the hindquarters.

When this movement is asked for in lower level dressage tests in some countries, concessions are made to allow the downward transition to be progressive, that is, the horse is permitted to come from canter to walk through a few steps of trot. Upward transitions are supposed to be direct. In my opinion, this is not actually helping the rider or the horse to progress. While the judges accept that a canter to walk transition through trot is still 'sufficient', riders will not bother to make clear canter to walk transitions. It is only if the judging fraternity states that canter/walk/canter is specifically required that riders will be forced to train for this sequence of transitions. I have always advocated that a horse should not compete in a dressage test until he can do canter/walk/canter! If it is required in the test, the riders will train the horses to do it.

Judging the Simple Change

To award a high mark, the judge will be looking for a general sense of fluency and submission in the transitions within the movement, and clear rhythm in the paces. The horse must remain straight in the transitions, and all other requirements for the particular transitions apply. If all the requirements can be satisfied, the marks can range from 'satisfactory' to 'excellent'. Examples of errors that can occur and their likely effects on the mark are as follows:

- If trot steps are shown the mark cannot be more than 'sufficient'.

- If no clear walk steps are shown the mark is always 'insufficient'.

- If the transitions are not straight, the mark cannot be more than 'satisfactory'.

The Flying Change

This is a movement that requires the horse to change canter lead in the moment of suspension of the canter. Flying changes are asked for individually, and also in sequences of every fourth, third and second stride, and every stride. In all cases, the horse should remain calm and light. The flying change should occur without a loss of impulsion. The jumps should be clearly forward and fluent, giving the appearance of the horse moving slightly 'uphill' (Figure 43). To perform a flying change, the horse must keep his balance and be strong enough to jump from one canter lead to the other whilst maintaining his self-carriage.

It is important that the quality and balance of the canter is maintained whether there is a single change, or a series of changes. The change must be 'clean', that is, the new leading fore and hind legs must come forward at the same time. The horse should remain on the bit throughout the movement. Whether performing a single change or a series of changes, the horse should remain straight and not 'swing' from side to side.

Figure 43 A correct flying change should look like this. The change appears to be forward and slightly 'uphill'.

It is important that the rider rides forward throughout the change or series of changes. The quality of the change is a reflection of the quality of the canter. Therefore, a canter without enough collection or impulsion is unlikely to produce a good quality flying change. In the beginning, many horses find the change exciting and have a tendency to run away. This results in the rider tending to hold the horse back during the change. Once this starts to happen, the change is no longer forward (Figure 44) and a frequent result is that the horse swings his hindquarters to one side as he performs the change. Swinging from side to side in the changes may also be caused by overuse of the rider's legs, or even the spurs. Not riding forward in the change, or not enough collection in the canter can also produce a flying change that is 'high behind', which means that the horse throws his hindquarters upwards during the change instead of bringing his hind legs under and forward (Figure 45).

Judging the Flying Changes

A horse showing the right number of strides and changes, and being straight in the movement, the changes clearly upwards and forward, should be awarded at least a 'good' mark and may even be 'very good' or 'excellent'. When judging the flying changes there are some problems that can occur. Some examples are as follows:

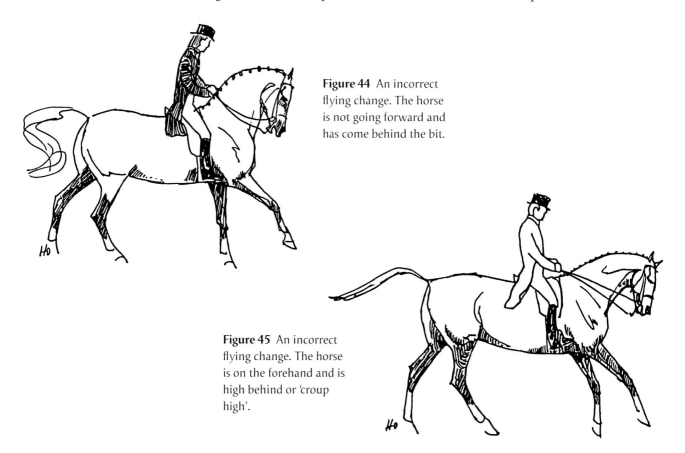

Figure 44 An incorrect flying change. The horse is not going forward and has come behind the bit.

Figure 45 An incorrect flying change. The horse is on the forehand and is high behind or 'croup high'.

A flying change clearly showing an 'uphill' tendency. Ulla Salzgeber riding *Rusty*. (Photo: HorseSource/ P. Llewellyn)

- A horse making no mistakes in a series and being moderately straight can be marked as 'fairly good'.

- A horse making no mistakes, but who is crooked (swinging or deviating sideways) may still be 'satisfactory'.

- A horse making one mistake in the changes can never be more than 'satisfactory'.

- More than one mistake occurring in a series of changes will always be 'insufficient'.

- A horse running onto the forehand and coming high behind ('croup high') in a single change is likely to receive a mark of no more than 'sufficient' (Figure 45).

- A horse not coming through with one hind leg, or being late behind or in front in a single change is 'insufficient'.

- When a flying change is required in medium canter and, as happens often, the rider slows and/or shortens the canter before the change and only rides forward after the change, the rider is more or less cheating and should not be given a high mark (never more than 'sufficient' or 'satisfactory')!

CHAPTER SEVEN

LATERAL MOVEMENTS AND EXERCISES

WORK ON TWO TRACKS ENCOMPASSES leg-yielding, shoulder-in, travers, renvers and half-pass. Why do we train the horse to perform these exercises? Because they increase the horse's obedience and make the horse supple. Specifically, they increase the freedom of his shoulders and the suppleness of his hindquarters. In addition, when performed correctly, the lateral movements (with the exception of leg-yielding) increase engagement and improve the horse's strength and balance.

Leg-yielding

Leg-yielding is primarily a training movement to supple and prepare the horse for collected paces and the more difficult lateral movements. Leg-yielding literally means that the horse is 'yielding to the leg' in response to the rider asking him to move away from sideways pressure of the leg. The movement is rarely required in dressage tests, except occasionally at the lower levels. There are different opinions on the usefulness, or otherwise, of this movement, as some trainers feel that it has little value and that it can confuse the horse. Leg-yielding can be performed at all paces and at different places in the arena (see Figure 46), depending on the result that the trainer wants to achieve. No matter where it is performed, the requirements of leg-yielding are the same and are as follows:

• The horse should be straight in his body, with a slight natural flexion at the poll.

• The horse looks away from the direction in which he is moving.

- The horse should move forwards and sideways fluently, without losing balance.

- The horse should cross his inside legs over in front of his outside legs as he moves sideways.

Riding a Correct Leg-yield

To ask for leg-yielding, the rider simply maintains a normal pace (trot, for example) and, whilst keeping the horse straight in the neck by maintaining a firm contact on the outside rein, he supples the horse to the inside with his inside hand and pushes the horse across to the outside with his inside leg. The outside leg remains in place. It might be necessary in the early stages to move the inside leg back a little to ensure

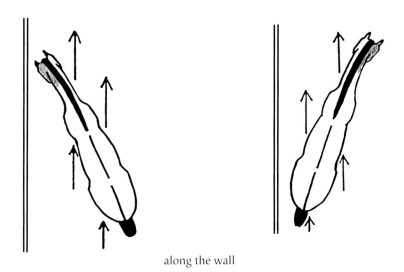

along the wall

Figure 46 Leg-yielding can be performed along the wall or away from the wall, or on the diagonal.

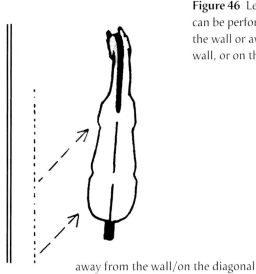

away from the wall/on the diagonal

that the hindquarters move across to the same extent as the forehand. If the rider is leg-yielding from the inside track to the wall, the aim should be to keep the horse's body parallel to the wall. This principle of parallel progression will apply wherever the movement is carried out.

In the early stages the horse may have difficulty coordinating his movement and may fall out through the shoulder. In this case the rider should stop asking for the leg-yield and ride forwards strongly. When the horse is again travelling forwards and straight, the rider should ask the horse for leg-yielding once more. In this way the rider may produce a few steps sideways followed by a few steps forwards. Only when the horse obeys the forwards and sideways driving aids respectively can he be said to be competent in the movement. Throughout the movement the horse should remain softly on the bit and should demonstrate a degree of self-carriage. The rhythm, speed and fluency should be maintained.

Principles of Other Lateral Movements

Shoulder-in, travers, renvers and half-pass are all movements that continually increase the engagement of the hindquarters. This is because, unlike leg-yielding, they all require a degree of bend in the horse's body. As a consequence of a combination of these two factors, they also result in an increase in collection. The experienced trainer can use any of these movements to help him in the process of producing the athletic horse that he needs to perform at the highest competitive levels. Depending on the direction in which the horse is travelling, one hind leg has to work continuously a little harder than the other in the different movements and the skill of the rider comes in knowing which particular movement is appropriate at any particular time, depending on the degree of progress in the horse's training. Shoulder-in, travers, renvers and half-pass can be ridden at all paces in training while, in competition, shoulder-in, travers and half-pass are all required in trot, but half-pass is also required in canter. Riding these movements in walk can be dangerous because the horse may lose his tendency to go forward.

As with all the exercises on two tracks, one evasion that the horse may attempt is to increase the tempo of the pace. The horse speeds up because he loses his balance, and he loses his balance because the rider asks too much. The rider must take care to ensure that he asks only as much as the horse is capable of doing without losing the quality of the pace.

Shoulder-in

As has already been explained, shoulder-in can be performed in walk and trot and, technically speaking, in canter. Shoulder-in in canter is used by some trainers but, in my experience, there is a danger that the horse may become used to not being straight in canter.

In dressage tests it is usually required in trot along the side of the arena, but it may also be asked for on the centre line. When performed correctly in trot, this movement should produce an improvement in the quality of the pace, which can be seen as an increase in the degree of elevation and suspension in the trot. The trot can be said to appear to 'grow' throughout the movement.

When performed in walk, shoulder-in can cause problems because the horse may lose activity and the desire to move forwards. Therefore, it should be used sparingly in walk especially when training a young horse.

The requirements of this movement are laid down in the FEI rules and can be summarized as follows:

- The horse should be slightly bent from the poll to the tail around the rider's inside leg and he should look away from the direction in which he is moving.

- The horse's inside foreleg should pass and cross in front of the outside foreleg.

The correct position of the horse with respect to the wall is shown in Figure 47. Figures 48(a) and (b) show how a correctly ridden shoulder-in should look when viewed from in front and behind respectively. The amount of bend should be such that three tracks can be clearly seen.

Riding a Correct Shoulder-in

Much confusion exists about shoulder-in but it is, in fact, quite a straightforward exercise. It depends entirely on the rider's ability to bend the horse. If the horse cannot bend correctly on an 8 m circle, he cannot be expected to perform a shoulder-in. Preparation for teaching the shoulder-in requires the horse to travel on an 8 m circle whilst developing and establishing the bend on that circle. Next, the rider should attempt to advance down the track keeping the same degree of bend. The rider does this by keeping everything the same and, as the horse takes the first step of what would be the next circle, the rider resists the tendency to circle with his outside hand and, at the same time, pushes the horse along the track with his inside leg (which is at the girth). In other words, the rider's position and aids are the same as if he were riding a circle, but the outside hand prevents the horse from moving onto a circle as soon as the forehand is on the inside track. The rider's inside leg at the girth pushes the horse forward along the track and maintains the bend while the outside leg stays

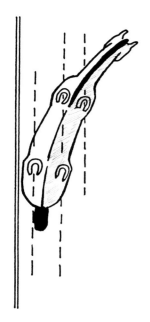

Figure 47 Shoulder-in. The bend should be such that three tracks can be clearly seen.

Figures 48 (a) and (b) Shoulder-in. The appearance of a correctly ridden shoulder-in when viewed from in front (a) and from behind (b).

a.

b.

back behind the girth. Shoulder-in could perhaps be described as riding forwards on a line with bend.

The inside leg should *never* push the hindquarters out and therefore should remain at the girth. Frequently, I have seen riders trying to produce a shoulder-in by taking their inside leg back behind the girth. This is completely incorrect, as they are effectively preventing the horse from bending and they are pushing the hindquarters to the outside. Also, the rider must never pull on the inside rein in an attempt to create, or maintain bend. Pulling just creates resistance, too much bend in the neck and blocks the action of the inside hind leg. All of these consequences are, in turn, liable to create irregularities and deterioration in the pace, which will be marked down by the judge.

Judging the Shoulder-in

Many things can go wrong during the execution of a shoulder-in and the judge must be aware of these problems so that his mark and comments can assist the rider in improving the quality of the movement.

A high mark can be given when the horse fulfils the requirements of the movement and maintains a cadenced, regular, good quality trot, showing suppleness and submission throughout. The angle of the horse to the track should not vary throughout the movement.

Depending upon where the judge is sitting, he may have very different views of the shoulder-in and it may be difficult for him to assess the movement. However, if he concentrates on seeing whether there is bend and whether the horse is moving regularly forward – aspects that can be seen from any position – he will be able to give a mark of at least 'satisfactory'.

How much bend is required? The correct degree of bend is the same as that required for an 8 m circle. Excessive bend and deviation from the straight line lead to irregularities in the pace and the horse consequently ceases to move forwards enough; thus the movement loses its fluency. Frequently, riders produce attempts at shoulder-in in which they have a lot of angle but very little bend. In such cases they are not really demonstrating shoulder-in; the movement is more like leg-yielding.

A horse who becomes irregular during a shoulder-in might not be supple enough; the rider may be sitting incorrectly; or the horse may be losing balance because he has not been trained correctly.

A horse who accelerates in shoulder-in, or indeed in any of the lateral movements, is not well balanced and tries to regain his balance by increasing the tempo of his steps.

Some of the problems that occur in the shoulder-in, and the likely effects on the marks awarded, are listed below:

- If the horse does not bend correctly, the mark can never be more than 'sufficient'.

- If the horse demonstrates head tilting (as a result of incorrect bend), the mark can never be more than 'sufficient'.

- If the horse loses the regularity of the basic pace, the mark can never be more than 'sufficient'.

- A shoulder-in showing a changing position (varying angle) can never be more than 'satisfactory'.

- When the horse clearly falls out through the shoulder (Figure 49), he does not show the correct bend and the mark cannot be 'sufficient'.

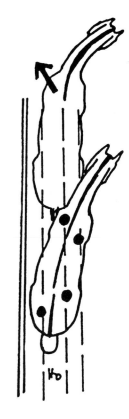

Figure 49 Shoulder-in showing the horse falling out through the shoulder.

Travers, Renvers and Half-pass — Relationship and Requirements

Travers, renvers and half-pass are, in principle, the same movement, described differently depending on its relationship to the track. The requirements for all of these movements are as follows:

- The horse is slightly bent around the rider's inside leg.

- The horse looks in the direction in which he is moving.

- The outside legs pass and cross in front of the inside legs.

- The same degree of cadence and balance should be maintained throughout the movement.

- The desire of the horse to go forwards should be clearly seen and has priority over the degree of sideways movement.

- The regularity and fluency of the basic pace throughout the whole movement is of great importance.

Travers

In travers, the forehand remains on the track whilst the hindquarters are displaced to the inside (Figure 50). The appearance of a correctly ridden travers, viewed from in front and from behind, is shown in Figures 51(a) and (b). The outside hind leg steps towards the horse's centre of gravity and, therefore, takes slightly more weight than the inside hind leg. Travers can demonstrate slightly more bend than shoulder-in and it is correct to see four tracks when it is viewed from in front. However, care should be taken not to bring the hindquarters too much to the inside, otherwise the horse can no longer move freely forwards and might lose the regularity of the pace.

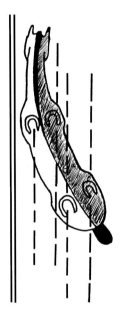

Figure 50 Travers.

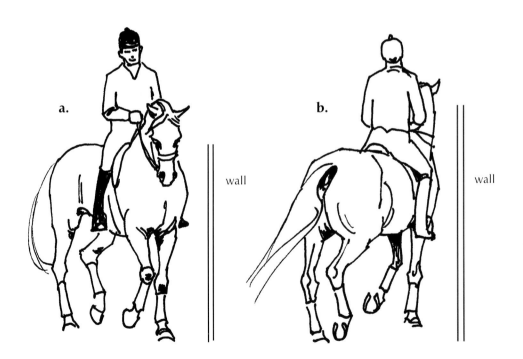

Figures 51 (a) and (b) Showing the appearance of a correctly ridden travers viewed from in front (a) and from behind (b).

Renvers

In renvers, the hindquarters remain on the track and it is the forehand that is displaced to the inside (Figure 52). Figures 53(a) and (b) show the appearance of a correctly ridden renvers viewed from in front and from behind. When renvers is ridden on the same rein as in the previous diagram of travers, because of the opposite bend, the outside hind leg is now the opposite one to that of the travers. So, it can be seen that the rider can work the hindquarters of the horse accordingly without changing rein.

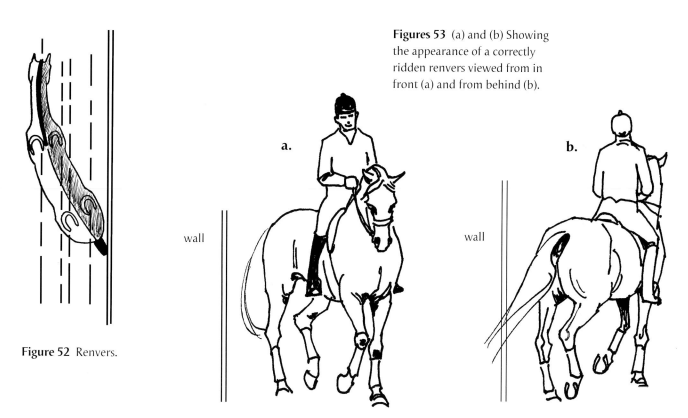

Figure 52 Renvers.

Figures 53 (a) and (b) Showing the appearance of a correctly ridden renvers viewed from in front (a) and from behind (b).

a.

b.

wall

wall

Half-pass

Half-pass is a variation of travers which is executed along the diagonal instead of along the wall (Figure 54). The horse's body should be almost parallel to the long side of the arena, however, the forehand should always be slightly in front of (leading) the hindquarters. The engagement of the hindquarters and the freedom of the shoulders are most important in this movement. The shorter the half-pass (that is, the steeper the angle of travel), the more bend is required. Figures 55(a) and (b) show the

Figure 56 Lateral work – the relationship between shoulder-in, travers, renvers and half-pass.

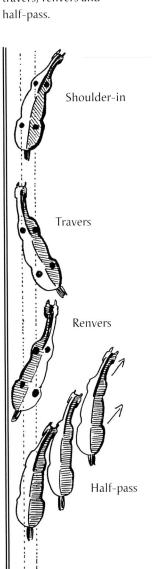

Shoulder-in

Travers

Renvers

Half-pass

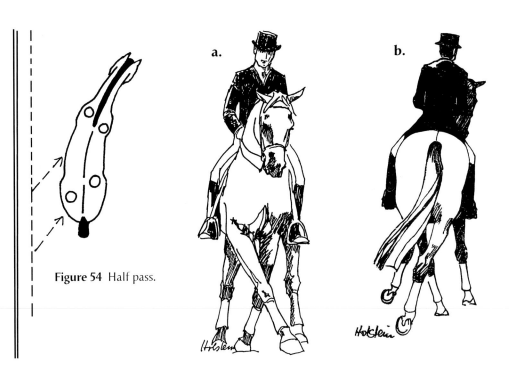

Figure 54 Half pass.

Figure 55 (a) and (b) Showing a correctly ridden half-pass viewed from the front (a) and from behind (b).

appearance of a correctly ridden half-pass viewed from both in front and behind respectively. Figure 56 shows the relationship between the three movements: travers, renvers and half-pass.

Riding a Correct Half-pass

As with the shoulder-in, the objective is to ride the movement with the horse correctly bent, moving forward on a line that, in this case, is the diagonal of the arena.

The rider should bend the horse by suppling him with the inside rein and should maintain a good contact on the outside rein, while tending to move his outside hand towards the withers. The outside hand should remain in a low position.

The rider should ride the horse strongly forwards and not be too preoccupied with riding the horse sideways. At the moment that the rider starts to simply ride sideways, the quality of the whole movement deteriorates and irregularities start to become apparent. In addition, the horse may start to lead with the hindquarters.

The rider's outside leg should be back while the inside leg remains at the girth, maintaining the bend and pushing the horse forward. The rider's outside shoulder should be slightly forward, following the outside foreleg of the horse, which is also slightly forward.

ABOVE Half-pass left. The horse and rider are in a very good position. Pia Laus on *Renoir*. ABOVE RIGHT Half-pass right. Pia Laus on *Renoir*. (Photos: H. Czerny)

From the beginning, the rider's weight must be positioned towards the inside. The rider must take care not to collapse his hips, and his shoulders should stay almost parallel to the horse's shoulders. In fact, the rider's position should be such that he looks towards the direction of travel of the horse (Figure 57).

Judging the Half-pass

A high mark can be given if the judge sees a clear bend in the horse, the pace is regular, the horse is in the correct position (forehand slightly in advance) and there is fluency in the whole movement. If these criteria are fulfilled, then the mark awarded is likely to be between 'fairly good' and

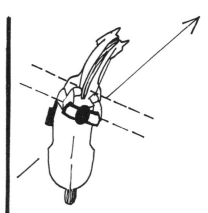

Figure 57 The rider's position in half-pass should be such that he looks in the direction of travel of the horse.

ABOVE Half-pass to the left showing the crossing of the hind legs. Christine Stückelberger riding *Aquamarin*. (Photo: K-H. Frieler)

ABOVE RIGHT Half-pass to the left showing the forelegs crossing. (Photo: E. Weiland)

'excellent'. If, in addition, the horse demonstrates a pace of high quality, which is expressive, with the freedom in the shoulders producing good crossing of both sets of legs, then a very high mark is appropriate.

Some of the problems that can occur during the execution of all the various lateral movements, but in particular the half-pass, are listed below, along with the likely effect on the judge's marks:

• A lack of regularity and/or fluency cannot produce a mark more than 'satisfactory'.

• A horse showing insufficient forward motion might possibly still be considered 'satisfactory'.

• A horse showing insufficient crossover in half-pass might possibly still be considered 'satisfactory'. The degree of crossover is related to the horse's athletic development, the freedom of the shoulders and his ability to take his weight on one or other hind leg. For a high mark, the judge wants to see as much crossover of both sets of legs as possible. Nevertheless, if everything else is correct and this is the only deficiency, a mark of 'satisfactory' would be acceptable.

- If, in the half-pass, the hindquarters are pushed across too much, the horse becomes wrongly positioned (the hind legs are leading) and he can no longer move regularly and fluently forwards. In such a case the mark cannot be more than 'sufficient'.

- If the horse shows insufficient bend or loses the bend during the movement, resulting in the hindquarters trailing, the mark cannot be more than 'sufficient'.

- When the movement is too hurried (losing balance) or irregular it cannot be considered 'sufficient'.

- A tilted head, as shown in Figure 58, indicates lack of bend and cannot be considered more than 'sufficient'.

- If the rider sits incorrectly by pushing the inside shoulder forwards or collapsing his hip (Figure 58), the horse stops moving forwards fluently and may even become irregular. This cannot be more than 'sufficient' and may even be less.

- A horse without clear bend should not be considered to be more than 'insufficient'.

The Counter-change of Hand

This is a movement in which the horse performs a half-pass in one direction followed immediately by a half-pass in the opposite direction. It can be performed in trot or in canter. In trot, the dressage test dictates the number of changes of direction required and the distance to be travelled laterally during each half-pass. In canter, the horse is required to perform a flying change at each change of direction after a prescribed number of strides of half-pass.

Riding a Correct Counter-change of Hand

As stated previously in the comments about the half-pass, the most important aspects of the movement in both paces are to keep the correct position, bend and fluency of the movement. The rider must take care to ride the horse forwards during the change of bend in the same way as in a change of direction, especially in trot. In canter, the moment created by the change of direction (bend) should be used for the flying change. When the rider makes a change of direction he should ensure that he brings the forehand of the horse towards the new direction immediately before he starts to bring the hindquarters in that direction. In the canter counter-change of hand, the change of leg should be made as the bend changes to bring the forehand over in the new direction.

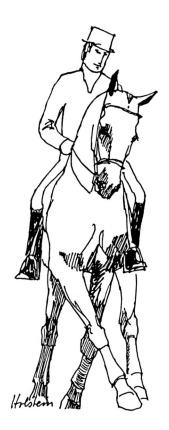

Figure 58 Half-pass showing a head tilt and the rider sitting in a faulty position, having collapsed his left hip.

Judging the Counter-change of Hand

For good counter-changes of hand in trot or canter, the correct position of the horse (hindquarters neither leading nor trailing) and the bend, regularity and fluency are the most important criteria. In trot, it is most important that the position and bend of the horse are correct and that there is an obvious fluency in the movement. In canter, the same criteria apply; in addition, the changes and the number of strides have to be correct. The balance must be maintained. If these conditions are fulfilled, a high mark ranging from 'satisfactory' to 'excellent' may be awarded.

Problems that may occur during the movement may affect the judge's marks as follows:

- In both trot and canter, a lack of fluency or regularity cannot lead to a higher mark than 'sufficient'.

- If the correct bend is not maintained, the mark cannot be more than 'sufficient'.

- If the horse makes a mistake in the flying changes, one mistake can result in the whole movement still being awarded a mark of 'satisfactory'. However, more than one mistake must result in a mark of 'insufficient' or lower.

- In trot, riding a few steps straight before the new bend is taken can still be considered to be 'satisfactory'; however, the movement appears much more fluent if the rider goes immediately from one bend to the other without any straight steps. The same applies to the half-pass in canter, where the change is sometimes made on a straight line.

Note for judges

When marking the counter-change in canter the judge should only start to count the strides after the first change, because it might not be absolutely clear when the rider starts the half-pass, that is, which stride is the first one of the half-pass.

THE PIROUETTES IN WALK AND CANTER

I N COMPETITIONS, PIROUETTES MAY BE performed in walk, when they are usually half-pirouettes, and in canter, where they may be half- or full pirouettes. They can also be shown in piaffe in freestyle tests. The principles of a pirouette are as follows:

- A pirouette is a small circle on two tracks, the forehand moving around the haunches.

- The horse should maintain activity (in walk) or impulsion and never move backwards or deviate sideways.

- The horse should show slight flexion to the inside.

- The inside hind foot forms the centre of the pirouette and should return to the same spot, or slightly in front of it, each time after leaving the ground.

- The regularity of the pace should be maintained throughout.

The Half-pirouette in Walk

Depending on the format of the dressage tests in individual countries, the half-pirouette in walk is usually introduced at the Elementary level of dressage tests and remains a requirement all the way through to Grand Prix. It is an important movement from the point of view of progressive training because it teaches the horse balance, increases engagement of the hind legs and improves suppleness. In the beginning, the half-pirouette is performed along the wall of the arena. Later, as the horse progresses in his physical control and self-carriage, it can be performed in the centre of the arena. The characteristics of half-pirouettes in walk are shown in Figures 59 and 60.

Riding the Half-pirouette in Walk

The most important aspect of the half-pirouette in walk is to have an active, good quality walk. In the beginning, when the rider is teaching the horse the movement, it is sufficient to ask for only a quarter of a pirouette. This will ensure that the horse does not lose the activity of the walk whilst performing the pirouette. The rider should maintain a good contact with his outside hand, suppling and slightly bending the horse with a soft inside hand. At the moment when the horse is asked to turn, the rider should move both hands, keeping them parallel, towards the inside. He should not pull on the reins.

At the moment that the horse starts to move to the inside, the rider should apply a strong outside leg behind the girth (to prevent the hindquarters from falling out);

Figure 59
Diagrammatic representation of a walk pirouette.

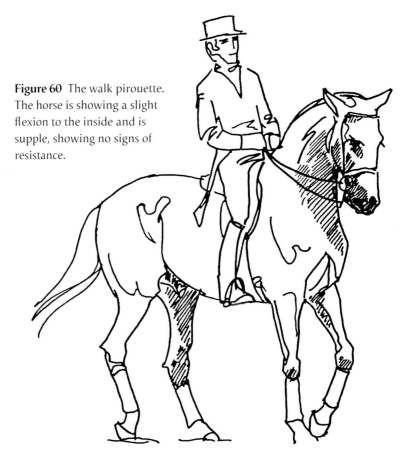

Figure 60 The walk pirouette. The horse is showing a slight flexion to the inside and is supple, showing no signs of resistance.

the inside leg remains at the girth. This means that the rider's inside leg can help to activate the steps. At all times the rider must maintain the forward movement. This is the most important aspect of the walk half-pirouette, indeed maintaining the forward impulse is the most important criterion of all forms of pirouette. In the beginning it is more important to keep the forward movement than it is to make the half-pirouette small. As the horse becomes more confident, the size of the circle marked by the hind legs can be reduced until the inside hind leg is marking time on the spot. The regularity of the pace must be maintained at all times.

Judging the Half-pirouette in Walk

During a half-pirouette in walk, the judge is looking for suppleness, a lack of resistance and regular footfalls. A high mark can be given when the steps are clearly shown and active, the circle described by the hind feet is very small, the horse's head is in the correct position and there is a fluency in the movement. If all these components are present, the judge would be likely to award a mark of 'good' or better. If the steps are correct while the circle described by the hind legs is a little bit large, the mark could still be 'satisfactory' and may even be 'fairly good' depending upon the level of the test being performed.

There are a number of mistakes that can occur during the execution of the half-pirouette and their likely effects on the judge's marks are as follows:

- If the horse moves backwards, the mark is always 'insufficient'.

- If the horse does not maintain the forward movement and misses one step the mark can never be more than 'sufficient'.

- If the horse does not mark the steps clearly ('screwing' or sticking with one hind foot), or misses more than one step, this is always 'insufficient'.

- If the horse steps out with one or both hind legs (that is, the hindquarters fall out) the mark will always be between 'insufficient' and 'bad'.

- If the pirouette is relatively large (for example, a circle described by the hind feet of up to about 60 cm), the mark can still be 'satisfactory' at the lower levels.

- If the horse looks to the outside, in other words, there is incorrect flexion, then the mark cannot be more than 'sufficient'.

- If the horse does not remain steady on the bit, the mark cannot be more than 'sufficient'.

The Half-pirouette and Full Pirouette in Canter

Half- and full pirouettes in canter are much more difficult movements than pirouettes performed in walk because of the innate energy of the canter. The rider must contain and collect the canter so that the horse can turn on a very small circle whilst maintaining the rhythm of the canter and the flexion. The horse should show suppleness, lightness of the forehand, cadence and regularity as well as good balance (Figure 61). For the half-pirouette 3–4 strides are required. For the full pirouette, the requirement is for 6–8 strides.

Riding the Half-pirouette and Full Pirouette in Canter

Pirouettes in canter depend on the quality of the canter and great strength in the horse's loins and hindquarters. In training for these movements, the rider must work to make the horse obedient to the collecting aids. The rider should, in principle, not attempt to make any sort of pirouette in canter until he can easily canter his horse almost on the spot without the use of the inside rein. The rider should shorten the canter strides with a straight horse by creating more tension on the outside rein and using a very light inside hand. The principle should be that the rider should aim to be able to canter the horse on the outside rein only, with the intention towards cantering on the spot.

In preparation for the pirouette, the horse should be slightly bent to the inside. The rider's outside leg should be back (holding the hind legs on the track) while his inside leg remains at the girth, pushing the horse forwards and maintaining the canter. The rider's shoulders and hips should stay parallel to the horse's and he should not collapse the inside hip.

I refer here back to the section on transitions and the rider's position in canter. It is in riding pirouettes that the importance of a correct position in canter will be appreciated by the intelligent rider. Without the correct position, a canter pirouette of any sort is impossible. As stated earlier, the smaller the circle being performed, the further in advance is the horse's inside shoulder. Consequently, in a pirouette in canter (this being the smallest circle possible for the horse to perform), the horse's inside shoulder is leading the way around the pirouette. Thus, the rider's inside shoulder should mirror that of the horse, and the rider should lead with his inside shoulder. If he does not do this, but brings his inside shoulder *back* to make the turn, he will block the action of the inside hind leg and the canter rhythm will be lost (Figure 62).

Throughout the pirouette, whether half or full, the rider should aim to have the horse as light as possible on the inside hand. The rider should keep the horse supple with a soft inside hand, not pulling the horse around. This allows the horse to step confidently forward with his inside hind leg, which is necessary if he is to keep his

Figure 61 The canter pirouette. The horse is correctly bent to the inside and is clearly taking weight on his hindquarters. The footfalls are correct.

Figure 62 Canter pirouette where the rider is pulling on the inside rein. The horse has become 'stuck' and has lost the canter rhythm because his inside hind leg is blocked by the rider's inside hand.

balance. If the rider pulls the horse around, he may fall out with his hind legs, break the canter, resist, lose the flexion, or simply stop.

During the execution of the half- or full pirouette, the horse may seem to slow down. To a certain extent this is a necessary function of the pirouette, as the horse needs to collect himself more and will slow down as he engages his hindquarters and takes more weight on them in preparation for the movement. The rider should prepare the horse correctly for the pirouette by shortening the canter on the straight line approaching the point where he wants to execute the pirouette. The horse should be more or less straight but with a slight bend to the inside going into and coming out of the pirouette. Some riders proceed into the pirouette rather as if they are decreasing the size of the circle. This is incorrect. The horse should be shortened on a straight line and then turn. It should be clear to the judge where the rider has started the pirouette.

Judging the Half-pirouette in Canter

The half-pirouette in canter is introduced at the Prix St Georges level of competition. The appearance of a horse performing a half- or full pirouette correctly in canter is shown in Figure 61. A horse cantering in a very short but clear three-beat canter, obviously taking the weight on his hindquarters, showing enough strides in the turn and maintaining a steady head position deserves a high mark. Depending upon the size of the circle described by the hind legs in canter, the mark may be lowered.

The mistakes that can occur during the canter half-pirouette and their effect upon the judge's marks are as follows:

- A clear deviation from the straight line can never be more than 'satisfactory'.

- If the horse makes a small half-circle, not taking the weight on the hindquarters, the mark cannot be more than 'sufficient'.

- If there are incorrect footfalls, for example, jumping with both hind feet together, the mark can never be more than 'sufficient'. However, if the horse changes the leading leg, the mark must be 'insufficient' or lower.

- Swinging the forehand around cannot be more than 'sufficient'.

- Falling out with the hind legs is always 'insufficient' to 'bad'.

- A horse bringing his head up cannot be more than 'satisfactory'. However, a horse coming clearly 'above the bit' must be considered to be 'insufficient' or lower.

BELOW This is an excellent example of a canter pirouette. The horse can clearly be seen to be taking almost all of his weight on his hindquarters as he turns. He clearly lowers his hindquarters and 'sits'. He is very well collected and is on the bit and correctly flexed. There is the appearance of controlled power and the rider is sitting in a good balance with his horse. Gylla Dallos on *Aktion*. (Photo: Mandorfi Bt/Mitrov Gabriella)

The beginning of a canter pirouette. Monica Theodorescu on *Grunox* at the Olympic Games, Altlanta 1996. (Photo: HorseSource/P. Llewellyn)

Another moment in the canter pirouette from a different viewpoint. Monica Theodorescu on *Grunox* at the Olympic Games, Altlanta 1996. (Photo: HorseSource/P. Llewellyn)

Judging the Full pirouette in Canter

The criteria for awarding a high mark for the full pirouette are similar to those for the half-pirouette. High marks are given for full canter pirouettes with clear, correct, short strides, a good position of the horse's head and in which the hind legs describe a very small circle. The appearance to the judge should be as if the horse could continue cantering and turning for so long as the rider desired him to do so. The horse and rider should be in a balance that demonstrates controlled power and the horse should show great engagement of the hind legs.

In a very highly collected canter, such as that required for a full pirouette, it can frequently be seen that the canter no longer has a clear three-beat rhythm; it becomes more like a four-beat rhythm. This can still be accepted as correct so long as the horse is clearly taking weight on his hindquarters and the footfalls are more or less correct (there should be no jumping together behind).

All errors as previously mentioned in half-pirouettes in walk and canter will apply, but I will repeat them here for ease of reference.

- A clear deviation from the straight line can never be more than 'satisfactory'.

- If the horse makes a small half-circle not taking the weight on the hindquarters, the mark cannot be more than 'sufficient'.

- If there are incorrect footfalls, for example, jumping with both hind feet together, the mark can never be more than 'sufficient'. However, if the horse changes the leading leg, the mark must be 'insufficient' or lower.

- Swinging the forehand around cannot be more than 'sufficient'.

- Falling out with the hind legs is always 'insufficient' to 'bad'.

- A horse bringing his head up cannot be more than 'satisfactory'. However, a horse coming clearly 'above the bit' must be considered to be 'insufficient' or lower.

In addition, other problems that can occur with particular respect to the full pirouette and their effect upon the marks are as follows:

- If, after a few correct strides, the horse takes a stride a little more forward, but the rest of the pirouette is correct, then the mark might still be 'satisfactory'.

- If the horse brings his head too high or becomes too short in the neck and behind the vertical, then the mark might still be considered to be 'satisfactory'.

- A horse clearly coming off the bit, or behind the bit, or throwing himself around can never be 'sufficient'.

HAUTE ÉCOLE: THE PASSAGE AND THE PIAFFE

The Passage

The passage is a very collected, highly elevated and very powerful cadenced trot with a prolonged period of suspension. The relationship of passage to the other forms of trot and the importance of the impulsion has been explained in Chapter 3. There should be pronounced engagement of the hindquarters. The height of the toe of the raised foreleg should be level with the middle of the cannon bone of the other foreleg. The neck should be raised, the poll the highest point (see Figures 63 and 64).

Riding the Passage

Passage is achieved as a consequence of the rider increasing the degree of collection and slowing the forward movement of the trot until the horse offers a few steps of passage in the first instance. In principle, it is the conversion of the forward movement of the trot into a more upward movement. Not all horses have the ability to produce the movement of passage as it requires great strength, coordination and balance. The rider must be able to sit in harmony with the movement of the horse, without stiffness in his body, as he develops the passage steps.

Once the passage has been created, in order to maintain it, the rider should apply pressure with both legs for every step in order to ask the horse for continuous engagement of the hindquarters. Both of the rider's legs should be slightly behind the girth in order to engage the hindquarters more. The rider's soft hands indicate the rhythm by a simultaneous light pressure of the hands, using only a supple wrist action. The rider's hands and arms should not move and should be *kept in a low position*.

The judge would like to see as little movement from the rider as possible. The horse should never be heavy in the rider's hands and should exhibit a high degree of self-carriage.

Figure 63 The appearance of a correct passage.

Figure 64 The appearance of a correct passage with a different type of horse from that shown in Figure 63.

In general, when training a horse to perform passage, help from another experienced person on the ground may be necessary.

Judging the Passage

To award a high mark for a good passage, the judge needs to see a clear moment of suspension, with regular movements and the horse steady on the bit. There should be pronounced engagement of the hindquarters. The regularity extends to the degree of lifting of each pair of legs. Both hocks should be raised by the same amount, as should each knee. There should be clear flexion of the horse's knees. The rider should barely appear to move. There should be an impression of controlled power, and considerable expression. It should not look as though the horse has to make a great effort to perform the movement; it should appear effortless for him to go forward in passage.

Pia Laus riding *Renoir* in passage. (Photo: H. Czerny)

BELOW Nicole Uphoff riding *Rembrandt* in passage. (Photo: HorseSource/ P. Llewellyn)

The judge will penalise any lack of impulsion and suspension in passage. These faults are often manifested by the horse more or less trotting with the hind legs! A well executed passage will only be demonstrated by a confident, powerful horse who has been correctly trained and who is being ridden by a rider who can sit in harmony in a relaxed manner without disturbing him.

A horse showing any of the following can never achieve a mark of more than 'sufficient' and in many cases it may be lower:

- A lack of suspension or sustained irregularity.

- An unsteady head.

- Not lifting enough.

- A lack of impulsion.

- Swinging the forelegs or crossing his fore or hind legs.

The Piaffe

The piaffe is a highly measured, collected, elevated and cadenced trot on the spot. The horse's hindquarters are slightly lowered while the haunches are well engaged, with active hocks. The steps should be elastic and regular. The forehand should be light, with most of the weight on the hindquarters. The horse should be light on the bit and should never be heavy in the rider's hand. The horse should demonstrate a perfect balance and confidence. There should be a lively impulsion, with the horse's desire to move forward apparent. This movement, whilst requiring great strength and control, should appear effortless and it should look as if the horse is dancing on the spot (Figures 65 and 66).

To perform the piaffe it is necessary for the horse to bring his hind legs well under his body and to flex his hocks. Consequently, he will round his back and lower his hindquarters. The degree of lowering for individual horses may vary according to their conformation and to their technique for performing the movement. In some cases there is a marked lowering, in others, only a slight lowering. Both can be considered correct so long as all of the other criteria are present. In both piaffe and passage, there are individual variations in technique.

How to Ride the Piaffe

As for the passage, when training the horse to perform the piaffe, it is a great help for the rider to have someone experienced to assist from the ground. There are many pitfalls and problems that can occur during the training for this movement. The aids to the horse for proceeding in piaffe can be as follows.

Figure 65 Piaffe showing good engagement of the hind legs and lowering of the hind-quarters. There is a complete lack of any resistance.

Figure 66 Piaffe showing a different technique from Figure 65 but still showing good engagement of the hind legs.

Out of walk or trot

The rider gives half-halts with both hands while his legs alternately touch the horse on the left and right sides. In some cases the rider's legs may be taken back slightly. During the piaffe, both hands should remain low and quiet. As soon as the horse stays more or less on the spot, the rider should release the tension of the reins and keep his hands still. So long as the movement is required, the rider should sit still and continue touching the horse with the left and right legs alternately in a regular rhythm.

Touching the horse with alternate legs makes the rider's intent clearer to the horse. However, the timing of these aids requires great sensitivity on the part of the rider. Many riders use both legs together to ask for the piaffe but this can often result

A nice piaffe. The horse is clearly showing a lowering of his hindquarters. Gylla Dallos on *Aktion*. (Photo: T. Holcbecher)

in the rider pushing the horse too fast and out of his rhythm in a desire to create the piaffe.

In the training for piaffe there are several options available depending on the horse's natural talent. Some horses offer a few piaffe steps easily when just touched slightly with alternate legs, others find this an extremely difficult exercise.

Energetic, active, forward-thinking horses can be asked for steps of piaffe straight from the walk. The rider collects the walk and asks for a trot that is almost on the spot. When the horse is waiting for the aid to move forwards, the rider can start to ask with his leg aids, synchronized with the half-halts with both hands. Early in training, the horse may offer a few small piaffe steps; immediately, he should be praised and then ridden forwards in walk or trot. It is important that the horse remains calm throughout, as it is then possible to keep a good rhythm. Any tension will destroy the rhythm and make the movement jerky and lacking in cadence.

A wonderful piaffe. Margit
Otto-Crepin riding *Corlandus*
in Hanover 1988.
(Photo: W. Ernst)

Out of passage

In some cases, it is easier for the rider to ask for piaffe by shortening the passage until
the horse is almost performing passage on the spot. This is perhaps the best option
for more phlegmatic horses, as the forward movement is maintained. Once a few
steps have been achieved, the rider should ride strongly forward again in passage and
then ask for piaffe again a little later.

Whether the piaffe is asked for out of the walk, trot or passage, in training the
piaffe itself should always be allowed to move a little bit forward (see below); this
ensures that the intent of the movement remains in a forward direction. Sometimes
the horse will start to swing from side to side in the piaffe. This is usually an indication
that he has difficulty balancing and that the movement is not forward. To correct this,
the horse should only be asked for a few steps before being ridden strongly forward in
trot. It is a serious mistake to allow any form of backward movement in the piaffe.

In the Intermediaire II test, when piaffe is first introduced, it is asked for out of
walk and then out of passage. At this level a degree of forward movement, up to one
metre, is allowed. However, at Grand Prix level the piaffe should be as close as
possible to on the spot, but a forward intention should remain.

Another good example of piaffe. Christine Stückelberger riding *Allga Bolino*.
(Photo: W. Ernst)

Proceeding forward from Piaffe into Passage

The rider uses both legs, in some cases slightly behind the girth, to urge the horse to engage the hind legs and move forward. He also indicates forward movement with the hand and the contact on the reins, following a short, good contact by releasing the tension of the reins, and proceeds forward in the passage as described earlier.

Judging the Piaffe

If the requirements above are more or less fulfilled, a high mark is deserved. The piaffe is introduced only at the highest levels of dressage test – Intermediaire II and Grand Prix. Because piaffe is a very difficult movement, there are many things that can go wrong. Listed below are some of the more common problems that can occur in piaffe and their likely effect upon the judge's marks:

- Irregular steps in piaffe (and passage) as well as in the transitions must be seen and penalized.

- If the horse moves even slightly backwards, the mark cannot be 'sufficient'.

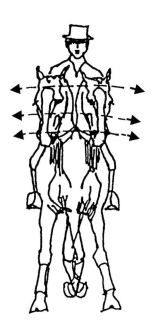

Figure 67 Piaffe swinging or balancing from side to side.

- If the horse shows sustained irregular steps *or;*

- crosses his forelegs *or;*

- swings his forehand or the quarters because he is trying to regain his balance (piaffe balancé – Figure 67) *or;*

- his forefeet stick to the ground, then in all these cases the movement would be considered to be 'insufficient' or lower.

- When hurried steps are shown without suspension, the movement cannot be more than 'sufficient'.

- If the hindquarters are not lowered, the movement can still be considered 'satisfactory' so long as the horse is clearly taking weight on his hindquarters.

- However, if the horse is dropping onto his forehand or staying high behind, then this cannot be more than 'sufficient' (Figure 68).

- A horse moving slightly forward (not more than about 60 cm) can still be 'satisfactory' (except in the cases where 1 m forwards is allowed as in Intermediaire II tests).

- The horse's hind feet should not come too far underneath his body and his forelegs must remain vertical when the foot is on the ground. Otherwise the picture will be

Figure 68 Piaffe with the horse heavy on the forehand and 'high behind'.

as shown in Figure 69, which is somewhat like the stance that an elephant would take when balancing on a ball. This is 'insufficient'. This stance in piaffe is an indication that the horse is unwilling to take weight on his hindquarters.

Figure 69 Piaffe showing the hind feet too far forward and the fore legs behind the vertical.

The Transitions Passage/Piaffe/Passage

From the judge's point of view, the transitions from passage to piaffe and piaffe to passage should be as smooth as possible. Any disturbance or irregularity should be penalized as described for the individual movements.

To achieve a high mark the horse should maintain the same rhythm that he demonstrates in piaffe throughout the transition and into the passage. These transitions, when executed well, are the ultimate demonstration of submission and self-carriage on the part of the well-trained dressage horse.

CHAPTER TEN

SUMMARY OF KEY PRINCIPLES

To summarize, there are a few points that I consider so important that they are worthy of being reiterated. It is only when the rider fully understands the way the horse functions, his biomechanics, that he can appreciate the simplicity behind my instructions for training. The rider should also make himself aware of the horse's psychology and his instincts so that he can use these to help himself make the training process easier. Alongside this, the rider should be constantly striving to improve the discipline of his own mind and body so that he is completely aware of what he is doing with any part of his own body at any one time. He must be able to sit in harmony with the horse's movements rather than disturb him. On the other hand, he must have a strong and correct position in the saddle so that he can resist any evasions that the horse may produce because, in reality, not all of the training of the horse will go as smoothly as the rider would wish. The horse may occasionally not want to work or cooperate with his rider, but the rider must be secure enough so that he can correct the horse without harming him by inadvertently pulling on his mouth or kicking him with the spur. It should be understood that, in principle, the horse is usually willing to cooperate if he can understand the rider.

There is no quick way to train a horse. The speed of learning is based largely on the rider's ability to avoid making mistakes. Of course, the horse has to play his part, but the majority of training problems arise because of riders' deficiencies. It has been said that it takes x repetitions to learn a skill but it takes at least $10x$ repetitions to unlearn a previously learned skill! Therefore, it is better to teach a horse correctly the first time. It makes no difference whether or not the rider aspires to Grand Prix or Elementary dressage tests. The system is the same and the aids for similar movements are the same.

There are some aspects of the training that are extremely important and I cannot emphasize them enough. These are the various transitions, and the riding of circles and turns. If these exercises are learned correctly, the horse can proceed more quickly to the higher levels. If they are not performed correctly, the rider will have to keep going back to the basics each time that he wants his horse to learn a new exercise. The lateral movements, for example, cannot be performed if the horse cannot bend. Riders should take the opportunity offered by every corner that they ride through to engage the horse more and so proceed towards greater collection. All too often, these basic requirements are ignored by the rider. In truth, it is often considered boring to ride around and around in one pace, continually riding transitions and circles and corners. Many riders these days only want to perform movements such as shoulder-in, travers and half-pass, flying changes, pirouettes and piaffe and passage. They are in too much of a hurry and want to do the exciting things, not the 'boring' ones upon which they are based. Consequently, many riders trying to train their own horses from the beginning get stuck, usually at about Medium level (or even before this), because they cannot make further progress and/or because they are getting low marks in dressage tests. If they have been reading their judges' comments they are likely to have seen repeatedly remarks such as: 'little bend'; 'more self-carriage required'; 'more engagement in transitions'; 'resistant transition', indicating to them that the fundamental principles are lacking. Comments of this sort from a judge should serve as a 'wake-up call' and alert the rider to the fact that something is seriously wrong with the basics.

The riding of a dressage test is a demonstration of the rider's training of his horse. He should only enter a dressage test if his horse can fulfil the requirements of that test. When in the arena, the rider has to perform the movements at the place prescribed, so it is a test of the horse's obedience and the rider's skill in getting the horse to cooperate.

The judge's job appears superficially to be straightforward but it requires a high degree of knowledge, expertise and concentration. The dressage judge is there to provide a commentary on the success or otherwise of the rider's progress in training his horse at that point in time. The judge should be able to see the performance in the context of the training of the horse towards Grand Prix and to point out to the rider in what respects he is succeeding, or where he has gone wrong.

The judge is not fulfilling the role of trainer, and therefore should not get involved with comments about training techniques, or attempt to give riding lessons when writing on the score sheet. The dressage judge is, in effect, the guardian of the standards of dressage. Poor judging, which ignores the importance of basic faults, allows horses and riders to progress to the higher levels before they are competent. This does nothing to help develop the individual rider and horse, nor does it help the sport, because riders then compete at higher levels and are at a loss to know why they consistently receive very low marks. Over-marking does no one any favours in the long run. The inevitable result is that the standard of performance in dressage tests will go down. Nevertheless, the judge should not be over-critical or destructive in his criticism. He should never be sarcastic; rather he should aim to help the rider to understand why he received a specific mark for a particular movement and what he needs to do to improve the movement in order to get a higher mark. The judges set the standards: it is up to the rider to conform.

I have alluded to the bad construction of certain dressage tests earlier in the text. Sometimes, the judges are in a unique position whereby they can change dressage tests, introducing exercises which they feel need attention and which may lead to improvements in the progressive development of the horse. If this opportunity ever befalls a particular judge, he must have a thorough understanding of the training process if he is to make a valid contribution.

In all his judgements, the dressage judge has to make sure that he uses the same point of view for all the riders performing, and ignores whatever he knows or has heard about a particular rider or the horse who is being presented in front of him. He should also be aware that there can be a considerable difference (for better or worse) in the performance of a particular horse and rider combination from one competition to the next – either horse or rider can have a good or a bad day.

During a performance the judge should retain in his head a running evaluation of the following factors:

- the submissiveness (acceptance of the bridle);

- the lightness and flexibility;

- the bend (flexion) on curved lines;

- the straightness on straight lines;

- the correct seat of the rider;

- the effect of the rider's aids;

- and, last but not least, the regularity, evenness and freedom of the paces.

CHAPTER ELEVEN

Freestyle Competitions

F REESTYLE DRESSAGE TO MUSIC HAS become a great attraction for spectators at dressage competitions. Spectators attract the media and sponsors and, in this way, freestyle competitions have done much to popularize the modern sport of dressage. In the 1996 Olympic Games, the Grand Prix Freestyle test was, for the first time, made compulsory, in addition to the Grand Prix and Grand Prix Special tests, for determining the medals. There was, initially, concern in some quarters about the introduction of the freestyle to music test, because it was perceived that this might lead towards accusations of 'circus', with horses merely performing tricks and showing a deteriorating level of technical performance. However, judicious use of the rules of dressage and a strict maintenance of the requirement for technical correctness has, so far, prevented too many accusations of this kind. However, I have some concerns about the influence of the various components of the 'artistic marks' (which comprise half of the total marks awarded in a freestyle test) and I believe that the modern freestyle test creates problems for the judges when assessing the artistic components of the test. It is, perhaps, appropriate at this stage to review the origins of the freestyle to music test.

Development of the Freestyle Tests

The popular spectator sport of ice-skating has always comprised both a test of compulsory figures and a freestyle programme. It was with the intention of developing a similar sort of interest in the sport that I supported the introduction of a dressage freestyle to music test in the early 1980s. There was much discussion in the Dressage Committee about the method of judging the freestyle test and finally we arrived at the format whereby the technical assessment comprises one half of the marks and the artistic assessment comprises the other.

In a freestyle test at any level, there are certain compulsory elements, some of which must be performed to at least a stipulated minimum extent. (For example, a test may require at least a certain number of consecutive one-time changes.) Where the rider has freedom is in the composition of the test and the relationships between movements. This gives an opportunity for the rider to show off his horse's abilities in the best possible light. He is completely free to choose the music which will accompany the test and his aim is to produce a rounded 'performance' for the judge to assess. Personally, I do not think that freestyle tests are suitable for the lower levels of training because there is little latitude for the rider regarding the movements that can be shown. The performance then frequently deteriorates to consist of just the paces with music and it has little artistic value. A minimum of Advanced standard (Prix St Georges) is more appropriate to this form of competition.

A freestyle programme is, in my view, an aesthetic, artistic performance, which demonstrates the unity and harmony between rider and horse. Impulsion and lightness of the horse, technically correct movements and a rider with a straight, upright yet supple seat, giving almost invisible aids, should be the highlights of a freestyle test. Thus, dressage transforms from technical craftsmanship into a live, creative art form.

The freestyle test is, therefore, a composition of various elements. It should be an exciting, breath-taking performance – never boring – showing a beautiful arrangement of different movements and well-placed figures, all of which allow the horse's athletic prowess to be exhibited. The rider is completely free to choose the format and the manner of the presentation. The spectator should be able to recognise clearly the rider's intentions in the various phases of the presentation that show his and the horse's abilities to the best possible extent.

Assessment of the Performance

The assessment of the performance has two sections: the technical marks and the artistic marks. The overall artistic marks have always been given the same weight as the technical marks in the total mark. When each compulsory movement is performed, the judge will mark it as in any other dressage test, out of a maximum of 10 marks. If the movement is repeated, the judge will mark it again. When the test has been completed, the judge will decide which mark he will allocate to those movements for which there have been two or more marks awarded; usually he will average the mark. This is quite straightforward and causes few problems. However, in current freestyle tests, allocation of the artistic marks causes problems for judges, riders and spectators alike because, in the first place, there are elements of the technical aspects included which cause confusion. In my opinion, this needs to be changed. When judging a freestyle test, it is clear that the final technical mark should reflect the sum of the marks for the compulsory movements as used in normal dressage judging. However, the artistic mark currently includes assessment of rhythm and energy, the harmony and lightness of the movements, the choreography, the degree of difficulty and the interpretation of the music. The judge for such a test should, therefore, also have an artistic empathy. He has to be able to evaluate and assess the relationship between the technical aspects (such as the degree of difficulty), the harmonious movement and the artistic presentation.

Today, two different methods of artistic presentation are commonly shown. In the first, basically, the horse is ridden to a background of music and shows, perhaps, a very good looking, smoothly executed programme with all the required movements present. In the second, the rider gives an *interpretation* of the music, which is naturally much more difficult because it needs, besides a very submissive horse, an especially high level of artistic feeling in the rider. This second type of performance, when successfully carried out, has a much higher artistic value than the first and should get the higher artistic mark. I certainly have the impression that this latter is more breathtaking than the former for the spectator. However, unlike the technical marks, it may be difficult for the judges to see, feel and quantify the difference. I believe that, in making his assessment, the judge should consider:

- the choreography;

- the degree of difficulty, and

- the pieces of music that were selected in view of their suitability with respect to the rhythm and to the movements.

For each of these factors he has to assess and evaluate the relative advantages and disadvantages. He also has to take into account such things as the rhythm, energy and elasticity of the horse as well as the degree of harmony between horse and rider. In a freestyle test, the judge is permitted to keep a record of the marks he has awarded in the artistic section. This is the only time that dressage judging incorporates a degree of comparison between performances. The judge is then comparing one performance to another in respect of these marks. This is why there is a limit (currently 12 for normal competitions and 15 for championships and Olympic Games) on the number of participants allowed in a freestyle competition.

In the beginning, when the freestyle test was introduced, there were only three components of artistic marks to be determined. However, the marking system had to be made simpler because the artistic marks were taking too long to produce. Therefore, the artistic marks were reduced to two components. It was essential to keep the marking system simple and easy for judges, riders and spectators to understand. In respect of judges, this was so that any judge could judge the freestyle and it would not be necessary to create a separate, specialized tier of judges especially for the freestyle. The test that was used in 1986 is shown in Figure 70, see opposite. It can be seen that there were two components for the artistic mark:

• Harmony between rider and horse. Ease of the movements. Rider's position and seat. Correctness and effect of the aids.

(These are the same components as for the 'submission' collective mark in a conventional dressage test)

• Composition of the programme, choreography, degree of difficulty and incorporation of the music.

The first component had a coefficient of 6 and the second, a coefficient of 10. The marks could be given in decimals. Thus, the 'harmony' component comprised 37.5% of the artistic mark whilst the rest of the artistic mark comprised 62.5%.

After I retired from the Committee, the format of the freestyle test was changed. The current Grand Prix Freestyle to Music Test (Figure 71, pages 126–127) has five artistic marks and there have been suggestions that these should be increased to eight! The artistic marks are awarded in comparison to each other and it is already very difficult to compare five marks, especially amongst twelve riders. How much more difficult would it be for the judges to compare eight! Another change has been that, whereas in the early days of freestyles, the artistic marks could be given in decimals, nowadays only half marks are allowed. Perhaps most significantly, in the current tests the first mark could be considered equivalent to the 'paces' collective mark in a normal dressage test. Theoretically, then, the judges are assessing an aspect of the technical side twice, thereby introducing a bias towards the technical mark. In my opinion, the marking system has become over-complicated. Judges and riders are confused. I would like to see a return to the simpler system of judging that we had in the beginning.

However, the five artistic marks in the current Grand Prix freestyle test are as follows:

• Rhythm, energy and elasticity.

• Harmony between horse and rider.

• Choreography. Use of the arena. Inventiveness.

• Degree of difficulty. Well-calculated risks.

• Choice of music and interpretation of the music.

The first two of the above carry a coefficient of three times the mark, the second two carry a coefficient of four times the mark and the final mark – the music mark – carries a coefficient of six times the mark.

FÉDÉRATION EQUESTRE INTERNATIONALE

Freestyle Test
(Grand Prix level)

Time allowed:
Performance to be finished between 5'30" and 6'

Event	Date	Judge & position	No in progr.	Competitor	Nation	Horse	No.

Compulsory movements	Marks	Points	Coeff	Final Marks
1. Walk (collected and/or extended minimum 20m)	10			
2. Collected trot including half-pass right and left	10			
3. Extended trot	10			
4. Collected canter including half-pass right and left	10			
5. Extended canter	10			
6. Flying changes every second stride (minimum 5 times consecutively)	10			
7. Flying changes every stride (minimum 5 times consecutively)	10			
8. Pirouette in canter right	10		2	
9. Pirouette in canter left	10		2	
10. Passage (minimum 20m)	10		2	
11. Piaffe (minimum 10 steps)	10		2	
12. Transitions from Passage to Piaffe and vice versa	10			
Total for technical execution	160			

Remarks

General Impression	Marks	Points	Coeff	Final Marks
13* Harmony between rider and horse / Ease of the movements / Rider's position and seat / Correctness and effect of the aids	10		6	
14* Composition of the programme, choreography, degree of difficulty and incorporation of the music	10		10	
Total for artistic presentation	160			

* Mark in decimals for No. 13 and 14 only

To be deducted
Time penalty:
more than 6' or less than 5'30" deduct 2 points from the total of artistic presentation

Score (see conversion table)		
Total for technical execution divided by 16	10	
Total for artistic presentation divided by 16	10	
Final score	20	

In case two competitors have the same final score, the one with the higher marks for artistic impression is leading

Signature of Judge

Figure 71 The current Grand Prix Freestyle to Music Test

OLYMPIC GAMES 2000

Freestyle Test (Kür) Grand Prix level (1999)

	Technical marks	Marks	Points	Coeff.	Final marks
1.	Collected walk (minimum 20m)	10			
2.	Extended walk (minimum 20m)	10			
3.	Collected trot including half-pass right	10			
4.	Collected trot including half-pass left	10			
5.	Extended trot	10			
6.	Collected canter including half-pass right	10			
7.	Collected canter including half-pass left	10			
8.	Extended canter	10			
9.	Flying changes every second stride (minimum 5 times consecutively)	10			
10.	Flying changes every stride (minimum 9 times consecutively)	10			
11.	Canter pirouette right	10		2	
12.	Canter pirouette left	10		2	
13.	Passage (minimum 20m)	10		2	
14.	Piaffe (minimum 10 steps)	10		2	
15.	Transitions from passage to piaffe and from piaffe to passage	10		2	
	Total for technical executions	**200**			

	Artistic marks*	Marks	Points	Coeff.	Final marks
16.	Rhythm, energy and elasticity	10		3	
17.	Harmony between horse and rider	10		3	
18.	Choreography. Use of arena. Inventiveness	10		4	

	Artistic marks*	Marks	Points	Coeff.	Final marks
19.	Degree of difficulty. Well calculated risks	10		4	
20.	Choice of music and interpretation of the music	10		6	
Total for artistic presentation		**200**			

To be deducted:
Time penalty: more than 6 minutes or less than 5 minutes 30 seconds, deduct 2 points from the total of the artistic presentation.

Total for technical execution divided by 20	10		
Total for artistic presentation divided by 20		10	
Final score		**20**	

World Cup:
In case two competitors have the same final score, the one with the higher marks for artistic impression is leading.

CDI***:
In case two competitors have the same final score, the one with the higher technical mark is leading.

In the original concept, the first, third, fourth and fifth components were combined in one mark with a coefficient of ten, which then comprised 63% of the artistic mark. By separating them out and giving them different coefficients, their influence on the artistic mark has been changed. Individually they are worth 15%, 20%, 20% and 30% of the artistic mark respectively. Collectively, they comprise 85% of the mark, whereas the relative importance of the 'harmony' mark has been reduced to only 15%. In addition, the judge can only award half marks in the artistic marks and not decimals. The judge gives his marks out of 10 in each case, but the different coefficients magnify the effect of a difference of half a mark in the various components to a different extent. Thus, if a judge is not consistent as to which component he should assign a certain aspect of the artistic marks, the artistic marks awarded by each judge may vary widely.

In addition, the high coefficient for the music mark makes it very difficult for the judge to keep track of this in his judging, and very easy for the result of the competition to be manipulated.

I do not agree with the format of the current tests because, first, in my opinion, the rhythm and the music cannot be separated. Second, there is a danger that the judge who has to give separate marks for the choice of music and its interpretation may be heavily influenced by his personal likes or dislikes in music. It is not a judge's job to judge the music itself. Furthermore, some judges think that the music should correspond to the conformation of the horse. I cannot agree with this because it is possible for a very heavy horse to show a fascinating performance to light music or, conversely, for a light, elegant horse to show a beautiful test to rather 'heavy' music. However, it is almost inevitable that a judge's personal taste will be a factor here. What is most important to me is that the rhythm of the horse's movements should harmonize well with the rhythm of the music in every situation. Third, it is the whole set-up of the composition, including the rhythm and the choreography as well as the degree of difficulty, which forms the artistic presentation. In addition and in particular, in an artistic presentation, the harmony between the rider and horse, the ease of the movements shown and the rider's discreet, almost invisible aids, form an essential part of the performance and should not be reduced in importance in the overall mark.

By separating all these points it becomes much more difficult to give marks that finally correspond to the artistic qualities of the presentation, especially since the coefficients are so different that the mark for the music alone can dominate the whole result. This dominance of the music mark can also lead to its use in manipulating the result one way or the other. The use of only two artistic marks, as was the case when the freestyle tests were introduced, made it easier for the judge to obtain a general artistic impression by comparing one test with another and ranking them. In addition, it took a much less time to give the marks, since it avoided the current possibility of the judge becoming confused as to what really has to be considered for each of the individual five marks. For example, the quality of the paces themselves and the degree of impulsion are already included in the technical mark for each compulsory movement. Is it, therefore, necessary to judge these again in a separate mark in the artistic section?

Guidelines for Judging the Artistic Element

Whilst I do not agree with the current format of freestyle tests, I think I should give some guidelines to riders and judges as to what should be included in the various marks on the artistic side. However, I should stress that, currently, each judge has to find his own method of interpreting the separate artistic components. Consequently, there will never be complete agreement amongst judges in a freestyle competition with regard to the actual marks given for each component.

Rhythm, Energy and Elasticity

The mark for this should reflect the quality of the paces demonstrated by the horse, combined with an assessment of the degree of impulsion. As in all dressage tests, the rhythm of all three paces must be clearly defined and maintained. The Grand Prix dressage horse is a highly trained athlete and, as such, should demonstrate the required level of collection and impulsion for this level of competition. The horse should demonstrate that he has developed the necessary power and strength to enable him to show clear transitions and powerful extensions with a great degree of suspension. However, these aspects have already been assessed in each of the compulsory movements. What could also be included here is an assessment of the relationship between the rhythm of the paces and the rhythm of the corresponding music. What proportion of this mark should be devoted to this aspect is entirely debatable: each judge must decide for himself how he intends to interpret this mark and must maintain this balance throughout the entire competition.

Harmony between Rider and Horse

This mark is easier to interpret since it is more like the collective mark for 'submission' in a normal competition. In the mark for 'harmony between rider and horse', the rider giving his aids discreetly, sitting almost motionless and displaying an easy-moving horse without any evident effort, should get a high mark; whereas the rather rough rider who moves about a lot in the saddle, with the horse showing some resistance, should be penalized accordingly.

The Choreography

This component includes factors such as the use of the arena and inventiveness. Here, the judge has to consider the outlines of the performance, such as well-placed movements (performed symmetrically if possible), whether or not the whole concept is fluent, and whether it is possible to recognize what the rider wants to show, or whether he just repeats the movements of a compulsory test. Does he use the whole of the arena? Are the same movements repeated several times, possibly even at the same spot? Is there a muddle of different movements and paces? Does he show some paces (except the walk) more often than others? Thus it can be seen that the judge has to be capable of considering concurrently a multitude of factors in order to produce the final mark.

The Degree of Difficulty

A fundamental consideration here is that of well-calculated risks. Does the rider take a risk without exceeding his or the horse's abilities? Can he show the difficult movements equally well on both reins, or can he show certain movements on one side only? Is he able to perform double pirouettes, piaffe-pirouettes or passage half-passes, or difficult but smooth transitions – for example a good extended trot to passage, or starting a pirouette out of walk?

The Music

Essential factors here are choice and interpretation. Is the music suitable for what the rider wants to show? Does it match the rhythm of the horse in trot, canter, passage, piaffe, walk and also in the pirouettes, or are the movements performed counter to the rhythm of the music? Here, there will be some inevitable overlap between the mark given for the music and the mark given for the 'rhythm, energy and elasticity'. The judge should not consider the music as such – which means that he should not be influenced by the rider's choice of the type of music, no matter what the judge likes personally, or whether he prefers classical music to modern. The judge is looking for a performance wherein the horse and rider appear to be dancing to the music. So, the clever use of movements that allow changes in musical emphasis to be matched by similar changes in the rhythm or power of a movement will result in a high mark, as the music is 'interpreted' by the horse and rider.

Specific Examples to Aid Assessment of Artistic Marks

I would like to conclude this section by mentioning some specific examples that might aid judges in their assessment of the artistic components of the marks.

- If a rider shows a double pirouette instead of a single full pirouette in canter, he increases the 'degree of difficulty'. So, if this double pirouette is good, the rider will get a high mark for the technical performance, but this can also be considered when the mark for the 'degree of difficulty' in the artistic value is given. However, if the double pirouette is badly executed, it affects not only the technical mark, but also has an influence on the artistic impression. That is, it would have an effect on both the 'harmony' mark as well as the 'degree of difficulty' mark and it may even have a bearing on the 'rhythm, energy and elasticity' mark. For example, this would certainly be the case if the horse loses impulsion, practically stops and is not able to maintain the canter. The same applies to the horse who shows clear resistance so that the whole movement is spoilt.

- If, however, the pirouette is performed with a slight technical error, which does not really affect the artistic quality of the movement (such as a slight error in the sequence of footfalls), or if the second pirouette becomes a slightly too big, the technical mark will be low but the rider should not be penalized a second time for this (or at least not by much), in the artistic marks. The piaffe pirouette should be marked in a similar way.

- It is of great importance to the artistic component of the test that the rider must demonstrate that he can keep to the same rhythm as the music, especially when showing collected, medium or extended trot. Here, it is possible to see clearly whether the steps are lengthened and that the rhythm is not increased. The same can be said for the half-passes and also for the corresponding canter work.

- A test in which the music is used simply as a background has very little artistic value, or even none, and must be marked as such. This would be reflected in a reduced 'rhythm' mark as well as in the 'music' mark.

The judge should derive much pleasure from watching a freestyle performance. However, I do feel that the recent changes in the format for assessing the artistic qualities of such a test do little to assist either the judges, riders or spectators in understanding the marking of the artistic elements. If the freestyle test is to maintain its popularity in the sport, and controversy over marking is to be avoided, then, as stated earlier, I believe that it would serve the sport better if we were to revert to a simpler method of assessment.

Nonetheless, I am convinced that the freestyle test will not endanger classical dressage, but will help to improve it while, at the same time, making dressage more pleasurable for the riders and more attractive for the spectators, which are essential components for the survival of dressage as a sport.

PART II

Dressage and the Olympic Games

EQUESTRIAN SPORT AND THE OLYMPIC GAMES

The Origins of the Modern Olympic Games

In 1889 Baron Pierre de Coubertin was entrusted by the French Government with the task of studying issues relating to the development of physical education at Universities. Whilst working on this project he came up with the idea of reviving the concept of the Olympic Games of antiquity. Baron de Coubertin presented his ideas to the public in a lecture entitled 'Rebirth of the Olympic Games' which he gave at the Sorbonne in 1892. In this lecture he explained that he wanted to bring this ancient institution back to life, but in a modern form.

In 1894, de Coubertin called for a Congress of the International Athletic Assembly at the Sorbonne. This comprised delegates from many different countries. After much discussion, the members of the Congress accepted de Coubertin's proposal, which was to hold, every four years, sporting competitions in accordance with the spirit of antiquity in which all nations would be invited to participate. So it was that the concept of the Modern Olympiad was born. In addition it was agreed that the first International Olympic Games should take place in Athens. The Greek people felt very honoured and anticipated various advantages for the country as a consequence of staging the Olympiad. However, members of the Greek government at the time were afraid of the financial implications and so they totally opposed the project, despite the popular enthusiasm for the Games.

It was the enthusiastic Baron de Coubertin who finally convinced enough influential people that Greece should be the first country to host this important event. Eventually, a provisional committee, under the honorary presidency of the Greek Crown Prince (who already had his own ideas about how to realize the proposal) was ready to take over the organization with a view to holding the Games in Athens. The prince replaced a number of the original committee members, who indicated that they wanted to retire, and created the positions of Secretary General and Secretary of Finances. Subsequently, in 1895, the Crown Prince was able to announce the commencement of work towards the first International Olympic Games, to be held in Athens in 1896. Corresponding to the programme already fixed by the Paris Assembly, the following committees were set up:

Committee of Athletics and Gymnastics
Committee of Shooting
Committee of Nautic Games
Committee of Arms and Fencing
Committee of Cycling
Committee of Lawn Games (e.g. tennis etc.)

There had been much discussion in the early meetings of the International Athletic Assembly of Paris (ICP) about the various sports and related issues. One of the first discussions dealt with the question of amateurism – no professionals were allowed to compete. The ancient Olympic Games had included athletics (track and field events) and chariot races, so it seemed logical to include some form of equestrian event in the modern Olympiad. The first record of discussions involving equestrian events dates back to the fifth session of the ICP in 1894 when the inclusion of a riding contest (polo) was proposed. Indeed, it was stated then that equestrian sport should always be included in future Olympic Games.

In the programme prepared for the first Olympic Games of the modern era, equitation was listed as one of the sports to be included (Figure 72). However, this particular competition never took place because Greece had no horse breeding of her own, there was no hippodrome in Athens and there was no money to pay for the building of one. Therefore, the Crown Prince finally proposed the cancellation of the equestrian element of the 1986 Games. Sports that were included were athletic sports, gymnastics, fencing and wrestling, shooting, nautical sports (yachting, rowing and swimming), cycling and 'athletic games' (cricket and lawn tennis).

For the equestrian sports, it had been planned to hold a competition based around school exercises in the arena with and without stirrups, a jumping competition, a voltige competition and a high school performance. Separate committees were even created to deal with each of these disciplines. Interestingly, it was clearly stated that they would not take into account the quality or value of the horse, only the ability of the rider!

However, as stated, although they were listed in the programme, these proposed equestrian events never took place. Equitation was not the only sufferer. Some other sports were also left out, although there were other athletic pursuits substituted in

2ᵉ Année. — Nᵒ 3.   Janvier 1895.

BULLETIN DU COMITÉ INTERNATIONAL
DES
JEUX OLYMPIQUES

PARIS, 229, Rue Saint-Honoré   *Citius — Fortius — Altius*   Rue Saint-Honoré, 229, PARIS

PROGRAMME
DES
JEUX OLYMPIQUES DE 1896
ATHÈNES

5-15 AVRIL 1896. — *(24 mars-3 avril, Style grec).*

SOUS LA PRÉSIDENCE DE

S. A. R. Monseigneur le Prince Royal, duc de Sparte

A. — SPORTS ATHLÉTIQUES

Courses à pied : 100 mètres, 400 mètres, 800 mètres et 1,500 mètres plat, 110 mètres haies. — Les règlements seront ceux de l'*Union des Sociétés françaises de Sports Athlétiques.*

Concours : Sauts en longueur et en hauteur *(running long et high jump)*; Saut à la perche *(Pole vault)*; Lancement du poids *(Putting the weight)* et du disque. — Les règlements seront ceux de l'*Amateur Athletic Association d'Angleterre.*

Course à pied, dite de Marathon, sur la distance de 48 kilomètres, de Marathon à Athènes, pour la coupe offerte par M. Michel Bréal, membre de l'Institut de France.

B. — GYMNASTIQUE

Exercices individuels : Corde lisse en traction de bras. — Rétablissements divers à la barre fixe. — Mouvements aux anneaux. — Barres parallèles profondes. — Saut au cheval. — Travail des poids.

Mouvements d'ensemble : (Les Sociétés ne pourront présenter d'équipes inférieures à 10 gymnastes).

C. — ESCRIME ET LUTTE

Assauts de fleuret, sabre et épée : Amateurs ; Professeurs (civils et militaires). — Un règlement spécial a été élaboré par la *Société d'encouragement de l'Escrime* (Paris).

Lutte : romaine et grecque.

D. — TIR

Par suite d'une difficulté imprévue, le programme du Tir ne pourra être publié qu'un peu plus tard.

E. — SPORTS NAUTIQUES

Yachting : Courses à la voile. — *L'Union des Yachts Français* a élaboré un règlement spécial.

Aviron : Un rameur : 2,000 mètres, sans virage, skiffs.
Deux rameurs de couple, sans virage, yoles et outriggers.
Quatre rameurs de pointe, sans virage, yoles.
Une course spéciale sera organisée pour les équipages des escadres.
Les règlements seront ceux du *Rowing Club Italiano.*

Natation : Vitesse : 100 mètres. Fond et vitesse : 500 mètres.
Fond : 1,000 mètres.
Jeu de water-polo.

F. — VÉLOCIPÉDIE

Vitesse : 2,000 mètres, sur piste, sans entraîneurs. 10,000 mètres, sur piste, sans entraîneurs.

Fond : 100 kilomètres sur piste avec entraîneurs.

Course de 12 heures sur piste, avec entraîneurs.

Les règlements suivis seront ceux de l'*International Cyclist's Association.*

G. — EQUITATION

Concours d'équitation : reprise de manège, avec et sans étriers, saut d'obstacles, voltige, haute école.

(Il ne sera tenu compte que de l'aptitude du cavalier et non de la valeur du cheval.)

H. — JEUX ATHLÉTIQUES

Lawn tennis : Simple. Double.

Cricket : Les règlements seront ceux de la *All England Lawn Tennis Association* et du *Marylebone Cricket Club.*

Fait à Athènes, le 12/24 novembre 1894.

Colonel MANO;
ETIENNE SOOULOUDIS, député, ancien ministre ;
A.-D. SOUTZO, chef d'escadron de cavalerie ;
RETZINAS, maire du Pirée,
  vice-présidents du Comité hellène.
PAUL SKOUSÈS, *trésorier.*
ALEXANDRE MERCATI, GEORGES M. MELAS, *secrétaires.*

APPROUVÉ :

D. BIKELAS. *président du Comité International.*
Baron PIERRE DE COUBERTIN, *secrétaire général.*
A. CALLOT, *trésorier.*

Page from the Bulletin of the International Olympic Committee containing the programme of the Olympic Games in 1896.

the programme. The organizers were permitted some flexibility in deciding the final programme.

The International Olympic Committee (IOC) had been formed some time after the Paris Congress of 1894 and before 1901, in which year there is a record of the fourth session of the IOC being held. This body established the Olympic Games Charter in 1906, which incorporated a requirement to make the inclusion of equestrian sports compulsory.

The first Olympic equestrian competition was, in fact, an individual jumping competition in the Olympic Games of 1900. There were no equestrian events in the 1904 and 1908 Games, despite the establishment of the Charter prior to the latter event. It appears that the problem was one of organization. The next time that equestrian sport was included in the Games was in 1912, when competitions in all disciplines of equestrian sport were held. There were individual and team jumping competitions, individual and team three-day eventing and an individual dressage competition. Since 1912, equestrian sport (showjumping, eventing and dressage) has been included in all the subsequent Olympic Games. Over the years the types of competition have varied; for example, in 1912 there were military, individual and team events while in 1920 the programme included long distance races and a mounted gymnastics competition. The latter was subsequently abolished.

The original concept of the Olympic Games was to encourage sport for the health and well-being of all persons involved. This was probably one reason why, in the early days, the amateur status of all competitors was so carefully guarded. Sadly, the acceptance of professional athletes into the Olympic Games since 1988 has changed the emphasis, so that money has become the driving force behind the modern Olympics. In recent times, rather than pursuing a healthy way of life, some athletes have even sacrificed their health in an attempt to succeed in their chosen sport.

Olympic Equestrian Sport

As stated earlier, the first Olympic equestrian competition was an individual jumping competition held at the Olympic Games of 1900. The next time that an equestrian sport was included in the Olympic Games was 1912. In 1912, the fifteenth session of the IOC defined equestrian sport as being 'indispensable' to the programmes of subsequent Olympic Games, thus securing the inclusion of equestrian sports for the future. However, this decree was slightly modified at a subsequent meeting held in Paris in 1924, when equestrian sport was more clearly defined and the inclusion of 'true' equestrian sport was declared to be 'compulsory', whereas polo was put onto a list of sports for 'optional' inclusion.

By 1928, the definitive programme of the Olympic Games was established in accordance with the classification adopted by the IOC, which included equestrian

FACING PAGE Page from the bulletin of the International Olympic Committee containing the programme of the Olympic Games in 1896.

sports. Since that time equestrian sports have always been included in the Olympic Games, despite the many changes which have been made to the criteria for inclusion of other sports. In the formative stages of the modern Olympic movement, one of the criteria for inclusion was that only sports that were practised in at least ten countries (six of which must enter the Olympiad) were admitted to the Games. In latter years these criteria for the admission of new sports have been further tightened, so that nowadays they should be practised in at least seventy-five countries and on four continents to be admissible for inclusion in the Olympic Games.

Originally, the only persons permitted to compete in equestrian events at the modern Olympic Games were commissioned officers and gentlemen. This restriction was not dropped until 1952. So strict were these criteria that, following the 1948 Games, the Swedish dressage team, which had won the gold medal, was disqualified a year after the event when it was discovered that one of its team members was in fact a non-commissioned officer! Although there was some resistance from the FEI, the IOC subsequently argued that all men should be able to compete on an equal basis and this rule was introduced in time for the 1952 Games.

Eighteen years earlier, at the thirty-third IOC session, held in Athens, an application was made for women to take part in a special jumping competition. This was rejected by the substantial majority of thirteen votes to two! A second application was made for the inclusion of women in the 1948 Games but was also rejected. Women continued to be debarred from equestrian events until 1952, when they were finally allowed to compete against men in the dressage events.

Dressage at the Olympic Games

The Olympic Dressage Competition has undergone numerous changes since its introduction in 1912. For example, team competitions were not organized until the 1928 Games.

The first Olympic Dressage Competition was entitled 'Individual Prize Riding' and the test was conducted in an arena measuring 40 x 20 m (Figure 73). There were seven judges for this test, which had a time allowed of 10 minutes. The test programme required the demonstration of all three paces of the horse plus some specific movements which included turns and small circles in trot and canter; collected and 'fast' paces; half-pirouettes; a single flying change and a sequence of flying changes. The required transitions were halt to canter, rein-back to trot and halt from 'fast gallop'. The movements of passage, piaffe and Spanish walk were not included in this test. Immediately after the dressage programme the rider was required to negotiate five 'high' jumps ranging from 80 cm to 1.1 m and one 'long' jump of 3 m. After this, the horse's bravery and obedience to the rider was '…tested by walking the horse up to, possibly over or through an object that has alarmed him'. However, it did state in the instructions for this phase of the test that there would be no firing of guns or beating of drums!

The principles of judging were specified and these indicated that the judges had to allocate marks from 0–10 for nine different aspects of the programme. Four of these were the horse's carriage when standing still, when walking, trotting and galloping. The others were the rider's seat in the saddle and his handling and management of the reins; the execution of the movements and the ability of the horse to turn and to jump and finally, the rider's management, exhibition and control of the horse.

The final results were based on the placings from each judge, that is, the winner was the rider who was placed first by the majority of judges, or who had the lowest place figure. The next placing was the next lowest value and so on.

This is a very different type of competition from the one in the modern Individual Olympic Dressage Competition, which currently entails riding three separate tests – the Grand Prix, the Grand Prix Special and the Grand Prix Kür, or Freestyle to Music tests.

The arena used in the 1912 Stockholm Games was 40 x 20 m and had markers as shown in Figure 73. The key markers that we use in dressage arenas today were introduced in the Three-day Event competition, which was held during the 1924 Olympic Games. This was the first time that a dressage arena measuring 60 x 20 m, with markers, was used for a Three-day Event competition. The locations of the key markers, which remain in use, are as shown in Figure 74.

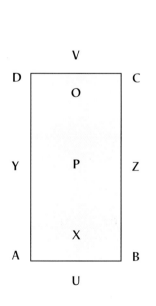

Figure 73 The dressage arena for the 1912 Olympic Games Dressage Competition (20 x 40m).

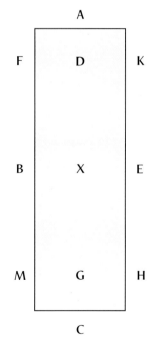

Figure 74 The dressage arena for the 1924 Three-day Event Dressage Competition (20 x 60m).

The 1920 and 1924 Dressage Competitions also used a 60 x 20 m arena, but with only the centre point and the centre line marked; additionally there were corner markers for the inside track – two metres in from the wall!

The modern Olympic tests evolved progressively over the years. In 1920 the test used was much more demanding than that used in the previous Games because it required half-pass in both trot and canter and flying changes every fourth, third and second stride and every stride. Tests with similar content and style were used in the two subsequent Olympic Games in 1924 and 1928.

A marked increase in the degree of difficulty occurred in 1932. The trot and canter counter-changes of hand were introduced at this stage, as was the schaukel. The passage, the piaffe and the canter half and full pirouettes also formed part of this test. Transitions from passage to extended trot and back were introduced. As on previous occasions, the test was timed and a time limit of 16 minutes was set. Penalties were incurred for taking longer than the time allowed. The test used in 1936 was of a similar type and had an even longer time limit of 17 minutes. Although not timed, the current Grand Prix test is expected to take approximately 7 minutes!

In 1948, the FEI removed the requirement for the passage and piaffe from the Olympic test but retained most of the other movements. However, passage and piaffe were restored for the Helsinki Games in 1952, the first year in which women were permitted to participate alongside men in the dressage events. The changes in 1956 were the introduction of the transitions from piaffe to extended trot and back to passage, along with flying changes in a set sequence on a 16 m circle.

The 1960 Grand Prix test was shorter than in previous Games (12 minutes) and incorporated most of the movements required in the current Grand Prix test. The changes on a circle were dropped, as were the transitions from piaffe to extended trot to passage. Another change in these Games was the absence of a team competition; also the five best-placed riders in the individual competition were required to perform a separate 'Ride-off' test in order to establish the winner. This 'Ride-off' test was the same as the Grand Prix test.

In 1964 a team competition was reintroduced: this used only the scores from the Grand Prix test which everyone was required to ride. The six best-placed riders in the Grand Prix test then went forward to the Ride-off test and the combined scores of both these tests decided the individual medal positions. In this Grand Prix test the trot counter-change of hand was made easier, but 8 m circles in passage were introduced at the end of the test. The Grand Prix test was still quite long, at more than 12 minutes, while the Ride-off test was now only about half as long.

A similar set of regulations was applied to the 1968 Games, which involved tests of a similar degree of difficulty. In 1972, the best twelve competitors in the Grand Prix test went forward to the Ride-off test but on this occasion, the Ride-off test results alone were used to determine the results of the individual competition. A similar situation applied to the 1976 Games but, on this occasion, the Ride-off test became the

'Grand Prix Special' test. This Grand Prix Special test included extensions on curved lines. In the controversial Games of 1980 the same tests were used. This was the year in which there was a boycott of the Moscow Olympic Games by the Western nations, resulting in only six countries and fourteen riders participating in the dressage event. As an alternative, a competition was held at Goodwood in England in the same year for those countries that did not participate in the Games. Full results of both events are included in this Appendix for the sake of completeness.

In the years before the 1984 Games there had been controversy over complaints of national bias on the part of judges from the nations that were expected to do well. So, it became an unwritten rule that no judges from Germany, Switzerland or Russia would be allowed to judge at Olympic Games, World Equestrian Games or World Championships. However, because I was then Chairman of the Dressage Committee, the Bureau insisted that I must judge. This led to the reintroduction of judges from these countries.

In 1984, the established formats for the team and individual competitions were maintained as per the 1972 Games, with Grand Prix and Grand Prix Special competitions. The Grand Prix was changed slightly to incorporate a transition from halt to medium trot, and the circles for the passage were increased to 10 m. The requirement to complete the test in a given time, with the potential to incur penalties, was dropped for this event.

In 1988 an unusual situation occurred. The regulations were changed actually during the Games to allow eighteen (which eventually became nineteen) riders to start in the Grand Prix Special. The original request came from the riders. There was a special meeting of the Bureau held solely for this purpose.

In 1992 the individual competition was opened to the best sixteen competitors from the Grand Prix test; however, a maximum of three riders per country were allowed to go forward (there were teams with a maximum of four riders). The circles in passage were dropped from the Grand Prix test.

1996 was the first time that a Freestyle to Music test was included in the competition. For the individual competition, the best twenty-four riders from the Grand Prix went forward to the Grand Prix Special and then the best twelve of those went forward once more to perform a Grand Prix Freestyle to Music test. The individual winner was the rider with the highest combined percentages from the Grand Prix Special and the Freestyle tests. Changes to the tests involved making the canter change of hand a little easier in the Grand Prix and, in the Grand Prix Special, transitions were required from passage to extended trot and back to passage.

The inclusion of the Freestyle to Music test caused some controversy. In the World Championships held before the 1996 Games, competitors had been free to choose which test they would elect to ride should they finish in the top twenty-four places in the Grand Prix. This arrangement produced two winners – one of the Grand Prix Special and one of the Freestyle to Music. However, at the Olympic

Games only one rider could win the gold medal so it was decided to make the Freestyle compulsory for the individual competition. The Freestyle to Music has become increasingly popular with riders and especially with the public and has done much to create a wide interest in the sport of dressage. In the 2000 Olympic Games, the individual winner was the rider with the highest combined percentages from the Grand Prix, Grand Prix Special and Grand Prix Freestyle competitions. This format is likely to be retained for the 2004 Olympic Games.

The material that follows comprises the records of all the dressage competitions held in all the Olympic Games since the first one in 1912. The data includes the names of the participants and the countries that they represented and, where appropriate, the names and numbers of teams. In addition, the types of competition and any special regulations that applied to them are given, along with the names of the judges and their judging positions, if known. Details of the size of the dressage arenas, plus their markings and the tests that were used are also given. The individual and team medal winners for each Olympic Games are listed, along with the full results for each participant. I hope that the reader finds this material an interesting guide through the historical development of our sport.

AN OLYMPIC GAMES ARCHIVE

Details of all Dressage Competions held in all
Olympic Games from 1912–2000

OLYMPIC GAMES 1912

STOCKHOLM, SWEDEN

Participating Countries: 8

Belgium	Norway
Denmark	Russia
France	Sweden
Germany	United States of America

Participating Riders: 21

Belgium – 2	Norway – 1
Denmark – 2	Russia – 1
France – 3	Sweden – 6
Germany – 5	United States of America – 1

Competitions

- Individual 'Prize Riding'.

- Maximum of 6 competitors per country (reserves not to exceed 3).

- No Team Competition.

Gold medallist Rittmeister Count Carl Bonde (SWE) on *Emperor*.
(Photo: courtesy of Max Ammann)

Special Regulations

- Open to all horses except those belonging to the army and attached to Government Riding Schools (not to individual officers) for the purpose of instruction.

- Every rider may enter 2 horses but may only ride 1.

- The prize will be awarded to the rider, not to the owner of the horse.

- Officers to wear uniforms without arms, others to wear high hat or hunting dress.

- Bitting: curb and snaffle; martingales or other special reins not allowed.

- Saddlery: optional.

Number of Judges: 7

Medal Winners

Individual

		Total of the placings of the seven judges
Gold	Rittmeister Count C Bonde (Sweden) *Emperor*	15
Silver	Maj G A Boltenstern (Sweden) *Neptun*	18
Bronze	Lt H von Blixen-Finecke (Sweden) *Maggie*	32

Arena: Rectangular court 40 x 20 m.

Markers:

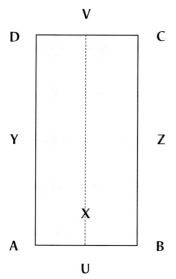

Judges

Lt Col Cederström (Sweden)
Maj Croneborg (Sweden)
Maj Karsten (Sweden)
Col Seiffert (Germany)

Rittm Bertrin (Russia)
Capt Chodron de Coursel (France)
Rittm Baumann (Norway)

DRESSAGE TEST – OLYMPIC GAMES 1912

Programme

- The rider shall enter at a gallop*, halt 10 metres in front of, and facing, the judges – salute.

- After halting, the horse shall stand still and 'at attention' until the signal is given, from which moment the rider is allowed 10 minutes for the performance of the movements specified below, at a walk, trot and gallop.

- The horse shall now be walked, trotted and galloped in the order named, each gait in an unbroken succession.

- All movements shall be exhibited alike from both sides in all the paces.

- The judges will not take into consideration such movements as passage, piaffe, Spanish trot, etc.

- Holding the reins, optional. When riding and holding the reins principally with one hand, 1 point extra will, however, be added to the number of points given for holding the reins during the walk and trot collectively; for the same in galloping, 2 points will be added.

The walk (about 1½ minutes) shall be free and long-striding.

The trot (about 3½ minutes) shall be ridden both 'collected' and 'fast'. From 'collected' trot a halt is made, then backing in a straight line (at least 6 metres at a stretch) and an immediate advance at a 'collected' trot; turns, voltes and facing about on the hindquarters without any previous halt.

The gallop (about 5 minutes) shall be ridden both 'collected' and 'fast', and the same movements as in the trot shall be displayed, and likewise: breaking into a gallop from a standstill; figure 8 with a diameter of about eight metres, in which the gallop shall be kept up alternately (left-handed) and changed both ways; change of gallop from one leg to another in a straight line at least four times; fast gallop, facing-about on hindquarters, fast gallop; a halt is made from fast gallop, followed immediately by trot.

5 obstacles to be taken at a gallop immediately after the performance of the programme.

- High jumps: one to be 0.8 metres high, two 1.0 metre and one 1.1 metre.

- Long jump: one to be 3 metres wide.

Obedience in the horse and controlling power of the rider will be tested by walking the horse up to, possibly over or through, the object, which has alarmed him. There will be no firing of guns, beating of drums, etc.

* 'Gallop' in this context implies canter: the French galop being used to describe both the three-beat canter and the four-beat gallop.

Principles for Judging

- Each judge shall give points from 0 to 10 for each of the following items:

1. The horse's carriage when standing still,
2. walking,

3. trotting,
4. galloping,
5. the rider's seat in the saddle,
6. handling and management of the reins,
7. the movements and ability of the horse to turn,
8. jumping and
9. the rider's management, exhibition and control of the horse.

- The horse shall, in all paces, move smoothly and be well on the bit with a steady head.

- In turning, the horse shall be set in the neck and have the trunk bent in the direction of the turn; when turning in the gallop, it shall be set to the right when riding a right gallop, in the opposite case to the left.

- When backing, the horse shall be well gathered together.

- The rider's seat shall be correct and must show a good, and supple grip of the horse, in unison with the motion of the horse, and without exaggerated movements.

- If the rider omits any of the movements stipulated in the programme, 1 point will be deducted. Should such omission be repeated, this will be considered a lack of training and occasion a deduction of 5 points.

- The judges are entitled to demand a repetition of any detail of the rider's performance, and an exhibition of any movements that may possibly have been omitted.

- In the event of a movement having been omitted, a judge is obliged to point this out to the other judges after the programme has been gone through.

Rules for Determining the Placing

- For each performance under the heading of 'Principles for Judging (1–9) a certain number of points will be allotted.

- All these figures will be added together for each competitor in the protocol of each of the judges, by which means the total number of points awarded to each competitor will be determined.

- After all the competitors have ridden, each judge will receive a summary of his protocols, in which the competitors are placed according to the total number of points by the respective judge. The judge awards the first place to the competitor who has obtained the highest number of points, the second to the next one, and so on.

- In case of two or more competitors obtaining the same total number of points, the judge will decide their respective places according to his impression of the performance of the competitors as a whole.

- The rider whom a majority of the judges have placed as No. 1 will be the winner. In case of there not being a majority in favour of any one competitor, the result will be obtained by adding the figures given by each judge, in which case the lowest figure will be declared the winner, the next lowest, second, and so on.

- If, in spite of this, the total number of all the points should remain equal for two or more competitors, the total of the points awarded by all the judges to the respective competitors will decide the award of the prizes, in which case the highest number of points will be No. 1, the next one No. 2, and so on. In the event of even such a procedure not giving a decision, the competitors with the same number of points shall draw lots.

EXAMPLE OF THE DISPLAY PROGRAMME

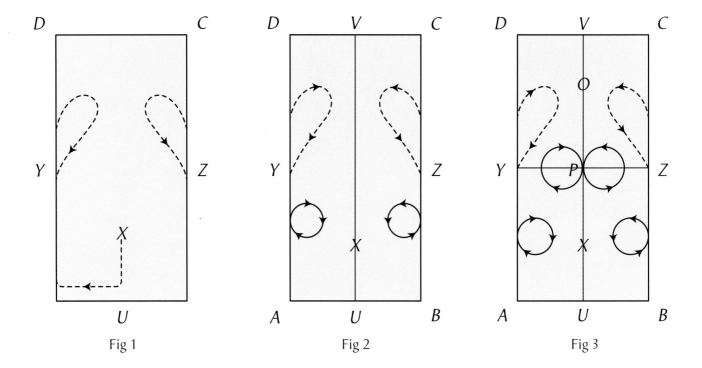

Fig 1   Fig 2   Fig 3

Walking (Fig 1)

Starting point = X. Follow the square to the right, between Y and D volte back, follow the square to the left, between Z and C volt back, follow the square to the right, 'collected' trot at U.

Trotting (Fig 2)

Between A and Y one volte, volte back between Y and D, between B and Z one volte, volte back between Z and C halt between Z and B, backing, 'collected' trot to Y, about-face, 'collected' trot to Z, halt, backing, 'collected' trot to Y, about-face, fast trot round the square to U, turn right up, at V follow the square to the left, at a fast trot, once round the square to V turn straight up and make a halt at X.

Gallop (Fig 3)

At X a 'collected' right gallop from standstill, at U follow the square to the right, between A and Y one volte. between Y and D volt back with change of gallop, halt between Y and A, from stand-still 'collected' left gallop, betwen B and Z one volte, between Z and C volte back with change of gallop, halt between Z and B backing, 'collected' right gallop, by Y about-face, 'collected' left gallop to Z, halt, backing, 'collected' left gallop to Y about-face, 'collected' right gallop, at V turn straight up to P, after which on figure 8. From figure 8 'collected' right gallop to U, follow the square to the right from U to V at a 'collected' gallop, turn straight up, 4 changes of gallop on the centre line to U, follow the square to the right at a fast gallop to V, turn straight up. Halt at O, right-about-face on the hind-quarters, fast left gallop to V and round the square to U turn straight up, at O left-about-face on the hind-quarters, right gallop. Halt at P, trot to U, halt, finish.

Count Carl Bonde
(SWE) performing
a compulsory jump.
(Photo: courtesy of
Max Ammann)

OLYMPIC GAMES 1912 RESULTS

Programme no.	Name of rider	Name of horse	Place figures							Total place figures	Placing
			Cederström Sweden	Croneborg Sweden	Karsten Sweden	Seiffert Germany	Chodron de Coursel France	Bauman Norway	Bertrin Russia		
47	**Carl Bonde**	*Emperor*	1	1	1	1	3	3	5	15	1
61	**Gustav A Boltenstern**	*Neptun*	1	2	2	2	3	3	5	18	2
55	**Hans von Blixen-Fineke**	*Maggie*	2	3	4	5	5	5	8	32	3
60	Karl von Oesterly	*Condor*	2	2	3	4	6	9	10	36	4
75	Carl Rosenblad	*Miss Hastings*	3	4	4	5	7	9	11	43	5
68	Oscar af Ström	*Irish Lass*	4	6	6	6	8	8	9	47	6
51	Felix Bürkner	*King*	1	2	6	7	8	13	14	51	7
57	Wilhelm Kruckenberg	*Kartusch*	4	6	7	8	8	8	10	51	8
64	Micael Ekimoff	*Tritonych XX*	3	7	7	10	10	12	13	62	9
41	G Seigner	*Dignité*	1	4	12	13	13	13	17	73	10
46	Andreas von Flotow	*Senta*	7	9	9	9	12	13	18	77	11
48	Carl von Moers	*New Bank XX*	10	10	11	11	11	15	15	83	12
63	Guy V Henry	*Chiswell*	9	12	12	13	14	15	18	93	13
39	Jean Cariou	*Cocotte*	5	7	11	15	17	19	20	94	14
69	Jens Chr B Falkenberg	*Hjördis*	12	14	14	14	16	16	17	103	15
56	R J G Keyper	*Kinley Princess*	12	14	15	15	17	18	20	111	16
50	Gaston de Trannoy	*Capricieux*	10	14	17	18	19	19	20	117	17
65	C H Saunte	*Steg*	11	15	16	16	20	21	21	120	18
45	D d'Astafort	*Castibalza*	11	17	18	18	19	19	21	123	19
58	John Montgomery	*Deceive XX*	16	17	18	19	19	20	21	130	20
54	Emmanuel de Blommaert	*Clonmore*	16	16	20	20	21	21	21	135	21

Olympic Games 1920

Antwerp, Belgium

Participating Countries: 5

Belgium
France
Norway
Sweden
United States of America

Participating Riders: 17

Belgium – 2
France – 6
Norway – 1
Sweden – 5
United States of America – 3

Competitions

- Individual.

- No Team Competition.

Special Regulations (same as Stockholm 1912).

- Open to all horses except those belonging to the army and attached to Government Riding Schools (not to individual officers) for the purpose of instruction.

- Every rider may enter 2 horses but may only ride 1.

- The prize will be awarded to the rider, not to the owner of the horse.

- Officers to wear uniforms without arms, others to wear high hat or hunting dress.

- Bitting: curb and snaffle; martingales or other special reins not allowed.

- Saddlery: optional.

Number of Judges: 4

Medal Winners

Individual

		Total points
Gold	Capt J Lundblad (Sweden) *Uno*	111.75
Silver	Lt K B Sandström (Sweden) *Sabel*	105.25
Bronze	Lt Count von Rosen (Sweden) *Running Sister*	100.50

Arena: Rectangle 50 to 60 metres x 20 metres. (Length given was approximate!)

Markers: Centre line and centre point marked.

Judges

Col Haegemann   (Belgium)
Col van Essen   (Sweden)
Cdt Haetjens   (France)
Maj Michelet   (Norway)

• No comparison of scores.

Test: Time allowed 10 minutes.

Note: One rider, Gustaf von Boltenstern, was disqualified because he used the arena before the competition, not knowing that this was not allowed.

BELOW The dressage arena in Antwerp. The rider is Lt Boudet (FRA) on *Ambleville*. (Photo: courtesy of Max Ammann)

DRESSAGE TEST – OLYMPIC GAMES 1920

Enter in canter, halt in front of the judges, immobility, salute (Fig 1).

A: Work in walk

- Proceed in free walk on a long rein, track to the right.
- On centre line towards judges, walk on the rein, collected walk.
- After the centre point, turn on the haunches in walk to the right.
- Continue on centre line, turn on the haunches to the left (Fig 2).
- Proceed in 'short trot' (collected trot) track to the right.

B: Work in trot

- Once around on the track with clear transitions from short trot (collected trot) to extended trot and vice versa. (In extended trot always rising, in short [collected] trot, sitting trot).
- On centre line towards the judges, half-pass to the right to the middle of the long side followed by half-pass to the left to the middle of the short side (Fig 3). Track to the left.
- One long side rising trot, turn on centre line towards the judges.
- Half-pass to the right and to the left of the centre line (3 steps, 7 x 6 steps, 3 steps, Fig 4).
- Track to the right.
- On the short side (entry), halt, immobility and proceed in short (collected) trot.

C: Work in canter

- Proceed on inner track 2 metres from the wall. (This distance has to be kept during all of the canter work.)
- Alternating – beginning on right rein in left canter – proceed in canter left and right out of trot, out of walk, out of rein-back. Every proceeding in canter should be executed in the middle of a long side.
- After the last proceeding in canter out of rein-back, on right rein a big circle in the middle of the arena. Change within the circle without changing leg, then a change of leg.
- Turn to the centre line in the direction of the judges.
- 10 metres before the short side, halt, immobility, 6 steps rein-back, proceed in canter right. Track to the right.
- On next long side, half-pass to the centre point of the arena.
- Halt, immobility, proceed in canter left and half-pass to the end of the same long side. Pass the corner without changing leg (Fig 5).
- Change of leg in the middle of the short side and serpentine 5 loops with change of leg when crossing centre line and 5 loops of counter-canter with change of leg when crossing the centre line. Finish in right canter, track to the left, before the corner change of leg (Fig 6).
- One long side extended canter, short side, short (collected) canter.

DISPLAY EXAMPLES OLYMPIC GAMES 1920

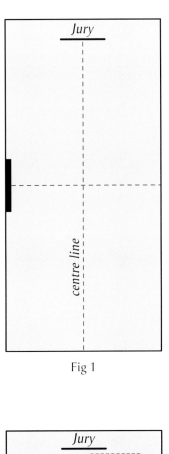

Fig 1

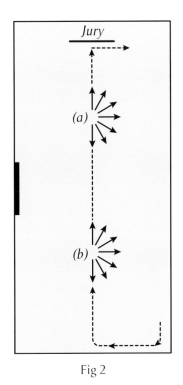

Fig 2

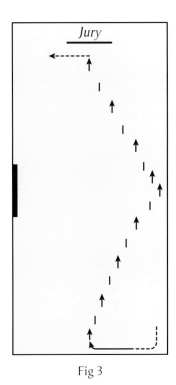

Fig 3

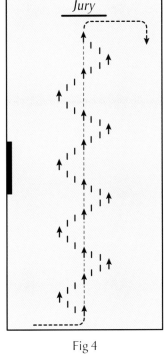

Fig 4

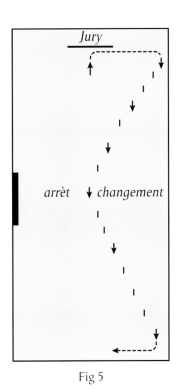

Fig 5

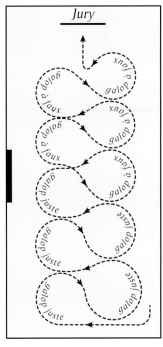

Fig 6

- ¾ of long side extended canter. Halt, rein-back, extended canter to ¾ of next long side. There short (collected) canter.

- On the centre line towards the judges, half-passes to the left and right with flying change at the end of every half-pass (3 strides, 5 x 6 strides, 3 strides). Track to the right.

- In the middle of the long side, turn right, at the centre point halt, immobility, 6 steps rein-back. Proceed in canter left, track to the left.

- On one long side 4 flying changes of leg every fourth stride (4-tempi).

- Next long side 6 flying changes of leg every third stride (3-tempi).

- On one long side 8 flying changes of leg every second stride (2-tempi).

- Next long side 16 flying changes of leg every stride (1-tempi).

- Turn to the centre line towards the judges. Proceed in walk, long reins, extended neck.

- At the centre point halt, salute.

- Exercises of the Haute École such as passage, piaffe and Spanish walk are not allowed to be shown.

- All the movements have to be shown at exactly the prescribed spot.

OLYMPIC GAMES 1920
Results – Grand Prix Test

Rider	Nationality	Horse	Judges' marks				Total	Average Value	Placing
			Belgium	France	Norway	Sweden			
Capt Janne Lundblad	Sweden	*Uno*	28.25	27.25	28.00	28.25	111.75	27.937	1
Lt Bertil Sandström	Sweden	*Sabel*	26.25	26.25	25.75	27.00	105.25	26.312	2
Lt Graf Hans von Rosen	Sweden	*Running Sister*	24.00	24.00	25.25	27.25	100.50	25.125	3
Capt Wilhelm von Essen	Sweden	*Nomeg*	25.75	22.25	24.25	27.25	99.50	24.875	4
Lt Hedoin Maille	France	*Chéribiribi*	25.50	23.25	23.00	24.00	95.75	23.937	5
Lt Michel Artola	France	*Plumard*	26.25	26.75	20.50	20.25	93.75	23.437	6
Cdt Gaston de Trannoy	Belgium	*Bouton d'Or*	25.50	21.50	21.75	23.75	92.50	23.125	7
Capt Jens Chr B Falkenberg	Norway	*Hjördis*	20.00	25.25	20.75	23.50	89.50	22.375	8
M Esnault-Peltière	France	*Saint James*	24.25	21.25	21.75	20.00	87.25	21.812	9
Lt Boudet	France	*Ambleville*	24.00	24.00	15.75	18.25	82.00	20.500	10
Lt E de Blommaert	Belgium	*Grizzly*	22.75	21.50	20.50	17.00	81.75	20.437	11
Lt Henri Mehu	France	*Gallypige*	23.00	19.25	16.25	22.00	80.50	20.125	12
Lt Marcel Blanchard	France	*Lenotre*	24.75	24.50	12.50	18.25	80.00	20.000	13
Maj Sloan Doak	USA	*Chiswell*	22.25	25.25	12.25	17.50	77.25	19.312	14
Capt Harry D. Chamberlain	USA	*Harebell*	22.25	23.75	14.75	16.50	77.25	19.312	14
Maj John A. Barry	USA	*Singlan*	21.00	25.00	16.75	14.50	77 25	19 312	14
Oberst Gustaf von Boltenstern [1]	Sweden	*Iron*	25.50	25.00	27.00	27.25	104.75	26.187	

1 Disqualified

OLYMPIC GAMES 1924

PARIS, FRANCE

Participating Countries: 9

Austria	Switzerland
Belgium	Sweden
Bulgaria	Czechoslovakia
France	Yugoslavia
Holland	

Participating Riders: 24

Austria – 2	Switzerland – 4
Belgium – 3	Sweden – 4
Bulgaria – 1	Czechoslovakia – 4
France – 4	Yugoslavia – 1
Holland – 1	

Competitions

- Individual 'Epreuve de Dressage'.

- No Team Competition.

Special Regulations

- Maximum of 4 riders per nation.

Number of Judges: 5

Gold medallist Ret Gen Ernst von Linder (SWE) on *Piccolomini*. (Photo: courtesey of Max Ammann)

Medal Winners

Individual

		Total points	Average
Gold	Gen E de Linder (Sweden) *Piccolomini*	1382	276.4
Silver	Lt K B Sandström (Sweden) *Sabel*	1379	275.8
Bronze	Capt François Lesage (France) *Plumarol*	1329	265.8

Arena: 60 x 20 m.

Markers: Centre line and centre point.

Judges

Gen Detroyat (President) (France)	Lt Col van Essen (Sweden)
Maj de Trannoy (Belgium)	Jonckher van Ufford (Holland)
Col Favre (Switzerland)	

- Four judges sitting at one table. After each test the judges compared the marks. If there were 3 or more points difference, the President of the Jury decided the final mark considering the majority verdict of the judges. The corresponding judges had to give the reason for the differences.

Test

- Total score maximum = 300 points per judge. To these points the extra points from the paces were added.

- Time allowed 10 minutes 30 seconds.

- (See also test from Amsterdam 1928; similar to test used at Antwerp 1920.)

The judges. Seated from left to right: Maj de Trannoy (BEL), Lt Col van Essen (SWE), unknown, Gen Detroyal (FRA), unknown, Col Favre (SUI), unknown. (Photo: courtesy of Max Ammann)

Dressage Test – Olympic Games 1924

Test time: 10 minutes 30 seconds

- Enter in canter towards the judges; halt; immobility, salute (Fig 1).

A: Work in walk

- Proceed in free walk on a long rein, track to the right.

- At the end of the arena, turn on the centre line towards the judges, collected walk.

- After the centre point, half turn on the haunches right. Continue on centre line. After a few steps, half turn on the haunches left (Fig 2) and proceed in short trot.

B: Work in trot

- Extend and shorten the trot on the track, 1½ tours of the arena by changing rapidly from short trot to extended trot and vice versa.

- Go on centre line towards the judges, half-pass right to the middle of the long side and half-pass left from there to the middle of the short side. (Fig 3). Track to the left.

- Rising trot on the long side.

- Go on centre line towards the judges and half-pass to left and right from centre line (3 steps, 7 x 6 steps, 3 steps) (Fig 4).

- Track to the right, halt on the short side, immobility, short trot.

C: Work in canter

- Track 2 metres from the wall.

- Proceed in canter, alternating right canter – left canter out of trot, walk, halt and rein-back. Every transition to be executed in the middle of the long side.

- Big circle on right rein in the middle of the arena.

- Change rein within the circle – counter-canter – flying change.

- Change rein within the circle – counter-canter – flying change.

- On centre line towards the judges – halt – immobility – rein-back.

- Proceed in canter right, track to the right.

- Half-pass on the diagonal, halt, immobility at centre point.

- Proceed in canter half-pass left – continue through the corner in counter-canter (Fig 5).

- Change of leg in the middle of the short side.

- Serpentine in canter (5 loops) with flying changes after every loop. Continue serpentine in counter-canter (5 loops) with flying change after every loop. Track to the right or to the left (Fig 6).

- Lengthening and shortening the canter – halt – proceed in extended canter – short canter.

- On centre line towards the judges.

Display examples Olympic Games 1924

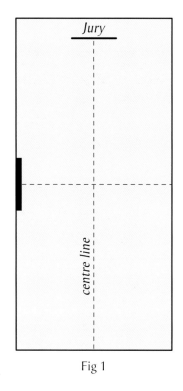

Fig 1

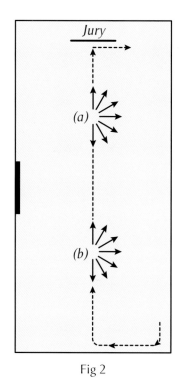

Fig 2

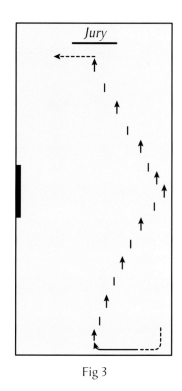

Fig 3

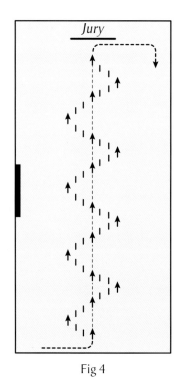

Fig 4

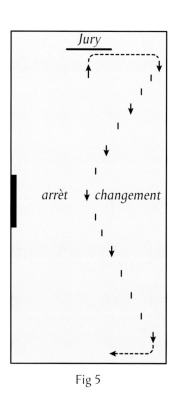

Fig 5

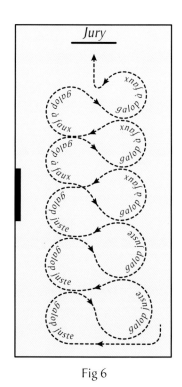

Fig 6

- Half-pass to right and left with flying changes (3 strides, 7 x 6 strides, 3 strides).

- Track to the right. In the middle of the long side turn right – halt at centre point – immobility – rein-back – proceed in canter left – track to the left.

- On the long sides, flying changes: 4 to 4-tempi; 6 to 3-tempi; 8 to 2-tempi and 16 to 1-tempi.

- Proceed to walk.

- Go on centre line, long reins – on centre point, halt, salute.

(It is not allowed to show movements from the Haute École like passage; piaffe; Spanish walk, etc.)

Note:

In principle this is the same test as that used in Antwerp in 1920 and Amsterdam in 1928. However, in Paris only, there were three extra marks given for the walk, trot and the canter as follows:

For walk   – maximum of 20 points

For trot   – maximum of 20 points

For canter – maximum of 20 points

For every clear mistake, 1 point or ½ point was deducted and the total average deducted from the total of all marks.

Example:

		Mistakes	Points	Average
Every Judge	Walk 20	1 1 ½	17½	
individually	Trot 20	1 ½ ½	18	
	Canter 20	1 1 ½ 1	16½	
			52	**17.33**

These average points were added to the overall marks for the test.

OLYMPIC GAMES 1924
Results

			Points allocated by the Judges								
Placing	Rider	Nationality	France	Holland	Sweden	Belgium	Switzerland	Total points	Average	Name of Horse	Age of Horse
1	**Ernst de Linder**	**Sweden**	**283**	**278**	**277**	**272**	**272**	**1382**	**276.4**	*Piccolmini*	**11**
2	**Bertil Sandström**	**Sweden**	**279**	**279**	**277**	**274**	**270**	**1379**	**275.8**	*Sabel*	**10**
3	**Xavier Lesage**	**France**	**283**	**265**	**255**	**265**	**261**	**1329**	**265.8**	*Plumard*	**12**
4	Wilhelm de Essen	Sweden	256	261	267	256	260	1300	260.0	*Zobel*	10
5	Victor de Ankarcrona	Sweden	239	267	255	250	272	1283	256.5	*Corona*	9
6	Emmanuel Thiel	Czechoslovakia	258	273	231	242	277	1281	256.2	*Ex*	8
	Not placed :										
	Robert Wallon	France	258	244	235	236	243	1216	243.2	*Magister*	9
	Henri Von der Weid	Switzerland	212	273	215	233	283	1216	243.2	*Uhlard*	11
	Georges Serlez	Belgium	238	242	245	244	241	1210	242.0	*Chong*	10
	L Paillard St-Fort	France	256	236	220	226	247	1185	237.0	*Roitelet VI*	NK
	Frantisek Donda	Czechoslovakia	251	254	228	206	241	1180	236.0	*Elan*	8
	Arthur von Pongracz	Austria	246	243	216	218	248	1171	234.2	*Aberta*	11
	Joseph Stevenart	Belgium	241	237	229	231	228	1166	233.2	*Paillasse*	13
	Jan van Reede	Holland	220	262	202	210	266	1160	232.0	*Slieve-Gallion*	14
	Albert Bourcier	France	258	205	231	241	205	1140	228.0	*Valentin*	9
	Adolphe-Ch. Mercier	Switzerland	212	226	214	215	251	1118	223.6	*Knabe*	13
	Vladimir-D Stoitcheff	Bulgaria	213	258	197	191	242	1101	220.2	*Pan*	10
	Otto Schoniger	Czechoslovakia	222	229	206	211	207	1075	215.0	*Fefé*	8
	Javosler Hanf	Czechoslovakia	213	235	193	193	233	1067	213.4	*Elegant*	6
	Werner Stuber	Switzerland	191	229	196	203	212	1031	206.2	*Queen-Mary*	7
	Charles Schlumberger	Switzerland	177	206	190	171	203	947	189.4	*Kincses*	13
	D von Sckullic-Vich	Austria	156	217	153	160	213	899	179.8	*Shagyax*	10
	Rojer Delrue	Belgium	164	184	155	169	182	854	170.8	*Kwango*	11
	Waldemar Seunig	Yugoslavia	179	175	152	149	183	838	167.6	*Benita*	9

OLYMPIC GAMES 1928

AMSTERDAM, HOLLAND

Participating Countries: 12

Austria	Denmark	Japan
Belgium	France	Norway
Bulgaria	Germany	Switzerland
Czechoslovakia	Holland	Sweden

Participating Riders: 29

Teams: 8 teams of 3 riders

Austria	Germany
Belgium	Holland
Czechoslovakia	Switzerland
France	Sweden

Individual Riders: 5

Bulgaria – 1	Denmark – 1
Japan – 2	Norway – 1

Competition

• Individual and Team Competitions – this was the first Olympic Team Competition.

• One test for the Team and Individual Competitions. The results of the 3 team riders gives the team result.

Special Regulations

• Maximum of 3 riders per nation (1 rider and 1 horse reserve optional).

• Only officers and gentleman riders (amateurs).

• The prizes will be awarded to the riders, not to the owners of the horses.

Number of Judges: 5

Medal Winners

Individual

		Total points	Average per judge
Gold	C F Frieherr von Langen (Germany) *Draufgänger*	1187.1	237.42
Silver	Col Charles Marion (France) *Linon*	1155.0	231.00
Bronze	Ragnar Olsen (Sweden) *Günstling*	1148.9	229.78

Teams

		Points	Placing
Gold	**Germany 3348.6 points**		
	C F Frieherr von Langen *Draufgänger*	1187.1	1
	Rittm H Linkenbach *Gimpel*	1121.3	6
	Maj E von Lotzbeck *Caracalla*	1040.2	11
Silver	**Sweden 3254.3 points**		
	Ragnar Olsen *Günstling*	1148.9	3
	J Lundblad *Blackmar*	1133.5	4
	C Bonde *Ingo*	971.9	19
Bronze	**Holland 3215.6 points**		
	J H van Reede *Hans*	1103.5	8
	P M R Versteegh *His Excellence II*	1082.2	9
	G W Leheux *Valérine*	1029.9	12

The Gold Medal-winning German Team. From left to right: Rittm Hermann Linkenbach (*Gimpel*) (placed 6th), Individual Gold Medallist Carl F Freiherr von Langen (*Draufgänger*), Maj Freiherr Eugen von Lotzbeck (*Caracalla*) (placed 11th). (Photo: courtesy of Max Ammann)

Arena: 60 x 20 m.

Markers: Centre line and centre point marked.

Judges

Jhr H van Reigersberg Versluys (Holland)
Frieherr von Holtzing-Berstett (Germany)
Baron G de Trannoy (Belgium)
E Wattel (France)
Count N Bonde (Sweden)

- The judges judge individually. The President of the Jury checks the judges' sheets after each test and asks for an explanation if the difference in marks is too big.

- In case of final equal points of 2 riders, the judges ask the rider to repeat 2 or 3 movements out of the test and decide afterwards.

Test

- Maximum points = 300 per judge.

- Time allowed 13 minutes.

DRESSAGE TEST – INDIVIDUAL AND TEAM – OLYMPIC GAMES 1928

	Test	Max. marks	Mark
1	Enter in canter. In front of the judges halt, immobility, salute.	4	
2	Proceed in free walk on a long rein, track to the right.	6	
3	On the centre line, walk on the bit, collected.	6	
4	On centre line after the centre point, turn on the haunches in walk to the right and to the left.	7	
		7	
5	Short trot.	6	
6	Transitions from extended to short trot and vice versa.	6+6	
7	On centre line, half-pass right to middle of long side, followed by half- pass left to middle of short side.	10	
8	One long side trot rising.	5	
9	On centre line, half-passes to the left and to the right (3 steps, 7 x 6 steps, 3 steps).	14	
10	Halt at the entry (middle of short side), immobility.	5	
	Proceed in short trot.	5	
11	On a track 2m inside of the wall.		
	Proceed in canter out of trot, first left	4	
	and then right.	4	

	Test	Max. marks	Mark
12	Proceed in canter out of walk, first left	4	
	and afterwards, right.	4	
13	Proceed in canter out of halt, first left	5	
	and afterwards right.	5	
14	Proceed in canter out of rein-back, first left	7	
	and afterwards right.	7	
15	Continue in canter on right rein. Big circle in the middle of the arena one full round, change	5	
	within the circle without changing leg.	5	
	– afterwards flying change of leg.	5	
	Circle on the left rein – change within the circle without changing leg – afterwards	5	
	flying change of leg.		
16	On centre line – halt, 6 steps rein-back, canter right – track to the right.	10	
17	Half-pass right to the centre point of the arena, halt at centre point.	10	
	Canter half-pass left to the end of the long side – through the corner without change of leg.		
	Middle of the short side flying change of leg.		
18	Serpentine through the arena, 5 loops with flying changes when crossing the centre line;	10	
	loops in counter-canter with flying changes when crossing the centre line.	15	
19	One long side, extended canter, short side, short canter.	15	
	¾ of long side short canter, halt, rein-back. Extended canter to ¾ of next long side.		
	From there short canter.		
20	On centre line, half-passes to left and to right with flying changes (3 strides, 5 x 6 strides, 3 strides)	18	
	end on right rein, track right.		
21	Turn right in middle of long side, at centre point, halt – immobility – 6 steps rein-back, proceed	7	
	in canter left, track to the left.		
22	On one long side 4 flying changes every 4th stride.	10	
23	Next long side 6 flying changes every 3rd stride.	12	
24	Next long side 8 flying changes every 2nd stride.	16	
25	Next long side 16 flying changes every stride.	20	
26	On centre line – proceed to walk – long reins. At the centre point halt, salute.	10	
	Position of the rider, seat, aids and use of the reins		
	Total	**300**	

For every movement missing, mark '0'.
Maximum time 13 minutes. For every full second over time deduct 2 points from total.

OLYMPIC GAMES 1928
Results – Team Competition

Country	Riders	Points	Total Points	Placing
Germany	Eugen von Lotzbeck	208.04		
	Herman Linkenbach	224.26	669.72	I
	Friedrich von Langen	237.42		
Sweden	Carl Bonde	194.38		
	Janne Lundblad	226.70	650.86	II
	Ragnar Olson	229.78		
Holland	Jan Hermanus van Reede	220.70		
	Pierre M R Versteegh	216.44	642.96	III
	Gerard W Leheux	205.82		
France	Pierre Marion	231.00		
	Robert Wallon	224.08	642.18	IV
	Pierre J Danloux	187.10		
Czechoslovakia	Javoslar Hanf	201.70		
	Emmanuel Thiel	225.96	637.94	V
	Otto Schöniger	210.28		
Austria	Arthur von Pongrácz de Szent-Miklós et Óvár	204.28		
	Wilhelm Jaich	204.16	606.40	VI
	Gustav Grachegg	191.96		
Switzerland	Werner Stuber	175.12		
	Oskar Frank	190.62	569.08	VII
	Adolphe Mercier	203.34		
Belgium	Roger G G Delrue	146.14		
	Henri J Laame	167.70	499.70	VIII
	Oswald G H Lints	185.86		

OLYMPIC GAMES 1928

Results – Individual Competition

Rider	Country	Judges Marks					Total points	Average points	Order of merit
		Holland	Germany	Belgium	France	Sweden			
Friedrich von Langen	**Germany**	**224.7**	**282.5**	**237.5**	**211.0**	**231.4**	**1187.1**	**237.42**	**1**
Pierre Marion	**France**	**210.4**	**258.6**	**245.9**	**236.1**	**204.0**	**1155.0**	**231.00**	**2**
Ragnar Olson	**Sweden**	**212.3**	**259.6**	**225.1**	**203.2**	**248.7**	**1148.9**	**229.78**	**3**
Janne Lundblad	Sweden	228.1	237.5	225.7	206.7	235.5	1133.5	226.70	4
Emmanuel Thiel	Czechoslovakia	227.9	223.2	246.0	224.8	207.9	1129.8	225.96	5
Herman Linkenbach	Germany	218.4	250.7	216.1	213.2	222.9	1121.3	224.26	6
Robert Wallon	France	207.7	219.5	240.3	261.4	191.5	1120.4	224.08	7
Jan Hermanus van Reede	Holland	237.0	243.0	224.7	187.6	211.2	1103.5	220.70	8
Pierre M R Versteegh	Holland	225.8	214.8	225.4	206.4	211.6	1082.2	216.44	9
Otto Schoniger	Czechoslovakia	220.4	233.2	223.4	190.5	183.9	1051.4	210.28	10
Eugen von Lotzbeck	Germany	189.7	239.8	207.0	201.0	202.7	1040.2	208.04	11
Gerhard W Leheux	Holland	245.3	204.9	209.0	182.4	187.5	1029.9	205.82	12
Arthur von Pongrácz de Szent									
Miklós et Óvár	Austria	208.7	240.2	198.0	187.3	187.2	1021.4	204.28	13
Wilhelm Jaich	Austria	201.6	232.5	206.2	170.5	210.0	1020.8	204.16	14
Adolphe Mercier	Switzerland	194.2	222.7	219.6	193.8	186.4	1016.7	203.34	15
Magnus Fog	Denmark	199.0	216.4	218.2	173.7	203.1	1010.4	202.08	16
Javoslar Hanf	Czechoslovakia	202.7	211.7	223.0	191.6	179.5	1008.5	201.70	17
Vladimir Stoitcheff	Bulgaria	219.5	205.5	218.9	163.6	196.3	1003.8	200.76	18
Carl Bonde	Sweden	185.1	201.8	188.1	169.8	227.1	971.9	194.38	19
Koichi Okada	Japan	191.7	212.9	208.0	178.6	184.5	968.5	193.70	20
Gustav Grachegg	Austria	200.5	210.4	204.8	176.4	167.7	959.8	191.96	21
Oskar Frank	Switzerland	188.1	189.4	208.1	187.5	180.0	953.1	190.62	22
Pierre J Danloux	France	227.0	225.2	252.7	267.2	l93.4	165.5	187.10*	23
Oswald G. H. Lints	Belgium	184.7	184.9	222.6	171.5	165.6	929.3	185.86	24
Werner Stuber	Switzerland	181.0	185.2	198.0	151.1	160.3	875.6	175.12	25
Paul Michelet	Norway	173.6	177.0	189.4	160.9	153.0	853.9	170.78	26
Henri J Laame	Belgium	171.8	174.9	176.4	153.3	162.1	838.5	167.70	27
Kohei Yusa	Japan	158.9	203.0	168.6	145.5	158.8	834.8	166.96	28
Roger G G Delrue	Belgium	135.8	143.4	175.4	132.5	143.6	730.7	146.14	29

*46 points deducted for loss of time

OLYMPIC GAMES 1932

LOS ANGELES, USA

Participating Countries: 4

France   Mexico   Sweden   United States of America

Participating Riders: 10

Teams: 3 teams of 3 riders

France   Sweden   United States of America

Individual riders: 1

Mexico – 1

Competition

- Grand Prix – one test for both Individual and Team Competition.

- The results from the 3 team riders are added for the team result.

Special Regulations

- Maximum of 3 riders per nation.

- Only officers and gentleman riders (amateurs).

Number of judges: 3

Gold Medallist Xavier Lesage (FRA) on *Taine*. (Photo: courtesy of Max Ammann)

Medal Winners

Individual

		Total points	Average	Placing
Gold	Col F Lesage (France) *Taine*	1031.25	343.75	6
Silver	Col Ch Marion (France) *Linon*	916.25	305.47	14
Bronze	H E Tuttle (USA) *Olympic*	901.50	300.50	14

Teams

		Total points	Total placings
Gold	**France 2818.75 points**		
	Col F Lesage *Taine*	1031.25	6
	Col Ch Marion *Linon*	916.25	14
	Col A Jousseaume *Sorelta*	871.25	17

		Total points	Total placings
Silver	**Sweden 2678.0 points**		
	B Sandström *Kreta*	964.00	9
	T Byström *Gulliver*	880.50	16
	G A Boltenstern *Ingo*	833.50	21
Bronze	**USA 2576.75 points**		
	H E Tuttle *Olympic*	901.50	14
	I L Kitts *American Lady*	846.25	17
	A H Moore *Water Rat*	829.00	20

Arena: 60 x 20 m.

Markers:

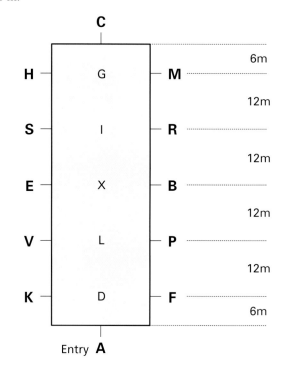

Judges

Lt Col Doak (USA)
Gen Lafond (France)
Counte Bonde (Sweden)

- No comparison of scores.

- Every judge marks every movement. Upon conclusion of the class each judge arranges the horses in order of merit (placing). The ratings (placings) of the judges are added and the rider with the smallest total is the winner.

- The winning team is that one the sum of whose ridersí individual places is the smallest.

Test

- Grand Prix – maximum score per judge = 400 points.

- Time allowed 16 minutes.

GRAND PRIX TEST – OLYMPIC GAMES 1932

Movements of the test	Directive ideas	Coefficients	Judges marks 0–10	Points obtained giving the classification	Observations
I	**I**				
Enter at the gallop. Halt at the centre; horse immobile; salute	Entering – no mark.				
II	**II**				
Move forward at the collected trot. Track to the right. From M to K – Change hands at the ordinary trot (posting). From K to F – Reins in one hand. From F to H – Change hands at the extended trot (sitting, reins in two hands). From H to C – Ordinary trot (posting).	Appreciation of the balance of the horse as a result of his suppleness in trot.	20			
III	**III**				
At C – Take right gallop (ordinary gallop). At M – Change hands changing lead at centre. From K to F – Collected gallop. From F to H – Change hands, ordinary gallop, reins in one hand, changing lead at centre. At C – Collected gallop, reins in two hands.	Appreciation of the balance of the horse as a result of his suppleness in gallop.	20			
IV	**IV**				
At B – Column right. At the centre, column right facing the Jury. At G – Halt, horse immobile 8 seconds.	Appreciation of the calmness of the horse and the absolute immobility.	10			
V	**V**				
Move forward at the collected trot, track to the right. After having passed M, half-turn on the haunches at the walk. Collected trot. After passing H, half-turn on the haunches at the walk. Collected trot.	Appreciation of the half-turns on the haunches.	10			
VI	**VI**				
From M to X to F – Counter change of hand on two tracks. At A – Column right.	Appreciation of the obedience and the mobility of the hindquarters.	10			

Movements of the test	Directive ideas	Coefficients	Judges marks 0–10	Points obtained giving the classification	Observations
VII	**VII**				
Two track seven times a distance two metres each side of the middle line, terminating the movement in such a manner as to take track to the left at C.	Suppleness and mobility of the horse in the half-passes.	30			
VIII	**VIII**				
At E – Column left. At X – Halt, back 3 steps, advance 6 steps, back 6 steps. Move forward at the collected trot. (All of these movements are to be made without perceptible halt in the transitions).	Proof of the mobility of the horse in his longitudinal axis.	20			
IX	**IX**				
At B – Track to the left. From M to H – the Passage. At H – Change hands at the extended trot (maximum extension – posting).	Perfect submission: in Passage	5			
At F – The Passage.	in Passage	5			
At A – The Piaffer from 10–20 steps.	in Piaffer	7½			
From A to E – The Passage.	in Passage	5			
At E – The Piaffer from 10–20 steps.	in Piaffer	7½			
From E to H – Collected trot.	in the Transitions	10			
(subtotal)		40			
X	**X**				
From H to M to X to K – Free walk. At K – Collect the horse, collected walk.	Appreciation of the free walk	10			
From F to E and M – Counter change of hands on two tracks. From M to E – Collected walk.	of the work on two tracks in walk	15			
At E – Column left.	in collected walk	10			
(subtotal)		35			
XI	**XI**				
At X – Collected gallop, right lead (at B, track to right). At A – Column right.	Proceeding in collected gallop	5			
At G – Demi-pirouette to the right. At X – Change leads.	Demi-pirouette right	10			
At D – Demi-pirouette to the left. At X – Change leads.	Demi-pirouette left	10			
(subtotal)		20			

Movements of the test	Directive ideas	Coefficients	Judges marks 0–10	Points obtained giving the classification	Observations
XII At G – Halt, back 6 steps. Collected gallop, left lead. Track left at C. At E – Collected trot. At A – Collected gallop.	**XII** Appreciation of the transitions from one pace to another in proceeding in gallop: from rein-back from trot	5 5			
XIII From F X to M – Counter changes of hands on two tracks, halting at X, with horse immobile. At C – Change leads.	**XIII** Degree of submission in the counter changes in gallop.	15			
XIV From H to K – Extended gallop. At K – Collected gallop.	**XIV** Perfection in the changes of speed.	5			
XV At A – Serpentine, five loops at the true gallop, changing leads at the middle line of the arena; five loops at the false gallop changing leads on the middle line of the arena; the diameter of the loops is 8 metres; terminate the movement so as to take track to the right hand changing leads at C.	**XV** Change of direction: serpentine in true gallop serpentine in false gallop	10 10	20		
XVI At M – Extended gallop. At F – Collected gallop.	**XVI** Perfection in the changes in speed.	5			
XVII At A – Column right, counter change of hand on two tracks to each side of the centre line, changing leads at each change of direction; the first and last two tracks are of three strides, the other five of two strides.	**XVII** Degree of perfection in the submission in the alternating half-passes.	30			

Movements of the test	Directive ideas	Coefficients	Judges marks 0–10	Points obtained giving the classification	Observations
XVIII	**XVIII**				
At C – Take track to the left hand. From H to K – Extended gallop. At K – Collected gallop.	Perfection in the changes in speed.	5			
XIX	**XIX**				
At A – Column left. Between D and X – Pirouette left. At X – Change leads. Between X and G – Pirouette right. At C – Change leads, track to the left.	Perfect submission: in the pirouette left / in the pirouette right	20 } 20 } 40			
XX	**XX**				
From H to K – 4 changes of leads in '4-time' From F to M – 6 changes of leads in '3-time' From H to F – 9 changes of leads in '2-time' From K to M – 15 changes of leads in '1-time'	Changes of leg: every 4th stride / every 3rd stride / every 2nd stride / every stride	5 5 10 20 } 40			
XXI	**XXI**				
From M to E – Ordinary left gallop. At E – Free walk.	Free walk.	5			
XXII	**XXII**				
At A – Column left. At X – Halt, facing the Jury. Salute.	No mark.				
XXIII	**XXIII**				
Correctness of position, seat, management of the horse.	General mark.	5			
Total		**400**			

Team Bronze medallists
(Left to right) Captain Hiram
E Tuttle on *Olympic*, Captain
Isaac L Kitts on *American Lady*
and Captain Alvin H Moore
on *Water Rat*.
(Photo: courtesy of Max
Ammann)

OLYMPIC GAMES 1932

Results – Individual

Rider	Horse	Doak	Laffont	Bonde	Total points	Average points	Place awarded by jury			Total	Final Place
							Doak	Laffont	Bonde		
Xavier Lesage (France)	*Taine*	335.50	368.50	327.25	1031.25	343.75	2	1	3	6	1
Pierre Marion (France)	*Linon*	263.25	363.25	289.75	916.25	305.42	7	2	5	14	2
Hiram Tuttle (United States)	*Olympic*	341.25	298.25	262.00	901.50	300.50	1	4	9	14	3
Thomas Byström (Sweden)	*Gulliver*	247.75	279.75	353.00	880.50	293.50	8	6	2	16	4
André Jousseaume (France)	*Sorelta*	276.75	316.50	278.00	871.25	290.42	6	3	8	17	5
Isaac L Kitts (United States)	*American Lady*	291.50	271.50	283.25	846.25	282.08	4	7	6	17	6
Alvin H Moore (United States)	*Water Rat*	281.50	267.50	280.00	829.00	276.33	5	8	7	20	7
Gustav A Boltenstern (Sweden)	*Ingo*	247.75	261.75	324.00	833.50	277.83	8	9	4	21	8
Gabriel G Jaramillo (Mexico)	*El Pravo*	195.75	208.00	197.75	601.50	200.50	10	10	10	30	9
Bertil Sandström (Sweden)	*Kreta*	298.00	291.25	374.75	964.00	321.33	3	5	1	9	10*

*Sandström placed in 10th place by the Jury of Appeal for a violation of an FEI rule for dressage.

OLYMPIC GAMES 1936

BERLIN, GERMANY

Participating Countries: 11

Austria	Germany	Sweden
Czechoslovakia	Holland	Switzerland
Denmark	Hungary	United States of America
France	Norway	

Participating Riders: 29

Teams: 9 teams of 3 riders

Austria	Germany	Norway
Czechoslovakia	Holland	Sweden
France	Hungary	United States of America

Individual Riders: 2

Denmark – 1
Switzerland – 1

Competitions

- Grand Prix – one test for Individual and Team Competition.

- Results from the 3 team riders added for the team result.

Special Regulations

- Maximum of 3 riders per nation.

- Only officers and gentleman riders (amateurs).

- Riders are not allowed to carry a whip.

- English saddle, bridle with snaffle-curb and curb-chain with padding if needed.

- Martingales, auxiliary reins, bandages, boots and blinkers of any kind were prohibited.

Number of Judges: 5

Medal Winners

Individual

		Total Marks	Total placings
Gold	First Lt H Pollay (Germany) *Kronos*	1760.0	15
Silver	Maj F Gerhard (Germany) *Absinth*	1745.5	18
Bronze	Maj A Podhajsky (Austria) *Nero*	1721.5	19

Team

		Marks	Final placing
Gold	**Germany 5074.0 points**		
	First Lt H Pollay *Kronos*	1760.0	1
	Maj F Gerhard *Absinth*	1745.5	2
	Capt v Oppeln-Bronikowski *Gimpel*	1568.5	10
Silver	**France 4846.0 points**		
	Capt Jousseaume *Favorite*	1642.5	5
	Lt de Ballorre *Débaucheur*	1634.0	6
	Col Gillois *Nicolas*	1569.5	8
Bronze	**Sweden 4660.5 points**		
	First Lt v Adlerereutz *Teresina*	1675.0	4
	Maj Colliander *Kal XX*	1530.5	11
	Capt Sandström *Pergola*	1455.0	15

Arena: 60 x 20 m.

Markers: Same as in Los Angeles 1932:

A-K-V-E-S-H-C-M-R-B-P-F [D-L-X-I-G].

Judges

Col Quarles van Ufford (Holland)
Gen Decarpentry (France)
Lt Col Baron v Henikstein (Austria)
Gen v Poseck (Germany)
Col Baron v Cederström (Sweden)

• No comparison of marks.

Test

• Maximum score per judge = 415 points.

• Time allowed = 17 minutes.

Gold medallist 1st Lt Heinz Pollay (GER) on *Kronos*. (Photo: courtesy of Max Ammann)

GRAND PRIX TEST – OLYMPIC GAMES 1936

Movements and Scoring

The movements had to be executed within 17 minutes in an arena of 60 x 20 m. In addition to further faults, any over-time was penalised by half a point for each second begun. The movements were:

I

Enter at the gallop.
Halt at the centre-points.
Immobility of horse. Salute.

II

Move on at the collected trot. Track to the right.

From M to K	Change hands at the ordinary trot (posting).
From K to F	Reins in one hand.
From F to H	Change hands at the extended trot (posting), reins in two hands.
From H to C	Ordinary trot (posting).

Coefficient: 20.

III

At C	Take ordinary gallop.
At M	Change hands, change of leg at centre-point.
From K to F	Collected gallop.
From F to H	Change hands, ordinary gallop, reins in one hand, change of leg at centre.
At H	Reins in two hands.
At C	Collected gallop.

Coefficient: 20.

IV

At B	Turn to the right. At the centre turn to the right facing the Jury.
At G	Halt, immobility of horse for 8 seconds.

Coefficient: 10.

V

Move on at the collected trot, at C track to the right.

After having passed M	Half-turn on the haunches at the walk. Collected trot.
After having passed H	Half-turn on the haunches at the walk. Collected trot.

Coefficient: 10.

VI

M to X to F	Counter-change of hands on two tracks.
At A	Turn on middle-line.

Coefficient: 10.

VII

Bending on two tracks seven times unto a distance of 2 metres each side of middle-line, terminating the movement in such a manner as to take track to the left at C (Fig. 2).

Coefficient: 30.

VIII

At E	Turn to the left.
At X	Halt. Back 3 paces, advance 6 paces, back 6 paces.
	Move on at the collected trot. (All of these movements must be executed without perceptible halt in the transitions).

Coefficient: 20.

IX

At B	Track to the right.
From F to K	The passage.
From K to M	Change hands at the utmost extended trot (sitting).

Coefficient: 5.

From M to C	The passage.

Coefficient: 5.

At C	The piaffe (10 to 20 paces).

Coefficient: 10.

From C to H	The passage.

Coefficient: 5.

From H to F	Change hands at the utmost extended trot (sitting) collect the horse and...

Coefficient: 5.

At A	Turn on middle-line, immediately beginning the passage, keeping it on, face to the Jury unto G.

Coefficient: 5.

At G	The piaffe (10 to 20 paces), facing the Jury, then move on at the collected trot.

Coefficient: 10.

At C	Track to the right, continuing collected trot unto B.

All transitions, coefficient: 10.

X

At B	Free walk.

Coefficient : 10.

At F	Turn to the right.

Coefficient: 15.

At K	Track to the left, collect the horse, collected walk.

Coefficient: 10.

F to E to M	Counter-change of hands on two tracks.
From M to E	Collected walk.
At E	Turn to the left.

XI

At X	Take collected gallop to right.
At A	Turn on middle-line.
	Coefficient: 5.
At G	Half-pirouette to the right.
	Coefficient: 10.
At X	Change of leg.
At D	Half-pirouette to the left.
	Coefficient: 10.
At X	Change of leg.

XII

At G	Halt. Back 6 paces. Move on at collected gallop to left.
	Coefficient: 5.
At E	Collected trot.
	Coefficient: 5.
At A	Collected gallop.

XIII

F to X to M	Counter-change of hands on two tracks.
	At X halt, immobility of horse.
At C	Change of leg.
	Coefficient: 15.

XIV

From H to K	Extended gallop.
At K	Collected gallop.
	Coefficient: 5.

XV

At A	Serpentine. 5 loops at the true gallop, changing leg on middle-line; 5 loops at the outer gallop, changing leg on middle-line; each loop of 8 metres in diameter, ending the movement so as to take track to the right; at C change of leg (Fig. 3).
	Coefficients: True gallop, 10, outer gallop, 10.

XVI

From M to F	Extended gallop.
F	Collected gallop.
	Coefficient: 5.

	XVII
At A	Turn on middle-line, counter-change of hands on two tracks to each side of middle-line, changing leg at each change of direction; the first and the last movement on two tracks are of 3, the other five movements of 6 strides. In this movement the auxiliary lines need not be respected. **Coefficient: 30.**

	XVIII
At C	Track to the left.
From H to K	Extended gallop.
At K	Collected gallop. **Coefficient: 5.**

	XIX
At A	Turn on middle-line.
Between D and X	Pirouette to the left. **Coefficient: 20.**
At X	Change of leg.
Between X and G	Pirouette to the right. **Coefficient: 20.**
At C	Change of leg, track to the left.

	XX
From H to K	4 changes of leg every 4th stride. **Coefficient: 5.**
From F to M	6 changes of leg every 3rd stride. **Coefficient: 5.**
On the diagonal from H to F	9 changes of leg every 2nd stride. **Coefficient: 10.**
On the diagonal from K to M	15 changes of leg every stride. **Coefficient: 20.**

	XXI
From M to E	Track to the left, ordinary gallop.
At E	Extended walk. **Coefficient: 5.**

	XXII
At A	Turn on middle-line.
At X	Halt facing the Jury. Salute. Leave the arena at the extended walk.

XXIII
Correctness of position, seat, management of the horse.
Coefficient: 5.

Scoring: The test had to be carried through by memory in the correct order of the movements. For each movement or group of movements a mark from 0 to 10 was given by each of the judges. Each mark was multiplied by the corresponding coefficient (for coefficients, see sections of movements). The total number of points which each horse was given by each judge decided the final placing. The rider with the lowest number of placing points was declared victor.

MOVEMENTS FROM GRAND PRIX TEST – OLYMPIC GAMES 1936

1. Arena for the
Dressage Test –
Pattern of the
movements

2. Movements,
Section VII

3. Movements,
Section XV

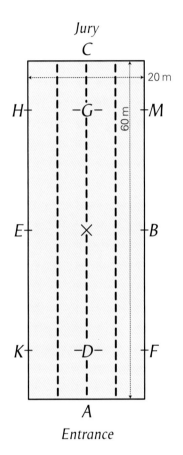

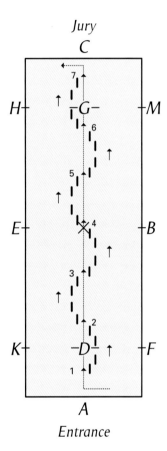

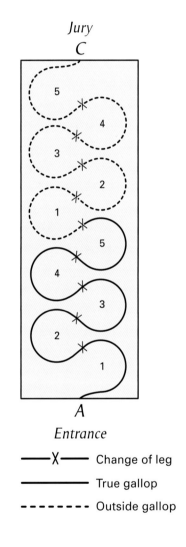

— X — Change of leg

——— True gallop

- - - - - - - Outside gallop

OLYMPIC GAMES 1936
Results – Individual Competition

Weather: August 12th: Dry, sunny day; temperature between 16° and 24° C. During the whole day a fairly perceptible wind prevailed, which occasionally disturbed the competition.

August 13th: Sunny and dry in the morning: temperature between 16° and 22° C. The wind became continuously stronger, its velocity increasing towards thc end of the competition to an extent which proved to be disturbing at times.

Judges: Col v Ufford (Holland), General Decarpentry (France), Lieut-Col v Henikstein (Austria), Baron General v Poseck (Germany), Col Baron v Cederström (Sweden).

			Judges					
Place	Rider, Country and Horse		Col Baron v Cederström (Sweden)	General Decarpentry (France)	Lt-Col v Henikstein (Austria)	Baron Gen v Poseck (Germany)	Col Qu v Ufford (Holland)	Totals
1	**First Lt Pollay (Germany)** *Kronos*	Judges' Marks	341.5	356.5	343.5	377.5	341.0	1760.0
		Points	4	1	4	1	5	15
2	**Maj Gerhard (Germany)** *Absinth*	Judges' Marks	346.0	333.5	345.0	376.5	344.5	1745.5
		Points	3	7	3	2	3	18
3	**Maj Podhajsky (Austria)** *Nero*	Judges' Marks	339.5	343.5	372.0	314.5	352.0	1721.5
		Points	5	4	1	7	2	19
4	First Lieut v Adlercreutz (Sweden) *Teresina*	Judges' Marks	372.0	334.5	351.5	307.0	310.0	1675.0
		Points	1	6	2	8	9	26
5	Capt Jousseaume (France) *Favorite*	Judges' Marks	309.0	339.5	315.0	325.5	353.5	1642.5
		Points	8	5	8	4	1	26
6	Lt de Ballorre (France) *Débaucheur*	Judges' Marks	309 0	353.5	340.5	316.0	315.0	1634.0
		Points	8	2	5	6	8	29
7	Capt Jensen (Denmark) *His Ex*	Judges' Marks	327.5	326.0	322.5	288.5	331.5	1596.0
		Points	7	8	7	11	6	39
8a	Capt Versteegh (Holland) *Ad Astra*	Judges' Marks	296.5	321.5	314.0	305.5	341.5	1579.0
		Points	13	9	9	9	4	44
8b	Comm Gillois (France) *Nicolas*	Judges' Marks	306.5	352.5	290.0	321.0	299.5	1569.5
		Points	10	3	13	5	13	44
10	Capt Oppeln-Bronikowski (Germany) *Gimpel*	Judges' Marks	294.5	291.5	326.5	348.5	307.5	1568.5
		Points	14	15	6	3	11	49
11	Maj Colliander (Sweden) *Kal XX*	Judges' Marks	337.5	316.5	303.0	285.5	288.0	1530.5
		Points	6	10	11	15	16	58
12	Lt-Col Dolleschall (Austria) *Infant*	Judges' Marks	284.5	308.0	314.0	286.0	283.5	1476.0
		Points	16	12	9	14	17	68

			Judges					
Place	Rider, Country and Horse		Col Baron v Cederström (Sweden)	General Decarpentry (France)	Lt-Col v Henikstein (Austria)	Baron Gen v Poseck (Germany)	Col Qu v Ufford (Holland)	Totals
13	Lt Jandl (Czechoslovakia) *Nestor*	Judges' Marks	270.5	314.0	285.5	286.5	296.5	1453.0
		Points	20	11	15	13	14	73
14	Gen v Pados (Hungary) *Ficsur*	Judges' Marks	277.0	293.0	289.0	288.0	277.0	1424.0
		Points	18	14	14	12	18	76
15a	Capt Sandström (Sweden) *Pergola*	Judges' Marks	348.0	275.5	277.0	284.0	270.5	1455.0
		Points	2	21	20	16	21	80
15b	Maj-Gen v Pongrácz (Austria) *Georgine*	Judges' Marks	273.0	289.5	303.0	268.5	296.0	1430.0
		Points	19	17	11	18	15	80
17a	Capt Quist (Norway) *Jaspis*	Judges' Marks	299.5	270.5	284.0	279.5	304.5	1438.0
		Points	12	23	17	17	12	81
17b	Col v Magashazy (Hungary) on *Tücsök*	Judges' Marks	284.0	289.5	277.5	291.0	273.5	1415.5
		Points	17	17	18	10	19	81
19	Maj Le Heux (Holland) on *Zonnetje*	Judges' Marks	288.5	286.5	270.0	268.0	309.0	1422.0
		Points	15	19	21	19	10	84
20	Capt Johansen (Norway) *Sorte Mand*	Judges' Marks	302.0	290.0	267.5	257.0	271.5	1388.0
		Points	11	16	22	22	20	91
21	Maj Camerling Helmolt (Holland) *Wodan*	Judges' Marks	258.5	268.0	277.5	253.5	323.5	1381.0
		Points	25	24	18	26	7	100
22	Lt Moser (Switzerland) *Revue*	Judges' Marks	265.0	293.5	285.5	255.0	238.0	1337.0
		Points	22	13	15	24	29	103
23	Capt Babcock jr (USA) *Olympic*	Judges' Marks	265.0	275.0	263.0	268.0	259.5	1330.5
		Points	22	22	23	19	23	109
24	Maj Pechmann (Czechoslovakia) *Idéal*	Judges' Marks	265.5	284.0	260.5	262.5	246.5	1319.0
		Points	21	20	24	21	28	114
25	Capt Kitts (USA) *American Lady*	Judges' Marks	246.0	265.5	246.0	256.5	251.0	1265.0
		Points	28	25	27	23	25	128
26	Lt-Col Kemery (Hungary) *Csintalan*	Judges' Marks	260.0	237.0	247.5	240.5	265.5	1250.5
		Points	24	28	26	29	22	129
27	Maj Tuttle (USA) *Si Murray*	Judges' Marks	254.5	226.0	239.0	254.5	259.0	1233.0
		Points	26	29	29	25	24	133
28	Capt Bjørnseth (Norway) *Invictus*	Judges' Marks	227.5	247.0	251.0	252.5	246.5	1224.5
		Points	29	27	25	27	26	134
29	Lt Col Schöniger (Czechoslovakia) *Helios*	Judges' Marks	246.5	265.0	242.0	251.0	249.5	1254.0
		Points	27	26	28	28	26	135

OLYMPIC GAMES 1936
Results – Team Competition

Place	Country, Rider and Horse		Col Baron v Cederström (Sweden)	General Decarpentry (France)	Lt-Col A v Henikstein (Austria)	Baron Gen v Poseck (Germany)	Col Qu v Ufford (Holland)	Total
					Judges			
1	**Germany**							
	Maj Gerhard *Absinth*		346.0	333.5	345.0	376.5	344.5	1745.5
	First Lt Pollay *Kronos*		341.5	356.5	343.5	377.5	341.0	1760.0
	Capt v Oppeln-Bronikowski *Gimpel*		294.5	291.5	326.5	348.5	307.5	1568.5
		Total	**982.0**	**981.5**	**1015.0**	**1102.5**	**993.0**	**5074.0**
2	**France**							
	Lt de Ballorre *Débaucheur*		309.0	353.5	340.5	316.0	315.0	1634.0
	Comm Gillois *Nicolas*		306.5	352.5	290.0	321.0	299.5	1569.5
	Capt Jousseaume *Favorite*		309.0	339.5	315.0	325.5	353.5	1642.5
		Total	**924.5**	**1045.5**	**945.5**	**962.5**	**968.0**	**4846.0**
3	**Sweden**							
	First Lt v Adlercreutz *Teresina*		372.0	334.5	351.5	307.0	310.0	1675.0
	Major Colliander *Kal XX*		337.5	316.5	303.0	285.5	288.0	1530.5
	Capt. Sandstrom *Pergola*		348.0	275.5	277.0	284.0	270.5	1455.0
		Total	**1057.5**	**926.5**	**931.5**	**876.5**	**868.5**	**4660.5**
4	**Austria**							
	Maj Podhajsky *Nero*		339.5	343.5	372.0	314.5	352.0	1721.5
	Lt Col Dolleschall *Infant*		284.5	308.0	314.0	286.0	283.5	1476.0
	Gen v Pongrácz *Georgine*		273.0	289.5	303.0	268.5	296.0	1430.0
		Total	**897.0**	**941.0**	**989.0**	**869.0**	**931.5**	**4627.5**
5	**Holland**							
	Capt Versteegh *Ad Astra*		296.5	321.5	314.0	305.5	341.5	1579.0
	Maj Le Heux *Zonnetje*		288.5	286.5	270.0	268.0	309.0	1422.0
	Maj Camerling-Helmolt *Wodan*		258.5	268.0	277.5	253.5	323.5	1381.0
		Total	**843.5**	**876.0**	**861.5**	**827.0**	**974.0**	**4382.0**
6	**Hungary**							
	General v Pados *Ficsur*		277.0	293.0	289.0	288.0	277.0	1424.0
	Col v Magashazy *Tücsök*		284.0	289.5	277.5	291.0	273.5	1415.5
	Lt-Col Kemery *Csintalan*		260.0	237.0	247.5	240.5	265.5	1250.5
		Total	**821.0**	**819.5**	**814.0**	**819.5**	**816.0**	**4090.0**
7	**Norway**							
	Capt Quist *Jaspis*		299.5	270.5	284.0	279.5	304.5	1438.0
	Capt Johansen *Sorte Mand*		302.0	290.0	267.5	257.0	271.5	1388.0
	Captr Bjørnseth *Invictus*		227.5	247.0	251.0	252.5	246.5	1224.5
		Total	**829.0**	**807.5**	**802.5**	**789.0**	**822.5**	**4050.5**
8	**Czechoslovakia**							
	Lt Jandl *Nestor*		270.5	314.0	285.5	286.5	296.5	1453.0
	Maj Pechmann *Ideal*		265.5	284.0	260.5	262.5	246.5	1319.0
	Lt Col Schöniger *Helios*		246.5	265.0	242.0	251.0	249.5	1254.0
		Total	**782.5**	**863.0**	**788.0**	**800.0**	**792.5**	**4026.0**
9	**USA**							
	Capt Babcock jr *Olympic*		265.0	275.0	263.0	268.0	259.5	1330.5
	Capt Kitts on *American Lady*		246.0	265.5	246.0	256.5	251.0	1265.0
	Maj Tuttle on *Si Murray*		254.5	226.0	239.0	254.5	259.0	1233.0
		Total	**765.5**	**766.5**	**748.0**	**779.0**	**769.5**	**3828.5**

OLYMPIC GAMES 1948

LONDON, GREAT BRITAIN

Participating Countries: 9

Argentina	Mexico	Sweden
Austria	Portugal	Switzerland
France	Spain	United States of America

Participating Riders: 19 (but one rider eliminated after the Games).

Teams: 4 teams of 3 riders

Argentina
France
Portugal
United States of America

(The Swedish team were eliminated because they entered one rider who was not qualified to compete.)

Gold Medallist Capt Hans Moser (SUI) on *Hummer*. (Photo: courtesy of Max Ammann)

Individual Riders: 4

Austria – 1
Mexico – 1
Spain – 1
Switzerland – 1

Competitions

- Grand Prix without piaffe and passage.

- One test for the Individual and Team competitions.

Special Regulations

- Maximum of 3 riders per nation.

- Only officers and gentleman riders (amateurs).

- The prescribed test must be carried out entirely from memory. Each competitor will be allowed 13 minutes to complete it. In the event of a rider failing to complete the test within the prescribed time he will lose half a point for every second over the time allowed.

- Teams will be placed according to the total number of points gained by the 3 riders of each team.

Medal Winners

Individual

		Points
Gold	Capt H Moser (Switzerland) *Hummer*	492.5
Silver	Col A Jousseaume (France) *Harpagon*	480.0
Bronze	Col G A Boltenstern (Sweden) *Trumf*	477.5

Team

		Points	Individual Placing
Gold	**France 1269 points**		
	Col A Jousseaume *Harpagon*	480.0	2
	J Paillard *Sous les Ceps*	439.5	6
	Capt M Buet *Saint Ouen*	349.5	15
Silver	**USA 1256 points**		
	R Borg *Klingsen*	473.5	4
	E Thomson *Pancraft*	421.0	8
	F Henry *Reno Overdo*	361.5	13
Bronze	**Portugal 1182 points**		
	F Pais *Matamas*	411.0	9
	F Valadas *Feitico*	405.0	10
	L Mena e Silva *Fascinante*	366.0	12

Arena: 60 x 20 m.

Markers: Same as Los Angeles and Berlin.

Judges

Gen Decarpentry (France) Col N Thommen (Switzerland) Count Bonde (Sweden)

• No comparison of scores.

Test

• Grand Prix – maximum of 200 points per judge.

• Time allowed 13 minutes.

Team prizegiving ceremony. The gold medal winners, Sweden, were subsequently disqualified and the gold medal was awarded to France. The bronze medallists were USA. (Photo: courtesy of Max Ammann)

GRAND PRIX TEST – OLYMPIC GAMES 1948

Test to be carried out in 13 minutes

		Directive ideas	Marks given by judge 0–10	Coefficients	Points obtained for classification	Remarks
I						
1		Entry at the canter. At X halt. Salute. Break into ordinary trot (rising in the stirrups).	Entry, Halt, Move off at the trot	5		
	At C	Track to the left.				
2	From H X F	Diagonally at the extended trot (rising in the stirrups).				
3	From F to K	Collected trot (sitting).				
4	At K	Reins in one hand.	The two extended trots	10		
	From K X M	Diagonally at the extended trot (rising in the stirrups).				
5	From M to E	Collected trot (sitting).	The two collected trots	10		
II						
6	At E	Turn, separate the reins.				
	At X	Circle to the right of 6 metres diameter, followed immediately by a circle of the same size to the left.				
	At B	Track to the right.	The two circles	5		
III						
7	At A	Turn down the centre line.				
8	From D to P	Traverse diagonally from left to right.				
	From P to S	From right to left.				
	From S to G	From left to right.				
	At G	Proceed direct to C.				
	At C	Track to the right and change to ordinary walk.	The traverses	10		
IV						
9	From MX K	Change the rein at extended walk.	The extended walk and the transition to the collected walk	10		
10	At A	Turn down the centre line at collected walk.				
11	At X	Traverse to the left on H the horse parallel to the long side of the arena.				
12	At H	Half-pirouette to the right and traverse with croup to the wall to the right to E.				

		Directive ideas	Marks given by judge 0–10	Coefficients	Points obtained for classification	Remarks
13	At E	Straighten out and proceed at ordinary walk straight to K.	The two traverses	10		
14	At A	Turn down the centre line. Collected walk.				
15	At X	Traverse to the right on M the horse parallel to the long side.				
16	At M	Half-pirouette to the left and traverse with croup to the wall to the left to B.				
17	At B	Straighten out and proceed straight at ordinary walk to F, following right-hand track.	The two half-pirouettes	10		
V						
18	At F	Move off at the collected canter on the left leg (false canter).				
19	At E	Change to ordinary walk.	Transition from the canter to the walk	5		
	At H	Turn down the centre line.				
20	At G	Halt. Rein-back 3 paces. Advance 3 paces. Rein-back 6 paces. Move off at the collected canter on the right leg.				
	At M	Right hand track.	Halt, Rein-back, Move off	10		
VI						
21	From KXM	Change the rein and extended canter.				
	At M	Collected canter, remaining on the right leg.				
	At C	Change leg.	The two extended canters	10		
22	At HXF	Change the rein and extended canter.				
	At F	Collected canter remaining on the left leg.				
	At A	Change legs. Turn down the centre line and counter-change the rein on two tracks to each side of the centre line changing leg at each change of direction. The first and last changes of direction are of 3 paces the five others being of 6 paces	Transitions to canter	15		
			Submission in the counter-changes	10		
VII						
23	At C	Track to the right.				
	At M	Change the rein.				
24	At X	Pirouette to the right.				
	At K	Change of leg (left).	Regularity and submission	10		
25	At F	Change the rein.				
26	At X	Pirouette to the left.				
	At H	Change leg (right).	Regularity and submission	10		

VII

		Directive ideas	Marks given by judge 0–10	Coefficients	Points obtained for classification	Remarks
27	At B	Make a figure of eight broadways on with X as the centre. No change of leg when changing the loop. Each loop to be 8 metres in diameter and the first loop should not be entirely closed (see diagram). Before finishing the second loop of the first figure eight, at X change leg and execute to the right and on the left leg the first loop of the second figure 8. Finish the second figure eight without changing leg, but the figure is complete and must be made lengthways. On finishing the last figure eight proceed direct to E.				
		Submission and correctness in the two figure eights		15		

IX

28	At E	Take the left-hand track to F.				
	At F	Change the rein and immediately make FIVE changes of leg every FOURTH stride. Finish on the right foot.		5		
29	At M	Change the rein and immediately make SEVEN changes of leg every two strides. Finish on the left leg.		10		
30	At F	Change the rein and make FIFTEEN changes of leg from stride to stride, the last on the right leg.		20		
		Continue the canter to B.				
31	At B	Change to extended walk.				
	At A	Turn down the centre line.				
32	At G	Halt and face the Jury. Salute. Exit at extended walk.		5		

X

33		The combined effect will be marked on the correctness of position, the seat of the rider and in the harmony and sympathy of his aids in controlling the horse.				
		Marking on the ensemble		5		
				Total 200		

MOVEMENTS FROM GRAND PRIX TEST – OLYMPIC GAMES 1948

Concours
de dressage
No. 22

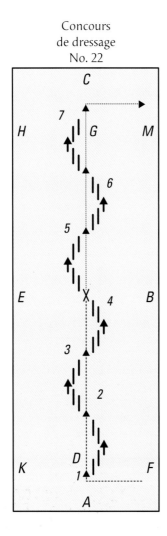

Concours
de dressage
No. 27

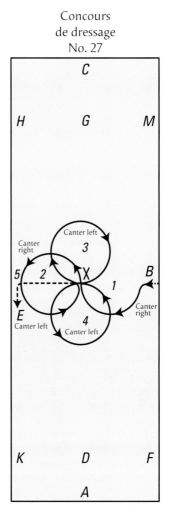

OLYMPIC GAMES 1948

Results - Individual Competition

				Judges' points			
				Decarpentry France	Bonde Sweden	Thommen Switzerland	Total points
Rank	Rider	Horse	Country				
1	Moser, Hans	*Hummer*	Switzerland	164.0	166.0	162.5	492.5
2	Jousseaume, André	*Harpagon*	France	176.0	157.0	147.0	480.0
3	Boltenstern, Gustaf	*Trumf*	Sweden	167.5	171.0	139.0	477.5
4	Borg, Robert J	*Klingson*	USA	179.0	147.5	147.0	473.5
5	St Cyr, Henri	*Djimm*	Sweden	144.5	170.0	130.0	444.5

Rank	Rider	Horse	Country	Judges' points			Total points
				Decarpentry France	Bonde Sweden	Thommen Switzerland	
6	Pailiard, Jean St-Fort	*Sous les Ceps*	France	162.5	151.0	126.0	439.5
7	Podhajasky, Alois	*Teja*	Austria	149.5	150.0	138.0	437.5
8	Thomson, Earl F	*Pancraft*	USA	146.0	145.0	130.0	421.0
9	Pais, Fernando	*Matamás*	Portugal	145.0	134.0	132.0	411.0
10	Valadas, Francisco	*Feitico*	Portugal	143.5	133.5	128.0	405.0
11	Iturralde, Justo J	*Pajarito*	Argentina	126.5	152.0	118.5	397.0
12	Mena e Silva, Luis Maena	*Fascinante*	Portugal	116.0	123.0	127.0	366.0
13	Henry, Frank S	*Reno Overde*	USA	129.5	126.0	106.0	361.5
14	Kirkpatrick, O'Donnell, C	*Yanta*	Spain	126.5	114.0	112.5	353.0
15	Buret, Maurice	*Saint Ouen*	France	132.0	90.0	127.0	349.0
16	Terzano, Humberto	*Bienvenido*	Argentina	111.5	106.5	109.0	327.0
17	Goulu, Oscar	*Grillo*	Argentina	96.0	98.5	87.0	281.5
18	Gracida Jaramillo, Gabriel	*Kamcia*	Mexico	83.5	87.5	77.5	248.5
	Persson, Gehnäll*	*Knaust*	Sweden	146.0	164.5	133.5	444.0

* Disqualified

OLYMPIC GAMES 1948

Results – Team Competition

	Rider/Country	Horse	Judges' marks			Total
			Decarpentry France	Bonde Sweden	Thommem Switzerland	
1	**France**					**1268.5**
	A Jousseaume	*Harpagon*	176.0	157.0	147.0	480.0
	J St-F Paillard	*Sous les Ceps*	162.0	157.0	126.0	439.5
	M Buret	*Saint Ouen*	132.0	90.0	127.0	349.0
2	**United States of America**					**1256.0**
	R J Bork	*Klingson*	179.0	147.5	147.0	473.5
	E F Thomsom	*Pancraft*	146.0	145.0	130.0	421.0
	F S Henry	*Rene Overdo*	129.5	126.0	106.0	361.5
3	**Portugal**					**1182.0**
	F Pais	*Matamás*	145.0	134.0	132.0	411.0
	F Valadas	*Feitico*	143.5	133.5	128.0	405.0
	L M Mena e Silva	*Fascinante*	116.0	123.0	127.0	366.0
4	**Argentina**					**1005.5**
	J Iturralde	*Pajarito*	126.5	152.0	118.5	397.0
	H Terzano	*Bienvenido*	111.5	106.5	109.0	327.0
	O Goulu	*Grillo*	96.0	98.5	87.0	281.5
	Sweden*					**1366.0**
	G Boltenstern	*Trumf*	165.5	171.0	139.0	477.5
	H St Cyr	*Djimm*	144.5	170.0	130.0	444.5
	G Persson*	*Knaust*	146.0	164.5	133.5	444.0

* Disqualified

OLYMPIC GAMES 1952

HELSINKI, FINLAND

Participating Countries: 10

Chile	Norway	Switzerland
Denmark	Portugal	United States of America
France	Soviet Union	
Germany	Sweden	

Participating riders: 27

Teams: 8 teams of 3 riders

Chile	Soviet Union
France	Sweden
Germany	Switzerland
Portugal	United States of America

Individual Riders: 3

Denmark – 2
Norway – 1

Competitions

- Grand Prix – one test used for both Individual and Team Competition.

- Results from the 3 team riders to be added together for the team result.

Special Regulations

- For the first time men and women competed for the same Olympic medals. (On this occasion, 4 out of the 27 competitors were women.)

- The restriction that only officers and gentlemen riders are allowed to compete is dropped.

- Amateur status is still required.

- The prescribed test had to be carried out entirely from memory. Each competitor was allowed 15 minutes to complete it. In the event of a rider failing to complete the test within the prescribed time half a point was deducted for every second over the time allowed.

Number of Judges: 5

Medal Winners

Individual

		Points
Gold	Henri St Cyr (Sweden) *Master Rufus*	561.0
Silver	Lis Hartel (Denmark) *Jubilee*	541.5
Bronze	André Jousseaume (France) *Harpagon*	541.0

Team

		Points	Placing in GP
Gold	**Sweden 1597.5 points**		
	Henri St Cyr *Master Rufus*	561.0	1
	Gustaf Boltenstern *Krest*	531.0	5
	Gehnäll Persson *Knaust*	505.5	9
Silver	**Switerland 1579.0 points**		
	Gottfried Trachsel *Kursus*	531.0	4
	Henri Chammartin *Wöhler*	295.5	6
	Gustaf Fischer *Soliman*	518.5	8
Bronze	**Germany 1501.0 points**		
	H Pollay *Adular*	518.5	7
	Ida von Nagel *Afrika*	503.0	10
	F Tiedemann *Chronist*	479.5	12

Gold medallist Col Henri St Cyr (SWE) on *Master Rufus*. (Photo: courtesy of Max Ammann)

Arena: 60 x 20 m.

Markers: Standard since 1932 Los Angeles.

Judges

Col N Thommen (Switzerland)
Col Baron S van Grovestins (Holland)
Mr M König (Sweden)
Maj Hanoteau (Belgium)
Col Challan-Belval (France)

• No comparison of scores. Highest and lowest score discounted.

Test

• Grand Prix – maximum score per judge = 255 points.

• Time allowed 15 minutes.

Gold, Silver and Bronze medallists: Col Henri St Cyr (SWE) (*Rufus*) (centre), Mrs Lis Hartel (DEN) (*Jubilee*) (right) and Col André Jousseaume (FRA) (*Harpagon*) (left). (Photo: courtesy of Max Ammann)

Grand Prix Test – Olympic Games 1952

			Directive ideas	Points awarded by judge 0–0	Coefficient	Points obtained
			I			
1		Enter in canter, X halt, salute Proceed in working trot (rising) Track to the left	Entry, halt, proceeding in trot		5	
2	HXF	Change rein in extended trot (rising)				
3	F – K	Collected trot (sitting)	The two extensions		10	
4	K	Reins in one hand				
	KXM	Change rein in extended trot (rising)				
5	M – E	Collected trot (sitting)	The two collections		10	
			II			
6	E	Turn left				
	X	Volte to the right 6m followed by volte to the left	The two voltes		5	
	B	Track to the right				
			III			
7	A	On centre line				
8	D – P	Half-pass on diagonal from left to right				
	P – S	Half-pass on diagonal from right to left				
	S – G	Half-pass on diagonal from left to right	The half-passes		10	
	G	Straight to C				
	C	Track to right and transition to medium walk				
			IV			
9	MXK	Change rein in extended walk	The extended walk and the transition to collected walk		10	
10	A	On centre line and collected walk				
11	X	Half-pass to H, horse parallel to long side				

		Directive ideas	Points awarded by judge 0–10	Coefficient	Points obtained
12	H	Track to the right to C			
	C	Half-pirouette to right and track to the left to V			
13	V	Turn left			
14	L	On centre line to X			
	X	Half-pass to the right to M, horse parallel to the long side			
	M	Track to the left	The two half-passes	10	
15	C	Half-pirouette to left and track to the right to B	The two half-pirouettes	10	
16	B	Proceed in sitting trot			
	A	Lengthen the trot			
	H	Shorten the trot	The transitions	5	
17	CMRSHG	Passage			
		V	**V**		
18	G	Piaffe 10 to 12 steps			
		Proceed in passage GMRISEX			
19	X	Piaffe 10 to 12 steps			
		Proceed in passage BIG			
20	G	Piaffe towards the Jury 10 to 12 steps	The four passages	30	
		Proceed in passage CHIX			
21	X	Piaffe 10 to 12 steps back to the Jury	The four piaffes	30	
22	X	Halt, immobility 6 to 8 seconds	Halt, immobility, transition to walk	5	
		Proceed in walk to L			
		VI	**VI**		
23	L	Turn left At P track to the right	Transition from walk into canter and from canter to walk	5	
		Proceed in collected counter-canter			
		Continue to E			
	E	Proceed in collected walk			

	Directive ideas	Points awarded by judge 0–10	Coefficient	Points obtained
H	Turn right			
G	Halt – rein-back 3 steps – forward 4 steps – rein-back 6 steps. Proceed in collected canter right			
M	Track to the right	Halt – rein-back and proceeding into canter	10	
	VII	**VII**		
24 KXM	Change rein in extended canter	The two extended canters	10	
M	Collected canter right			
C	Change of leg			
25 HXF	Change rein in extended canter	The transitions in canter	10	
F	Collected canter left			
A	Change of leg			
	On centre line and counter changes half-pass to either side of centre line, changing leg for every change of half-pass The first and the last half-passes of 3 strides, the 5 others of 6 strides	Submission in the counter changes	10	
	VIII	**VIII**		
26 C	Track to the right			
M	Change rein			
27 X	Pirouette right	Regularity and submission in the two pirouettes	20	
K	Change of leg			
28 F	Change rein			
29 X	Pirouette left			
H	Change of leg			
	IX	**IX**		
30 B	Turn right	Submission and correctness of the two voltes	10	
X	Volte left canter right			
X	At the end of the volte change leg and volte to right in canter left			
X	At the end of the volte to E and track left			

		Directive ideas	Points awarded by judge 0–10	Coefficient	Points obtained
		X			
31	E	Track to the left to F			
	F	Change rein and immediately 5 changes of leg every 4th stride; end on right leg	Correctness of the changes every 4th stride	5	
32	M	Change rein and immediately 7 changes of leg every second stride; end on left leg	Correctness of the changes every 2nd stride	10	
33	F	Change rein and 15 changes of leg every stride, the last change to the right leg. Continue in canter to B	Correctness of the changes every stride	15	
34	B	Proceed in extended walk			
	A	On centre line	The extended walk, the halt, salute	5	
35	G	Halt towards the Jury, salute, leave the arena in extended walk			
		XI			
36		The combined effect will be marked on the correctness of position, the seat of the rider and the harmony and sympathy of his aids in controlling the horse	General mark	5	
				Total 255	

MOVEMENTS FROM GRAND PRIX TEST – OLYMPIC GAMES 1952

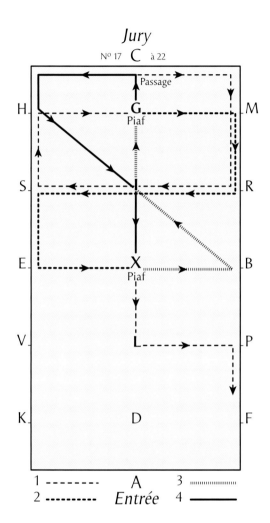

Jury

Nº 17 **C** à 22

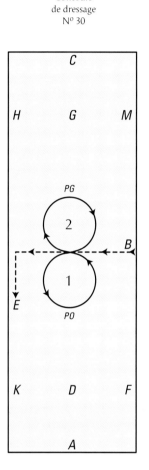

Concours
de dressage
Nº 30

OLYMPIC GAMES 1952

Results – Individual Competition

	Rider	Horse	Country	Total points
1	**St Cyr, H**	*Master Rufus*	**Sweden**	**561.0**
2	**Hartel, L**	*Jubilee*	**Denmark**	**541.5**
3	**Jousseaume, A**	*Harpagon*	**France**	**541.0**
4	Trachsel, G	*Kursus*	Switzerland	531.0
5	Boltenstern, G	*Krest*	Sweden	531.0
6	Chammartin, H	*Wöhler*	Switzerland	529.5

	Rider	Horse	Country	Total points
7	Pollay, H	*Adular*	Germany	518.5
8	Fischer, G	*Soliman*	Switzerland	518.5
9	Persson, G	*Knaust*	Sweden	505.5
10	von Nagel, I	*Afrika*	Germany	503.0
11	Borg, R	*Bill Biddle*	USA	492.0
12	Thiedemann, F	*Chronist*	Germany	479.5
13	Peitevin de Saint-André, J	*Vol Au Vent*	France	479.0
14	Larrain, J	*Rey de Oros*	Chile	473.5
15	Christophersen, E	*Diva*	Norway	459.0
16	Clavel, H	*Frontalera*	Chile	452.0
17	Haines, M	*The Flying Dutchman*	USA	446.0
18	Jensen, Chr	*Odense*	Denmark	439.0
19	Raspopov, V	*Imeninnik*	USSR	433.5
20	Reymao Nogueira, A	*Napeiro*	Portugal	429.5
21	Valadas Junior, F	*Feitiço*	Portugal	422.0
22	Silva, E	*Viarregio*	Chile	415.0
23	Saint-Fort Paillard, J	*Tapir*	France	403.5
24	Tihonov, V	*Pevec*	USSR	395.0
25	Sitjko, N	*Cesar*	USSR	377.0
26	Silva Paes, F	*Matamás*	Portugal	346.0
27	Pauley, H	*Reno Overdo*	USA	315.5

Results – Team Competition

Country	Rider	Horse	Points	
1 Sweden	H St Cyr	*Master Rufus*	561.0	
	G Boltenstern	*Krest*	531.0	
	G Persson	*Knaust*	505.5	
			1597.5	
2 Switzerland	G Traschel	*Kursus*	531.0	
	H Chammartin	*Wöhler*	529.5	
	G Fischer	*Soliman*	518.5	
			1579.0	
3 Germany	H Pollay	*Adular*	518.5	
	Ida von Nagel	*Afrika*	503.0	
	F Thiedemann	*Chronist*	479.5	
			1501.0	

OLYMPIC GAMES 1956

MELBOURNE, AUSTRALIA (Equestrian Events held in Stockholm, Sweden)

Participating countries: 17

Argentina	Finland	Norway	Switzerland
Austria	France	Portugal	United States of America
Bulgaria	Germany	Romania	
Canada	Great Britain	Soviet Union	
Denmark	Holland	Sweden	

Participating Riders: 36

Teams: 8 teams of 3 riders

Denmark	Romania
France	Soviet Union
Germany	Sweden
Norway	Switzerland

Individual Riders: 12

Argentina – 1	Canada 1	Holland – 1
Austria – 2	Finland – 1	Portugal – 1
Bulgaria – 1	Great Britain – 2	United States of America – 2

Competitions

- Grand Prix – one test for Individual and Team Competitions.

- One ride-off test for use in case of equal results in the Grand Prix (not used).

Special Regulations (Same as for Helsinki, 1952.)

- Both men and women competing for the same Olympic Medals.

- Amateur status still required.

- The prescribed test had to be carried out entirely from memory. Each competitor was allowed 16 minutes to complete it. In the event of a rider failing to complete the test within the prescribed time half a point was deducted for every second over the time allowed.

Medal Winners

Individual

		Points
Gold	Henri St Cyr (Sweden) *Juli*	860
Silver	Lis Hartel (Denmark) *Jubilee*	850
Bronze	Liselotte Linsenhoff (Germany) *Adular*	820

Team

		Points	Individual placing
Gold	**Sweden 2475 points**		
	Henri St Cyr *Juli*	860	1
	Gehnäll Persson *Knaust*	821	4
	Gustaf Boltenstern *Krest*	794	7
Silver	**Germany 2346 points**		
	Liselotte Linsenhoff *Adular*	832	3
	Hamelore Weygand *Perkunos*	785	9
	Anneliese Küppers *Afrika*	729	14
Bronze	**Switzerland 2346 points**		
	Gottfried Trachsel *Kursus*	807	6
	Henri Chammartin *Wöhler*	789	8
	Gustaf Fischer *Vasello*	750	10

Arena: 60 x 20 m.

Markers: Standard since 1932 Los Angeles.

Judges

Baron de Trannoy (Belgium)
Gen Berger (Germany)
Lt Gen Colliander (Sweden)
Gen Yañez (Chile)
Col Fog (Denmark)

• No comparison of scores.

Test

• Grand Prix – Maximum score per judge = 228.

• Time allowed 16 minutes.

Team Gold Medallists Sweden: Individual Gold Medallist Col Henri St Cyr *Juli* (centre) with Gehnäll Persson on *Knaust* and Gustaf Boltenstern on *Krest*. (Photo: courtesy of Max Ammann)

Grand Prix Test (1955) – OLYMPIC GAMES 1956

To be carried out in 16 minutes

	Movement	Remarks	Marks
A – G	Enter at ordinary canter		
At G	Halt – Immobility – Salute –		
	Proceed at collected walk		
At C	Track to the right		
MX	Change rein at ordinary walk	Impulsion, ease	
XKF	Extended walk	and freedom of the	12
FB	Collected walk	paces	
BMC	Ordinary trot		
CHXF	Extended trot (rising)		
At F	Ordinary canter (right)		
KEHM	Extended canter		
MBXI	Collected canter		
At I	Halt		

Movement		Remarks	Marks
Work at the Walk			
At I	Proceed at collected walk		
At C	Track to the right		
MXK	Change rein at extended walk with maximum extension	The extension	6
At F	Collected walk	The 2 collected walks	6
FL	On two tracks (to the left)		
LX	On centre line	The two tracks to the left	6
XH	On two tracks (to the left)		
At C	Turn down centre line		
At X	Half-pirouette to the left	The 2 half-pirouettes	6
At G	Half-pirouette to the right		
At A	Track to the right		
KL	On two tracks (to the right)	The two tracks to the right	6
LX	on centre line		
XM	On two tracks (to the right)		
At C	Halt – Rein-back 6 steps		6
Work at the Trot			
CHXF	Change rein at collected trot(sitting)	The collection	6
At A	Turn down centre line		
DP	On two tracks (to the right)	The two tracks to the right	6
PXS	On two tracks (to the left)		
SG	On two tracks (to the right)	The two tracks to the left	6
At C	Track to the right		
CMRIG	Passage (first)	First passage	6
At G	Piaffer (10 to 12 steps)	First piaffer	6
	Transition from passage to piaffer		6
GCHEV	Extended trot (rising)	The extension	6
VLPRI	Passage (second)	Second passage	6
At I	Piaffer (10 to 12 steps)	Second piaffer	6
	Transition from extended trot to passage		6
ISHC	Passage (third)	Third passage	6
At C	Halt – Rein-back 3 steps – Advance 4 steps – Rein-back 6 steps		6

	Movement	Remarks	Marks

Work at the Canter

	Movement	Remarks	Marks
At C	Collected canter right		
MXK	Change rein – At X pirouette to the right	First pirouette	6
At K	Change leg (left)		
KBMC	Extended canter with maximum extension	The extension	6
At C	Collected canter	The collected canters	6
HXF	Change rein – At X pirouette to the left	Second pirouette	6
At A	Turn down centre line		
At D	Seven counter-changes of hand on two tracks to either side of the centre line with change of leg at each change of direction. The first and the last counter-changes (to the right) are of 3 strides, the other five of 6 strides	The seven counter-changes	6
At G	On centre line		
At C	Track to the right		
MXK	Change rein and make on the diagonal 5 changes of leg every fourth stride, finishing on the left leg	Changes every fourth stride	6
FXH	Change rein and make on the diagonal 7 changes of leg every third stride, finishing on the right leg	Changes every third stride	6
MBFA	Extended canter with maximum extension		
At A	Collected canter		
KXM	Change rein and make on the diagonal 9 changes of leg every second stride, finishing on the left leg	Changes every second stride	6
HXF	Extended canter	The extended canters	6
FAD	Collected canter	The collected canters	6
DG	15 changes of leg every stride	Changes every stride	6
At C	Track to the right		

Movement	Remarks	Marks

Work on the Circle

At B	On a circle of 16 metres diameter with X as the centre, execute at collected canter on the right rein:	
	4 strides left – 4 strides right	
	3 strides left – 3 strides right	
	2 strides left – 2 strides right	6
	1 stride left –1stride right	
	Change rein on the circle with change of leg at X.	
	On the circle on the left rein execute:	
	4 changes of leg every stride	
	3 changes of leg every second stride	
	2 changes of leg every third stride	6
	2 changes of leg every fourth stride	
	Continue the circle.	
At L	Turn down centre line towards C	
IG	Passage (fourth)	Fourth passage	6
At G	Halt – Salute	

General Impression

1.	The paces have been marked at the beginning of the test.	
2.	Suppleness and lightness of the horse execution of the movements.	12
3.	Position and seat of the rider. Correctness of the application of the aids.	12

Total 228

OLYMPIC GAMES 1956

Test to be used in case of a 'ride-off' in the Grand Prix de Dressage.

	Enter at the canter
At G	Halt – salute
	Proceed at collected canter left
At C	Track to the left
HXF	Change rein – at X pirouette to the left
At F	Collected trot
At A	Turn down centre line
IG	Passage
At G	Piaffer (12 steps)
At C	Track to the right – extended trot
MXK	Change rein
At A	Collected trot
BESR	Passage
At R	Track to the right – extended canter right
BFKE	Extended canter
At E	Collected canter
At S	Turn to the right
AT I	Pirouette to the right
AT R	Turn to the right
RBFA	Extended canter
KM	Change rein – canter on a loose rein
MCHIB	Walk on a loose rein
BXG	Collected walk
At G	Halt – salute

General Impression

The correctness of the presentation.

Mark: A single mark of 12 for the whole of the test.

OLYMPIC GAMES 1956
Results – Individual

Place	Rider	Horse	Nation	de Trannoy (Belgium)	Berger (Germany)	Colliander (Sweden)	Yañes (Chile)	Fog (Denmark)	Total	Time*
						Judges' marks				
1	**H St Cyr**	*Juli*	**Sweden**	**160.0**	**159.0**	**192.0**	**177.0**	**172.0**	**860.0**	
2	**L Hartel**	*Jubilee*	**Denmark**	**157.0**	**161.0**	**166.0**	**177.0**	**189.0**	**850.0**	
3	**L Linsenhoff**	*Adular*	**Germany**	**147.0**	**174.0**	**160.0**	**173.0**	**178.0**	**832.0**	
4	G Persson	*Knaust*	Sweden	154.0	153.0	190.0	147.0	177.0	821.0	
5	A R Jousseaume	*Harpagon*	France	166.0	150.0	165.0	167.0	166.0	814.0	
6	G Trachsel	*Kursus*	Switzerland	157.0	155.0	158.0	171.0	166.0	807.0	
7	G Boltenstern	*Krest*	Sweden	149.0	158.0	173.0	155.0	159.0	794.0	
8	H Chammartin	*Wöhler*	Switzerland	150.0	154.0	155.0	151.0	179.0	789.0	
9	H Weygand	*Perkunos*	Germany	138.0	168.0	149.0	167.0	163.0	785.0	
10	G Fischer	*Vasello*	Switzerland	144.0	148.0	142.0	156.0	160.0	750.0	
11	S Filatov	*Ingas*	Soviet Union	144.0	145.0	155.0	143.0	158.0	744.0	
12	A Pereira deAlmeida	*Feitiço*	Portugal	140.0	142.0	153.0	151.0	157.0	743.0	
13	E Christophersen	*Diva*	Norway	142.0	139.0	164.0	135.0	159.0	739.0	
14	A Küppers	*Afrika*	Germany	124.0	163.0	144.0	158.0	140.0	729.0	+16
15	A Vtorov	*Repertoir*	Soviet Union	130.0	132.0	152.0	161.0	151.0	726.0	
16	G Teodorescu	*Palatin*	Romania	140.0	137.0	153.0	139.0	152.0	721.0	
17	R J Borg	*Bill Biddle*	USA	139.0	135.0	145.0	149.0	152.0	720.0	
18	N Sitko	*Skatchek*	Soviet Union	129.0	132.0	145.0	151.0	143.0	700.0	
19	H Zobel	*Monty*	Denmark	127.0	122.0	133.0	139.0	152.0	673.0	
20	L R Lafond	*Rath Patrick*	Canada	125.0	117.0	150.0	131.0	134.0	657.0	
21	H L Johnstone	*Rosie Dream*	Great Britain	128.0	129.0	139.0	127.0	132.0	655.0	
22	J A Brau	*Vol d'Amour*	France	132.0	122.0	129.0	131.0	134.0	648.0	
23	I Lemvigh-Müller	*Bel Ami*	Denmark	111.0	113.0	141.0	126.0	153.0	644.0	
24	N Mihalcea	*Mihnea*	Romania	120.0	116.0	134.0	126.0	129.0	625.0	
25	L B Williams	*Pilgrim*	Great Britain	131.0	116.0	118.0	119.0	132.0	616.0	
25	R Lattermann	*Danubia*	Austria	116.0	128.0	115.0	127.0	130.0	616.0	
27	A L Kielland	*Clary*	Norway	102.5	119.5	127.5	124.5	127.5	601.5	
28	A Pantchoulidzew	*Lascar*	Holland	119.5	118.5	120.5	111.5	116.5	586.5	+5
29	B Russ	*Corona*	Norway	108.0	118.0	120.0	113.0	113.0	572.0	
30	E S Watt	*Connecticut Yankee*	USA	113.0	118.0	112.0	115.0	110.0	568.0	
31	M Roiha	*Laaos*	Finland	111.0	114.0	112.0	114.0	111.0	562.0	
32	J Salmon	*Kipling*	France	111.0	102.0	112.0	107.0	122.0	554.0	+40
33	N Marcoci	*Corvin*	Romania	102.0	107.0	98.0	106.0	103.0	516.0	
34	A Sagadin	*Cyprius*	Austria	92.0	112.0	100.0	96.0	113.0	513.0	
35	J H Cavoti	*Carnavalito*	Argentina	95.5	92.5	89.5	110.5	95.5	483.5	+33
36	K G Lekarsky	*Edgard*	Bulgaria	67.5	77.5	82.5	84.5	84.5	396.5	+89

* Number of seconds over time allowed (16 minutes). There was a half-point penalty for every second taken over this time.

OLYMPIC GAMES 1956

Results – Team Competition

Country	Rider	Horse	Total Marks	Individual Place
1. Sweden	H St Cyr	*Juli*	860.0	1
	G Persson	*Knaust*	821.0	4
	G Boltenstern	*Krest*	794.0	7
			Total 2475.0	
2. Germany	L Linsenhoff	*Adular*	832.0	3
	H Weygand	*Perkunos*	785.0	9
	A Küppers	*Afrika*	729.0	14
			Total 2346.0	
3. Switzerland	G Trachsel	*Kursus*	807.0	6
	H Chammartin	*Wöhler*	789.0	8
	G Fischer	*Vasello*	750.0	10
			Total 2346.0	
4. Soviet Union	S Filatov	*Ingas*	744.0	11
	A Vtorov	*Repertoir*	726.0	15
	N Sitko	*Skatchek*	700.0	18
			Total 2170.0	
5. Denmark	Lis Hartel	*Jubilee*	850.0	2
	H Zobel	*Monty*	673.0	19
	I Lemvigh-Müller	*Bel Ami*	644.0	23
			Total 2167.0	
6. France	A R Jousseaume	*Harpagon*	814.0	5
	J A Brau	*Vol d'Amour*	648.0	22
	J Salmon	*Kipling*	554.0	32
			Total 2016.0	
7. Norway	E Christophersen	*Diva*	739.0	13
	A L Kielland	*Clary*	601.5	27
	B Russ	*Corona*	572.0	29
			Total 1912.5	
8. Romania	G Theodorescu	*Palatin*	721.0	16
	N Mihalcea	*Mihnea*	625.0	24
	N Marcoci	*Corvin*	516.0	33
			Total 1862.0	

OLYMPIC GAMES 1960

ROME, ITALY

Participating Countries: 11

Argentina	Great Britain	Switzerland
Bulgaria	Portugal	United States of America
Czechoslovakia	Soviet Union	
Germany	Sweden	

Participating Riders: 17

Argentina – 1	Great Britain – 2	Switzerland – 2
Bulgaria – 1	Portugal – 2	United States of America – 2
Czechoslovakia – 1	Soviet Union – 2	
Germany – 2	Sweden – 2	

Competitions

- Individual Competition only, maximum of 2 riders per nation.

- One Grand Prix test.

- One ride-off test for the 5 best placed riders from the Grand Prix (same test as the original Grand Prix).

Special Regulations (Same as Helsinki 1952)

- Men and women amateurs

- The prescribed test had to be carried out entirely from memory. Each competitor was allowed 12 minutes to complete it. In the event of a rider failing to complete the test within the prescribed time half a point was deducted for every second over the time allowed.

Number of Judges: 3

Medal Winners

Individual

		Points in GP	Ride-off	Total
Gold	Sergey Filatov (Soviet Union) *Absent*	1074	1070	2144
Silver	Gustaf Fischer (Switzerland) *Wald*	1052	1035	2087
Bronze	Josef Neckermann (Germany) *Asbach*	1071	1011	2082

Arena: 60 x 20 m.

Markers: Standard since 1932 Los Angeles.

Judges

Col Le Heux (Holland) A
Col Margot (France) B
Gen Yañez (Chile) C

Comparison of marks

• Every performance was filmed. It took two days before all the judges arrived at the final score for the Grand Prix. All the judges were chosen from those countries that had no chance of winning (i.e. from countries not taking part).

Test

• Maximum score per judge for each test = 520 points.

• Time allowed 12 minutes.

Medal ceremony. (Left to right) Bronze medallist Josef Neckermann (GER) (*Asbach*), Gold medallist Sergey Filatov (USSR) (*Absent*), Silver medallist Gustaf Fischer (SUI) (*Wald*).

Gold Medallist Sergey Filatov (USSR) on *Absent*.

Grand Prix Test – Olympic Games 1960

		Test	Directive ideas	Points	Coeff	Total	Remarks
1	A	Enter in collected trot	The entry	10			
	X	Halt – Immobility – Salute	The correctness of the halt				
		Proceed in ordinary trot (sitting)					
2	C	Track to the right	The extension and transition	10			
	MXK	Change rein in extended trot					
	K	Ordinary trot sitting					
3	A	Ordinary walk	The lengthening and	10			
	FXH	Change rein in extended walk	the transition				
4	HC	Collected walk	The collection	10			
	C	On centre line					
5	X	Half-pirouette right	The 2 half-pirouettes	10			
	G	Half-pirouette left					
6	I	Collected trot	The collection	10			
	A	Track to the left					
	B	Turn left					
7	X	Halt – rein-back 3 steps, forward 6 steps, rein-back 6 steps and immediately proceed in collected trot	The halt and the rein-back	10			
8	E	Turn to the left	The 6 counter changes	10			
	A	On centre line					
	DG	6 counter changes in half-pass to the left and to the right of the centre line. The first and the last to the right 2 metres, the others 4 metres					
	C	Track to the left					
9	HEK	Ordinary trot sitting	The extension and the regularity	10			
	KAF	Collected trot					
	FXH	Extended trot sitting					
10		The transitions		10			
11	HC	Collected walk	The collection and transition	10			

	Test	Directive ideas	Points	Coeff	Total	Remarks
12	CMBX	First passage	The passage	10			
13	X	First piaffe 10 to 12 steps	The piaffe	10	2		
14	XEHC	Second passage	The passage	10			
15	C	Second piaffe 10 to 12 steps	The piaffe	10	2		
16		The transitions from passage to piaffe and from piaffe to passage		10			
17	CMXK	Extended trot sitting	The extension	10			
18	KA	Collected trot	The collection and transition	10			
19	A	On centre line					
	X	Third passage and immediately volte of 8m to the right	The passage	10			
20	X	Third piaffe 10 to 12 steps	The piaffe	10	2		
21	X	Fourth passage and immediately volte of 8m to the left, back to X and continue to G	The passage	10			
22		The transitions from passage to piaffe and from piaffe to passage		10			
23	G	Proceed in canter right	The proceeding in canter	10			
	C	Track right					
24	B	Turn right	The halt, the rein-back and the proceeding in canter	10			
	X	Halt – rein-back 3 steps and immediately proceed in collected canter left					
25	DG	7 counter changes in half-pass. The first and the last of 3 strides to the left, the others of 6 strides	The 7 counter changes and the half-pass	10	2		
	G	Straight on centre line					
	C	Track to the left					
26	CHK	Extended canter	The extension	10			
	KA	Collected canter	The collection				
	A	On centre line	The transition				

211

	Test		Directive ideas	Points	Coeff	Total	Remarks
27	L	Pirouette left	The pirouette	10	2		
	X	Flying change of leg					
28	I	Pirouette right	The pirouette	10	2		
	G	Flying change of leg					
	C	Track to the left					
29	HXF	On the diagonal 7 flying changes every third stride	The 3-tempi changes	10	2		
	FAK	Collected canter					
30	KHC	Extended canter	The extension				
	CM	Collected canter	The transition	10			
31	MXK	On the diagonal 9 flying changes every second stride. Finish in canter left	The 2-tempi changes	10	2		
	KAF	Collected canter					
32	FXH	On the diagonal 15 flying changes every stride. Finish in canter right	The changes every stride	10	3		
	HCB	Collected canter					
33	B	Collected trot	The transition	10			
	A	On centre line					
	D	Fifth passage	The passage				
	G	Halt – salute	The halt – salute				
		Leave arena at walk on a long rein					

Collective marks:

	Points	Coeff
1. Paces and impulsion	10	4
2. Submission, lightness and elasticity of the horse	10	3
3. Position of the rider, seat, effect of the aids	10	3

Total 520

To be deducted:

Penalty for exceeding the time allowed: for each commenced second, ½ point

Errors: 1st time = 5 points

2nd time = 15 points

3rd time = Elimination

OLYMPIC GAMES 1960
Results – Individual

Place	Rider	Horse	Nation	Le Heux (Holland) Test		Margot (France) Test		Yañez (Chile) Test		Total Test		Final points
				1st	2nd	1st	2nd	1st	2nd	1st	2nd	
1	**S Filatov**	*Absent*	**Soviet Union**	347	360	358	353	369	357	1074	1070	2144
2	**G Fischer**	*Wald*	**Switzerland**	353	344	342	337	357	354	1052	1035	2087
3	**J Neckermann**	*Asbach*	**Germany**	349	325	363	333	359	353	1071	1011	2082
4	H Saint Cyr	*L'Etoile*	Sweden	336	340	337	342	363	346	l036	1028	2064
5	I Kalita	*Korbey*	Soviet Union	338	329	336	323	336	345	1010	997	2007
6	P Galvin	*Rath Patrick*	USA	330		312		353		995		995
7	R M Springer	*Doublette*	Germany	311		334		340		985		985
8	H Chammartin	*Wolfdietrich*	Switzerland	331		326		321		978		978
9	Y Viebke	*Gaspari*	Sweden	316		328		331		975		975
10	A Nogueira	*Greek Warrior*	Portugal	301		314		333		948		948
11	L B Williams	*Little Model*	Great Britain	315		309		315		939		939
12	A J Newberry	*Forstrat*	USA	312		303		312		927		927
13	J Hall	*Conversano Caprice*	Great Britain	289		259		290		838		838
14	F Sembera	*Ivo*	Czechoslovakia	271		287		274		832		832
15	J Cavoti	*Vidriero*	Argentina	293		247		288		828		828
16	G Lekarski	*Edgard*	Bulgaria	237		280		282		799		799
17	L Mena e Silva	*Adonis*	Portugal	246		269		260		775		775

OLYMPIC GAMES 1964

TOKYO, JAPAN

Participating Countries: 9

Argentina	Great Britain	Sweden
Canada	Japan	Switzerland
Germany	Soviet Union	United States of America

Participating Riders: 22

Teams: 6 teams of 3 riders

Germany	Sweden
Japan	Switzerland
Soviet Union	United States of America

Individual Riders: 4

Argentina – 1
Canada – 2
Great Britain – 1

Competitions

- Both Individual and Team Competitions.

- Grand Prix and ride-off test for the 6 best placed competitors in the Grand Prix. The combined scores from the two tests to give the final result.

- For the Team Competition, only the Grand Prix scores to count.

Special Regulations (same as for Stockholm 1956)

- Men and women amateurs.

Number of Judges: 3

Medal Winners

Individual

		Points in GP	Ride-off	Total
Gold	Henri Chammartin (Switzerland) *Woermann*	870	634	1504
Silver	Harry Boldt (Germany) *Remus*	889	614	1503
Bronze	Sergey Filatov (Soviet Union) *Absent*	847	639	1486

Team

		Points in GP	Placing in GP
Gold	**Germany 2558 points**		
	Harry Boldt *Remus*	889	1
	Reiner Klimke *Dux*	837	6
	Josef Neckermann *Antoinette*	832	5
Silver	**Switzerland 2526 points**		
	Henri Chammartin *Woermann*	870	2
	Gustaf Fischer *Wald*	854	3
	Marianne Gossweiler *Stephan*	802	7
Bronze	**Soviet Union 2311 points**		
	Sergey Filatov *Absent*	847	4
	Ivan Kizimov *Ikhor*	758	10
	Ivan Kalita *Moar*	706	15

Arena: 60 x 20 m.

Markers: Standard.

Judges

F Jandl (Czechoslovakia) President
Col Margot (France)
Col Nyblaeus (Sweden)

Tests

- Grand Prix – Maximum score per judge = 410 points.
  Time allowed 12 minutes 30 seconds.

- Ride-off Test – Maximum score per judge = 300 points.
  Time allowed 6 minutes 30 seconds.

Gold Medallist Henri Chammartin (SUI) on *Woermann*.
(Photo: courtesy of Max Ammann)

GRAND PRIX TEST (1963) – OLYMPIC GAMES 1964

		Test	Directive ideas	Marks	Coeff.
1	A X	Enter at collected canter Halt – Immobility – Salute Proceed at collected trot	Entry. Correctness of the halt.	10	
2	C MXK KA	Track to the right Change rein at extended trot rising Ordinary trot sitting	The trot.	10	
3	A FXH HC	Ordinary walk Change rein at extended walk Ordinary walk	The walk.	10	
4	C MXK FXH	Proceed at ordinary canter right Change rein with change of leg at X Change rein with change of leg at X	The canter.	10	
5	H C X	Collected walk Down centre line Half-pirouette to the right	The half-pirouette.	10	
6	G	Half-pirouette to the left	The half-pirouette.	10	
7	X A B	Collected trot Track to the left Turn left	The collected trot.	10	
8	X E	Halt – Rein-back 3 steps – advance 6 steps – rein-back 6 steps. Immediately proceed at collected trot Track to the left	The halt, the rein-back, the transition to the trot, connection between these movements.	10	
9	A DV VXR RG C	Down centre line On two tracks On two tracks On two tracks Track to the left	The two tracks.	10	
10	HK KF FXH	Ordinary trot sitting Collected trot Change rein at extended trot sitting	The extension. The transitions.	10	
11	H HCM	Collected walk Collected walk	The collected walk.	10	
12	MRB XESI	 First passage	The passage.	10	

		Test	Directive ideas	Marks	Coeff.
13		The transition from the walk to the passage	The transition.	10	
14	I	First piaffer 10 to 12 steps	The piaffer.	10	
15		The transition from the passage to the piaffer	The transition.	10	
16	IRMCH	Second passage	The passage.	10	
17		The transition from the piaffcr to the passage	The transition.	10	
18	HXF F	Extended trot sitting Collected trot	The extension. The transitions.	10	
19	A L X B	Down centre line Halt – Rein-back 3 steps, immediately proceed at collected canter on the right leg Turn right Track to the right	The halt, the rein-back. The transition to the canter. The connection between thesse movements.	10	
20	A G	Down centre line – 7 counter-changes of hand on two tracks to either side of the centre line, with change of leg at each change of direction. The first and the last are of 3 strides to the right, the five others of 6 strides. Change of leg	The two tracks and changes of leg.	10	
21	C HK K	Track to the left Extended canter Collected canter	The extension. The transitions.	10	
22	A L	Down centre line Pirouette to the left	The pirouette.	10	
23	X I	Change of leg Pirouette to the right	The pirouette.	10	
24	C MF F KHC	Track to the right Ordinary canter Collected canter Extended canter	The extension. The transitions.	10	
25	C	Halt. Immobility 6 seconds. Proceed at collected canter right	The halt, the immobility, the Transition from the halt.	10	
26	MXK	On the diagonal, 9 changes of leg every second stride, finishing on the left leg	The changes of leg every 2nd stride.	10	

		Test	Directive ideas	Marks	Coeff.
27	FXH	On the diagonal, 15 changes of leg every stride. finishing on the right leg	The changes of leg every stride.	10	
28	B A L X	Collected trot Down centre line Third passage Circle to the right 8 metres	The passage.	10	
29	X	Second piaffer 10 to 12 steps	The piaffer.	10	
30	X	Fourth passage and immediately circle to the left, 8 metres on returning to X proceed to G	The passage.	10	
31		The transitions from the passage to the piaffer and from the piaffer to the passage	The transitions	10	
32	G	Halt – immobility – salute Leave arena at the walk on a long rein	The halt, the immobility	10	

Collective Marks

		Marks	Coeff.
1. Paces		10	2
2. Impulsion.		10	2
3. Submission, suppleness and lightness of the horse		10	3
4. Position, seat of the rider, correct use of the aids		10	2
	Total	**410**	

To be deducted:

a. For every commenced second exceeding the time allowed: $^1/_2$ mark

b. Errors of the course and omissions are penalised

lst time   =   5 marks
2nd time   =   10 marks
3rd time   =   15 marks
4th time   =   Elimination

RIDE-OFF TEST – OLYMPIC GAMES TOKYO 1964

		Test	Directive ideas	Marks	Coeff.
1	A	Enter at collected canter	The entry, correctness of the halt, the	10	
	X	Halt – Immobility – Salute – Proceed at collected trot	transition from the halt		
2	C	Track to the left	The extension		
	HXF	Change rein at extended trot sitting	The collected trot	10	
	F	Collected trot			
3	VXR	On two tracks	The two tracks	10	
4	CHS	Extended trot sitting	The extension		
	SEV	Collected trot	The transitions		
	VKA	Extended trot sitting		10	
	A	Collected trot			
5	PXS	On two tracks	The two tracks	10	
6	H	Collected walk	The collected walk		
	HCMG	Collected walk		10	
7	G	First piaffer 10–12 steps	The piaffer	10	
8	GHSIRBX	First passage	The passage	10	
9		The transitions from the collected walk to the piaffer and from the piaffer to the passage	The transitions	10	
10	X	Second piaffer 10–12 steps	The piaffer	10	
11	XEVLPFA	Second passage	The passage	10	
12		The transitions from the passage to the piaffer and from the piaffer to thc passage	The transitions	10	
13	A	Extended trot sitting	The extension		
		KXM Change rein at extended trot sitting	The transitions	10	
	M	Collected trot			
14	C	Ordinary walk	The extension		
	HXF	Change rein at extended walk	The transitions	10	
	F	Collected walk			
15	A	Proceed at collected canter right	The changes of leg every second stride	10	
	KXM	On the diagonal, 9 changes of leg every second stride, finishing on the left leg			
16	HXF	On the diagonal, 15 changes of leg every stride, finishing on the right leg	The changes of leg every stride	10	

		Test	Directive ideas	Marks	Coeff.
17	A	Down centre line	The pirouette	10	
	D	Pirouette to the right			
18	Between D and G	9 changes of leg every stride, finishing on the left leg	The changes of leg every stride	10	
19	G	Pirouette left	The pirouette	10	
	C	Track to the left			
20	HK	Extended canter	The extension		
	K	Collected canter	The transitions	10	
	A	Down centre line			
21	D	Collected trot	The passage	10	
	L	Third passage, advance to G			
22	G	Third piaffer 10–12 steps	The piaffer	10	
23	G	After the piaffer, Halt – Immobility – Salute Leave arena at walk on a long rein	The halt and immobility	10	

Collective marks

1. Paces		10	2
2. Impulsion		10	2
3. Submission, suppleness and lightness of the horse		10	2
4. Position, seat of the rider, correct use of the aids		10	1
		Total 300	

To be deducted:

For every commenced second exceeding the time allowed, ½ mark

Errors of course and omissions are penalised:

1st time = 5 marks
2nd time = 10 marks
3rd time = 15 marks
4th time =   Elimination

OLYMPIC GAMES 1964

Results – Individual

Place	Name	Country	Horse	Points	Ride off Points	Total Points
I	**Chammartin, Henri**	**Switzerland**	*Woermann*	**870.0**	**634.0**	**1504.0**
2	**Boldt, Harry**	**Germany**	*Remus*	**889.0**	**614.0**	**1503.0**
3	**Filatov, Sergey**	**Soviet Union**	*Absent*	**847.0**	**639.0**	**1486.0**
4	Fischer, Gustav	Switzerland	*Wald*	854.0	631.0	1485.0
5	Neckermann, Josef	Germany	*Antoinette*	832.0	597.0	1429.0
6	Klimke, Reiner	Germany	*Dux*	837.0	567.0	1404.0

Place	Name	Country	Horse	Points	Ride off Points	Total Points
7	Gossweiler, Marianne	Switzerland	*Stephan*	802.0		802.0
8	De La Tour, Patricia G	USA	*Rath Patrick*	783.0		783.0
9	Hamilton, William	Sweden	*Delicado*	777.0		777.0
10	Kizimov, Ivan	Soviet Union	*Ikhor*	758.0		758.0
11	Wikne, Hans	Sweden	*Gaspari*	753.0		753.0
12	Hall, Johanna Sybille	Great Britain	*Conversano Caprice*	743.0		743.0
13	D Alessandri, F Obdulio	Argentina	*Vidriero*	734.0		734.0
14	Newberry, Anne Jessica	USA	*Forstrat*	707.0		707.0
15	Kalita, Ivan	Soviet Union	*Moar*	706.0		706.0
16	Inoue, Kikuko	Japan	*Katsunobori*	648.0		643.0
17	Mcintosh, Karen Stuart	USA	*Malteser*	640.0		640.0
18	Fischer-Credo, lnez	Canada	*Gordina*	597.0		397.0
19	Okabe, Nagahira	Japan	*Seiha*	589.5		589.5
20	Hanson, Christilot	Canada	*Jonbeur*	549.0		549.0
21	Matsudaira, Yorisuke	Japan	*Hamachidori*	542.0		542.0
22	Ljungquist, Bengt	Sweden	*Karat*	538.0		538.0

OLYMPIC GAMES 1964

Results – Team Competition

Place	Country	Name	Horse	Points
1	**Germany**	Boldt, Harry	*Remus*	889.0
		Klimke, Reiner	*Dux*	837.0
		Neckermann, Josef	*Antoinette*	832.0
			Total	**2558.0**
2	**Switzerland**	Chammartin, Henri	*Woermann*	870.0
		Fischer, Gustav	*Wald*	854.0
		Gossweiler, Marianne	*Stephan*	802.0
			Total	**2526.0**
3	**Soviet Union**	Filatov, Sergey	*Absent*	847.0
		Kizimov, Ivan	*Ikhor*	758.0
		Kalita, Ivan	*Moar*	706.0
			Total	**2311.0**
4	USA	De La Tour, Patricia G	*Rath Patrick*	783.0
		Newberry, Anne Jessica	*Forstrat*	707.0
		Mcintosh, Karen Stuart	*Malteser*	640.0
			Total	2130.0
5	Sweden	Hamilton, William	*Delicado*	777.0
		Wikne, Hans	*Gaspari*	753.0
		Ljungquist, Bengt	*Karat*	538.0
			Total	2068.0
6	Japan	Inoue, Kikuo	*Katsunobori*	648.0
		Okabe, Nagahira	*Seiha*	589.5
		Matsudira, Yorisuke	*Hamachidori*	542.0
			Total	1779.5

Olympic Games 1968

Mexico City, Mexico

Participating Countries: 9

Canada	German Democratic Republic	Soviet Union
Chile	Great Britain	Switzerland
Germany	Mexico	United States of America

Participating Riders: 26

Teams: 8 teams of 3 riders

Canada	Great Britain
Chile	Soviet Union
Germany	Switzerland
German Democratic Republic	United States of America

Individual Riders: 2

Mexico – 2

Competitions

• Grand Prix test and Ride-off test for the 7 best riders from the Grand Prix.

• The total of the scores from the two tests gives the final individual score.

• For the team competition, only the results from the Grand Prix to count.

Special Regulations: (same as for Stockholm 1956)

• Men and women amateurs.

Number of Judges: 3

Medal Winners

Individual

		Points in GP	Ride-off	Total
Gold	Ivan Kisimov (Soviet Union) *Ichor*	908	664	1572
Silver	Josef Neckermann (Germany) *Mariano*	948	598	1546
Bronze	Reiner Klimke (Germany) *Dux*	896	641	1537

Team Gold medallists
Germany: (Left to right) Josef
Neckermann (*Mariano*),
Liselotte Linsenhoff (*Piaff*) and
Reiner Klimke (*Dux*).

Team Competition

		Points in GP	Placing in GP
Gold	**Germany 2699 points**		
	Josef Neckermann *Mariano*	948	1
	Reiner Klimke *Dux*	896	3
	Liselotte Linsenhoff *Piaff*	855	8
Silver	**Soviet Union 2657 points**		
	Ivan Kisimov *Ichor*	908	2
	Ivan Kalita *Absent*	879	4
	Elena Petushkova *Pepel*	870	6
Bronze	**Switzerland 2547 points**		
	Gustav Fischer *Wald*	866	7
	Henri Chammartin *Wolfdietrich*	845	9
	Marianne Gossweiler *Stephan*	836	10

Arena: 60 x 20 m.

Markers: Standard.

Judges

	Position along short side
Col Margot (France) President	A
Jaap Pot (Holland)	B
Simpson Vigil (Chile)	C

• Comparison of scores.

Tests

• Grand Prix – maximum score per judge = 440 points.
  Time allowed 12 minutes 30 seconds.

• Ride-off – maximum score per judge = 300 points.
  Time allowed 6 minutes 45 seconds.

GRAND PRIX TEST (1967) – OLYMPIC GAMES 1968

		Test	Directive ideas	Marks	Coeff.
1	A	Enter at collected canter	The entry	10	
		Halt – Immobility – Salute			
	X	Proceed at collected trot	The halt and the transition from the halt		
2	C	Track to the right			
	MXK	Change rein at extended trot sitting	The extensions		
	KA	Ordinary trot sitting	The transitions	10	
3	A	Ordinary canter left	The extension, the calmness and the change of leg	10	
	FXH	Change rein with change of leg at X			
4	MXK	Change rein with change of leg at X	The extension, the calmness, the change of leg and	10	
	K	Collected canter	the transition		
	A	Turn down centre line			
5	X	Collected walk	The regularity of the half-pirouette	10	
	G	Half-pirouette to the left			
6	X	Half-pirouette to the right	The regularity of the half-pirouette	10	
7	I	Collected trot	The transition	10	
	C	Track to the right	The collection		
	B	Turn to the right			
8	X	Halt – rein-back 3 steps	The halt, the 2 rein-backs, the advance and the	10	
		– advance 6 steps	connection between these movements		
		– rein-back 3 steps			
		Immediately proceed at collected trot			
	E	Track to the left			

		Test	Directive ideas	Marks	Coeff.
9		The transitions from the collected trot to the halt and from the rein-back to the collected trot	The transitions	10	
10	A	Down centre line	The correctness and the regularity of the two tracks	10	
	DV	On two tracks left	The bearing and flexion of the horse		
	VXR	On two track right			
	RG	On two tracks left			
	C	Track to the left			
11	HK	Ordinary trot sitting	The extension	10	
	KF	Collected trot	The transitions		
	FXH	Change rein at extended trot sitting			
12	HCM	Collected walk	The collection and the regularity	10	
13	MBX	First passage	The cadence	10	
			The regularity		
14	X	First piaffe 10 to12 steps	The cadence	10	
			The regularity		
15	X	Proceed in passage – the transitions from the passage to piaffe and from the piaffe to the passage	The transitions	10	
16	XESI	Second passage	The cadence	10	
			The regularity		
17	I	Second piaffe 10 to 12 steps	The cadence	10	
			The regularity		
18	I	Proceed in passage – the transitions from the passage to piaffe and from the piaffe to the passage	The transitions	10	
19	IRMCH	Third passage	The cadence	10	
			The regularity		
20	HXF	Change rein at extended walk	The extension	10	
	F	Ordinary walk			
21	A	Turn down centre line	The halt and the rein-back		
	L	Halt – rein-back 3 steps. Immediately proceed at collected canter right	The straightness of the transition		
	X	Turn to the right			
	B	Track to the right			

		Test	Directive ideas	Marks	Coeff.
22	A	Down centre line. 5 counter changes of hand on two tracks to either side of the centre line, with change of leg at each change of direction. The first on two tracks to the right and the last to the left are of 3 strides, the 4 others of 6 strides.	The correctness and regularity of the 6 on two tracks and the 5 counter changes. The bearing and the flexion of the horse	10	
	G	Finishing on the left leg			
	C	Track to the left	The extension	10	
	HK	Extended canter	The transitions		
	K	Collected canter			
24	A	Down centre line	The regularity of the pirouette	10	2
		Pirouette to the left			
25	X	Change of leg	The regularity of the pirouette	10	2
		Pirouette to the right			
26	C	Track to the right	The extension, the collection and the transitions	10	
	MF	Ordinary canter			
	FK	Collected canter			
	KHC	Extended canter			
	C	Collected canter			
27	MXK	On the diagonal, 9 changes of leg every second stride, finishing on the left leg	The correctness and the straightness of the changes of leg	10	
28	FXH	On the diagonal, 15 changes of leg every stride, finishing on the right leg	The correctness and the straightness of the changes of leg	10	
29	B	Collected trot	The cadence	10	
	A	Down centre line	The regularity		
	L	Passage	The flexion of the horse		
	X	Circle to the right 8 metres			
		Fourth passage (LXX)			
30	X	Third piaffe 10 to 12 steps	The cadence	10	
			The regularity		
31	X	Immediately circle to the left 8 metres	The cadence	10	
		On returning to X, proceed to G	The regularity		
		Fifth passage (XXG)	The flexion of the horse		
32		The transitions from the passage to piaffe and from the piaffe to the passage	The transitions	10	
33	G	Halt – Immobility – Salute	The halt, the immobility	10	

Leave arena at the walk on a long rein

			Marks	Coeff.
Collective Marks				
1. Paces (freedom and regularity)			10	2
2. Impulsion			10	2
3. Submission, suppleness and lightness of the horse			10	3
4. Position, seat of the rider, correct use of the aids			10	2
		Total	**440**	

To be deducted:

for every second over the time allowed ½ mark

Errors:

1st = 5 marks

2nd = 10 marks

3rd = 15 marks

4th = Elimination

RIDE-OFF TEST – OLYMPIC GAMES 1968

		Test	Marks
1	A	Enter in collected canter	10
	X	Halt – Salute – Proceed in collected trot	
2	C	Track to the left	10
	HXF	Change rein in extended trot	
	F	Collected trot	
3	VXR	Half-pass to the right	10
4	CHS	Extended trot	10
	SEV	Collected trot	
	VKA	Extended trot	
	A	Collected trot	
5	PXS	Half-pass to the left	10
6	H	Collected walk	10
	HCMG	Collected walk	
7	G	First piaffe 10 to 12 steps	10
8	GHSIRBX	First passage	10
9		Transitions from collected walk to piaffe and from piaffe to passage	10
10	X	Second piaffe 10 to 12 steps	10

		Test	Marks
11	XEVLPFA	Second passage	10
12		Transitions from passage to piaffe and from piaffe to passage	10
13	A KXM M	Extended trot Change rein in extended trot Collected trot	10
14	C HXF F	Medium walk Change rein in extended walk Collected walk	10
15	A KXM	Collected canter right On the diagonal, 9 changes of leg every second stride, ending on left canter	15
16	HXF	On the diagonal, 15 changes of leg every stride, ending on right canter	10
17	A D	On centre line Pirouette right	10
18	Between D and G	9 flying changes every stride ending in left canter	10
19	G C	Pirouette left Track to the left	10
20	HK K A	Extended canter Collected canter On centre line	10 10
21	D L	Collected trot Third passage – continue to G	10
22	G	Third piaffe 10 to 12 steps	10
23	G	After the piaffe – Halt – Salute	10
		Leave arena in walk on a long rein	

Collective marks

1. Paces (freedom and regularity)	10	(x2)
2. Impulsion	10	(x2)
3. Submission, suppleness and lightness of the horse	10	(x2)
4. Position, seat of the rider, correct use of the aids	10	

Total 300

To be deducted:

a. For every commenced second exceeding the time allowed, ½ mark

b. Errors of the course and omissions are penalised

1st time   =   5 marks
2nd time   =   10 marks
3rd time   =   15 marks
4th time   =   Elimination

OLYMPIC GAMES 1968

Results – Individual

Rider, horse and country	Grand Prix marks (placing)				Ride-off marks (placing)				Grand total
	A	B	C	Total	A	B	C	Total	
1. Ivan Kisimov *Ichor* (Soviet Union)	313 (1)	307 (3)	288 (6)	908	221 (1)	224 (1)	219 (1)	664	1572
2. Josef Neckermann *Mariano* (Germany)	305 (2)	315 (1)	328 (1)	948	193 (7)	201 (4)	204 (5)	598	1546
3. Reiner Klimke *Dux* (Germany)	293 (4)	309 (2)	294 (4)	896	204 (4)	220 (2)	217 (2)	641	1537
4. Ivan Kalita *Absent* (Soviet Union)	296 (3)	291 (5)	292 (5)	879	214 (2)	211 (3)	215 (3)	640	1519
5. Horst Köhler *Neuschnee* (German Democratic Republic)	289 (6)	289 (6)	297 (2)	875	200 (5)	200 (5)	200 (6)	600	1475
6. Elena Petuschkova *Pepel* (Soviet Union)	293 (4)	294 (4)	283 (8)	870	208 (3)	194 (6)	199 (7)	601	1471
7. Gustav Fischer *Wald* (Switzerland)	288 (7)	282 (8)	296 (3)	866	199 (6)	193 (7)	207 (4)	599	1465
8. Liselott Linsenhoff *Piaff* (Germany)	286 (9)	285 (7)	284 (7)	855					
9. Henri Chammartin *Wolfdietrich* (Switzerland)	288 (7)	280 (10)	277 (10)	845					
10. Marianne Gossweiler *Stephan* (Switzerland)	272 (10)	281 (9)	283 (8)	836					
11. Domini Lawrence *San Fernando* (Great Britain)	259 (11)	263 (12)	271 (12)	793					
12. Gerhard Brockmüller *Tristan* (German Democratic Republic)	248 (13)	267 (11)	274 (11)	789					
13. Lorna Johnstone *El Guapo* (Great Britain)	259 (11)	252 (14)	266 (13)	777					
14. Johanna Hall *Conversano Caprice* (Great Britain)	244 (15)	261 (13)	257 (14)	762					
15. Ines Fischer-Credo *Marius* (Canada)	245 (14)	231 (17)	256 (15)	732					
16. Guillermo Squella *Colchaguine* (Chile)	223 (18)	235 (16.)	235 (19)	693					

Rider, horse and country	Grand Prix marks (placing)				Ride-off marks (placing)				Grand total
	A	B	C	Total	A	B	C	Total	
16. Wolfgang Müller *Marios* (German Democratic Republic)	216 (21)	237 (15)	240 (17)	693					
18. Federico Serrano *Marko* (Mexico)	236 (16)	211 (20)	242 (16)	689					
19. Christiot Hanson *Bonheur* (Canada)	234 (17)	222 (18)	221 (22)	677					
20. Antonio Piraino *Ciclon* (Chile)	219 (19)	214 (19)	239 (18)	672					
21. Kyra Downton *Cadet* (USA)	217 (20)	211 (20)	229 (21)	657					
22. Patricio Escudero *Prete* (Chile)	208 (23)	209 (23)	233 (20)	650					
23. Edith Master *Helios* (USA)	214 (22)	211 (22)	221 (22)	646					
24. Donnan Plumb *Attache* (USA)	207 (24)	197 (24)	212 (24)	616					
25. Zoltan Sztehlo *Virtuose* (Canada)	201 (25)	193 (25)	209 (25)	603					
26. Julio Herrera *Otard* (Mexico)	173 (26)	170 (26)	194 (26)	537					

Judge A: Col. Margot (France) President   Judge B: Jaap Pot (Holland)   Judge C: Simpson Vigil (Chile)

OLYMPIC GAMES 1968

Results – Team

		GP points
Gold	**Germany 2699 points**	
	Josef Neckermann *Mariano*	948
	Reiner Klimke *Dux*	896
	Liselotte Linsenhoff *Piaff*	855
Silver	**Soviet Union 2657 points**	
	Ivan Kisimov *Ichor*	908
	Ivan Kalita *Absent*	879
	Elena Petushkova *Pepel*	870
Bronze	**Switzerland 2547 points**	
	Gustav Fischer *Wald*	866
	Henri Chammartin *Wolfdietrich*	845
	Marianne Gosswiler *Stephan*	836

OLYMPIC GAMES 1972

MUNICH, GERMANY

Participating Countries: 13

Brazil	Great Britain	Sweden
Canada	German Democratic Republic	Switzerland
Denmark	Holland	United States of America
France	Japan	
Germany	Soviet Union	

Participating Riders: 33

Teams: 10 teams of 3 riders

Canada	Holland
Denmark	Soviet Union
Germany	Sweden
German Democratic Republic	Switzerland
Great Britain	United States of America

Individual Riders: 3

Brazil – 1
France – 1
Japan – 1

Competitions

- Grand Prix and Ride-off test for the 12 best riders from the Grand Prix.

- The Ride-off test forms the final of the Individual Competition.

Special Regulations

Article 512 – Participation

- Each nation may enter 3 riders, each with 2 horses. However, only 1 of these horses may be ridden in this competition.

- The Dressage Grand Prix is open to all horses, without restriction.

- No horse may take part In the Dressage Grand Prix which has been schooled mounted in the saddle by anyone other than the competitor, during the eight days preceding this competition and for the duration of the whole competition itself. Lungeing, work in hand, etc. by someone else are therefore permitted during this period.

Number of Judges: 5

Medal Winners

Individual

		GP	Ride-off
Gold	Liselott Linsenhoff (Germany) *Piaff*	1763	1229
Silver	Elena Petushkova (Soviet Union) *Pepel*	1747	1185
Bronze	Joseph Neckermann (Germany) *Venetia*	1706	1177

Team

		Points in GP	Placing in Ride-off
Gold	**Soviet Union 5095 points**		
	Elena Petushkova *Pepel*	1747	2
	Ivan Kizimov *Ikhor*	1701	4
	Ivan Kalita *Tarif*	1647	6
Silver	**Germany 5083 points**		
	Liselott Linsenhoff *Piaff*	1763	1
	Joseph Neckermann *Venetia*	1706	3
	Karin Schlüter *Liostro*	1614	9
Bronze	**Sweden 4849 points**		
	Ulla Hakanson *Ajax*	1649	5
	Ninna Swaab *Casanova*	1622	7
	Maud von Rosen *Lucky Boy*	1578	11

Arena: 60 x 20 m.

Markers: Standard.

Judges

	Position
Col Gustav Nyblaeus (Sweden) President	C
Col H Pollay (Germany)	E
J Herrera (Mexico)	H
Col du Breuil (France)	M
Jaap Pot (Holland)	B

Tests

- Grand Prix – maximum score = 500 per judge.
  Time allowed 10 minutes.

- Ride-off test – maximum score = 340 per judge.

Team Gold Medallists the USSR. (Left to right) Ivan Kalita on *Tarif*, Elena Petushkova on *Pepel* and Ivan Kizimov on *Ikhor*.
(Photo: courtesy of Max Ammann)

BELOW Individual Gold medallist Liselotte Linsenhoff (GER) on *Piaff*.
(Photo: courtesy of Max Ammann)

GRAND PRIX TEST (1971) – OLYMPIC GAMES 1972

		Test	Directive ideas	Marks	Coeff.
1	A X	Enter at collected canter Halt – Immobility – Salute Proceed at collected trot	The entry. The halt and the transition from the halt.	10	
2	C MXK KA	Track to the right Change rein at extended trot Ordinary trot	The extension. The transitions.	10	
3	A FXH	Ordinary canter Change rein with change of leg at X	The extension, the calm- ness and the change of leg.	10	
4	MXK K	Change rein with change of leg at X Collected canter	The extension, the calm- ness, the change of leg and the transition.	10	
5	A FXH H	Collected trot Change rein at extended trot Ordinary trot	The extension. The transitions.	10	
6	HCMBX	Ordinary trot	The extension. The balance.	10	
7	X E	Halt – rein-back 4 steps Advance 4 steps Rein-back 6 steps Immediately proceed at ordinary trot Track to the left	The halt, the 2 rein-backs, the advance and the connection between these movements.	10	
8		The transitions from the ordinary trot to the halt and from the rein-back to the ordinary trot		10	
9	XEKA A	Ordinary trot Collected trot	The extension. The balance. The transition.	10	
10	FE	On two tracks	The correctness and the regularity. The bearing and the flexion of the horse. The balance.	10	
11	EM	On two tracks	The correctness and the regularity The bearing and the flexion of the horse. The balance.	10	
12	MCH	Collected walk	The collection. The regularity.	10	

		Test	Directive ideas	Marks	Coeff.
13	HXF FAK	Change rein at extended walk Ordinary walk	The extension. The transition.	10	2
14	K V Between L and P	Collected walk Turn to the right Half-pirouette to the right	The regularity of the half-pirouette.	10	
15	Between L and V	Half-pirouette to the left	The regularity of the half-pirouette.	10	
16		The collected walk KV (P) (V) L	The collection. The regularIty.	10	
17	LPBX	First passage	The cadence. The regularity.	10	
18	X	First piaffer 10 to 12 steps	The cadence. The regularity.	10	
19	X	Proceed in passage. The transitions from the passage to the piaffer and from the piaffer to the passage.		10	
20	XESI	Second passage	The cadence. The regularity.	10	
21	I	Second piaffer 10 to 12 steps	The cadence. The regularity.	10	
22	I	Proceed in passage. The transitions from the passage to the piaffer and from the piaffer to the passage.		10	
23	IRMG	Third passage	The cadence. The regularity.	10	
24	G H	Proceed at collected canter left Track to the left	The straightness and the calmness of the transition from the passage.	10	
25	HK K	Extended canter Collected canter	The extension, the straightness the transition.	10	
26	A G	Down centre line – 5 counter-changes of hand on two tracks to either side of the centre line with change of leg at each change of direction. The first on two tracks to the left and the last to the right are of 3 strides, the 4 others of 6 strides Finishing on the right leg	The correctness and the regularity of the 6 on two tracks and the 5 counter-changes. The bearing and the flexion of the horse. The balance.	10	
27	C MXK K	Track to the right Change rein at extended canter Collected centre and change of leg	The extension, the collection, the transitions and the change of leg.	10	
28	A L	Down centre line Pirouette to the left	The regularity of the pirouette.	10	2

		Test	Directive ideas	Marks	Coeff.
29	X I	Change of leg Pirouette to the right	The regularity of the pirouette.	10	2
30	C MXK	Track to the right On the diagonal. 9 changes of leg every second stride (finishing on the left leg)	The correctness and the straightness of the changes.	10	
31	FXH	On the diagonal. 15 changes of leg every stride (finishing on the right leg)	The correctness and the straightness of the changes.	10	
32	MF F	Ordinary canter Collected canter	The extension, the balance, the straightness, the transition.	10	
33	A L	Down centre line Halt – Rein-back 4 steps – immediately proceed at the fourth passage	The halt. The rein-back.	10	
34		The transitions from the collected canter to the halt and from the rein-back to the passage		10	
35	X	Circle to the right 8 metres diameter followed by the same circle to the left	The regularity of the two circles. The cadence and the regularity of the passage. The flexion of the horse.	10	
36	I	Third piaffer 10 to 12 steps	The cadence. The regularity.	10	
37	I	Proceed in passage. The transitions from the passage to the piaffer and from the piaffer to the passage		10	
38	G	Halt – Immobility – Salute	The halt, the immobility.	10	

Leave arena at a walk on a long rein.

Total 410

Collective marks

	Marks	Coeff.
1. Paces (freedom and regularity)	10	2
2. Impulsion (desire to move forward, elasticity of the steps, suppleness of the back and engagement of the hindquarters)	10	2
3. Submission (attention and confidence; harmony, lightness and ease of the movements; acceptance of the bridle and lightness of the forehand)	10	3
4. Position, seat of the rider, correct use of the aids	10	2

Total 500

To be deducted:

For every commenced second exceeding the time allowed: ½ mark
Errors of the course and omissions are penalised:

1st time = 2 marks
2nd time = 4 marks
3rd time = 8 marks
4th time = Elimination

RIDE-OFF TEST – OLYMPIC GAMES 1972

		Test	Directive ideas	Marks	Coeff.
1	A X	Enter at collected canter Halt – Immobility – Salute – Proceed at collected trot	The entry. The halt and the transition from the halt.	10	
2	C HXF F	Track to the left Change rein at extended trot Collected trot	The extension. The transitions.	10	
3	VXR	On two tracks	The regularity. The bearing and the flexion of the horse. The balance.	10	
4	CHS SEV VKA A	Extended trot Collected trot Extended trot Collected trot	The extension, the collection. The transitions.	10	
5	PXS	On two tracks	The regularity. The bearing and the flexion of the horse. The balance.	10	
6	H HCMG	Collected walk Collected walk	The collection. The regularity.	10	
7	G	First piaffer 10 to 12 steps	The cadence. The regularity.	10	
8	GHSI RBX	First passage	The cadence. The regularity.	10	
9		The transitions from the collected walk to the piaffer and from the piaffer to the passage		10	
10	X	Second piaffer 10 to 12 steps	The cadence. The regularity.	10	
11	XEVL PFA	Second passage	The cadence. The regularity.	10	
12		The transitions from the passage to the piaffer and from the piaffer to the passage		10	
13	A KXM M	Extended trot Change rein at extended trot Collected trot	The extension. The transitions.	10	
14	C HXF F	Ordinary walk Change rein at extended walk Collected walk	The extension. The transitions.	10	

		Test	Directive ideas	Marks	Coeff.
15	A KXM	Proceed at collected canter right On the diagonal, 9 changes of leg every 2nd stride, (finishing on the left leg)	The correctness and the straightness of the changes.	10	
16	HXF	On the diagonal 15 changes of leg every stride, (finishing on the right leg)	The correctness and the straightness of the changes.	10	
17	A D	Down centre line Pirouette to the right	The regularity of the pirouette.	10	2
18	Between D and G	9 changes of leg every stride (finishing on the left leg)	The correctness and the straightness of the changes	10	
19	G C	Pirouette to the left Track to the left	The regularity of the pirouette.	10	2
20	HK K A	Extended canter. Collected canter. Down centre line	The extension, the straightness The transition.	10	
21	D L	Collected trot Third passage advance to G	The cadence. The regularity.	10	
22	G	Third piaffer 10 to 12 steps.	The cadence. The regularity.	10	
23		The transition from the passage to the piaffer		10	
24	G	After the piaffer, Halt – Immobility – Salute.	The halt, the immobility.	10	
		Leave arena at a walk, on a long rein	**Total**	**260**	

Collective marks

	Marks	Coeff.
1. Paces (freedom and regularity)	10	2
2. Impulsion (desire to move forward elasticity of the steps, suppleness of the back and engagement of the hindquarters)	10	2
3. Submission (attention and confidence; harmony, lightness and ease of the movements; acceptance of the bridle and lightness of the forehand)	10	2
4. Position, seat of the rider, correct use of the aids.	10	2
Total	**340**	

To be deducted:

For every commenced second exceeding the time allowed : $1/2$ mark.
Errors of the course and omissions are penalised:

1st time = 2 marks
2nd time = 4 marks
3rd time = 8 marks
4th time = Elimination

OLYMPIC GAMES 1972
Results – Grand Prix

	Rider	Nation	Horse	Time	E	H	C	M	B	Total Points
1.	Linsenhoff, Liselott	Germany	*Piaff*	8:27	368	367	326	343	359	1763
2.	Petushkova, Elena	Soviet Union	*Pepel*	8:14	323	360	362	365	347	1747
3	Neckermann, Josef	Germany	*Venetia*	8:09	350	355	314	347	340	1706
4.	Kizimov, Ivan	Soviet Union	*Ikhor*	8:29	340	342	322	357	340	1701
5.	Hakanson, Ulla	Sweden	*Ajax*	8:31	321	357	331	311	329	1649
6.	Kalita, Ivan	Soviet Union	*Tarif*	8:32	325	336	326	338	322	1647
7.	Swaab, Ninna	Sweden	*Casanova*	8:37	319	313	316	333	341	1622
8.	Hanson, Christilot	Canada	*Armagnac*	8:24	326	300	303	344	342	1615
9.	Schlüter, Karin	Germany	*Liostro*	8:13	319	289	328	347	331	1614
10.	Mikkelsen, Aksel	Denmark	*Talisman*	8:50	324	319	313	313	328	1597
11.	von Rosen, Maud	Sweden	*Lucky Boy*	8:52	309	304	313	332	320	1578
12.	Johnstone, Hilda Lorna	Great Britain	*El Farruco*	7:52	313	307	307	349	300	1576
13.	Brockmüller, Gerhard	GDR	*Marios*	8:34	306	281	313	310	335	1545
14.	Petersen, Ulla	Denmark	*Chigwell*	8:47	319	301	307	306	301	1534
15.	Stückelberger, Christine	Switzerland	*Granat*	8:18	305	305	296	311	311	1528
16.	Müller, Wolfgang	GDR	*Semafor*	8:43	306	284	308	315	308	1521
17.	Köhler, Horst	GDR	*Imanuel*	8:55	301	287	297	273	328	1486
18.	van Doorne, Annie	Holland	*Pericles*	8:21	301	289	274	311	305	1480
19.	Master, Edith	USA	*Dahlwitz*	8:59	292	289	274	322	303	1480
20.	Ingemann, Charlotte	Denmark	*Souliman*	8:03	278	288	291	314	304	1475
21.	Dür, Hermann	Switzerland	*Sod*	8:16	298	271	301	299	297	1466
22.	Winnett, John	USA	*Reinald*	8:16	283	283	279	308	305	1458
23.	le Rolland, Patrick	France	*Cramique*	9:03	270	332	262	306	281	1451
24.	Loriston-Clarke, Jennifer	Great Britain	*Kadett*	8:00	291	292	270	298	299	1450
25.	M. de Rezendae, Sylvio	Brazil	*Othelo*	8:21	289	279	262	304	297	1431
26.	Neale, Cecil	Canada	*Bonne Année*	8:33	293	274	267	283	307	1424
27.	Benedictus, Friederike	Holland	*Turista*	7:45	280	266	278	295	301	1420
28.	Swaab, John	Holland	*Maharadscha*	8:23	281	273	260	300	295	1409
29.	Aeschbacher, Marita	Switzerland	*Charlamp*	8:18	247	277	286	301	278	1389
30.	Stubbs, Lorraine	Canada	*Venezuela*	8:18	273	270	263	296	277	1379
31.	Stephens, Lois	USA	*Fasching*	9:12	254	278	274	277	262	1345
32.	Inoue, Kikuko	Japan	*Don Carlos*	8:30	264	252	258	270	269	1313
33.	Lawrence, Margret-Domini	Great Britain	*San Fernando*	9:11	243	267	239	239	254	1242
	(d'Alessandri, Francisco)	Argentina	*Comalero*							
	(Vargas, Juan Jose)	Argentina	*Pincen*							

OLYMPIC GAMES 1972
Ride-off test results – Individual Competition

	Rider	Nation	Horse	Time	E	H	C	M	B	Total points
						Judges' Marks				
1.	**Linsenhoff, Liselott**	**Germany**	*Piaff*	**6:27**	**254**	**257**	**232**	**245**	**241**	**1229**
2.	**Petushkova, Elena**	**Soviet Union**	*Pepel*	**6:14**	**230**	**243**	**220**	**257**	**235**	**1185**
3.	**Neckermann, Josef**	**Germany**	*Venetia*	**5:58**	**247**	**240**	**211**	**245**	**234**	**1177**
4.	Kizimov, Ivan	Soviet Union	*Ikhor*	6:25	223	243	224	244	225	1159
5.	Kalita, Ivan	Soviet Union	*Tarif*	6:33	223	226	219	238	224	1130
6.	Hakanson, Ulla	Sweden	*Ajax*	6:31	227	233	226	215	225	1126
7.	Schlüter, Karin	Germany	*Liostro*	6:14	233	217	205	230	228	1113
8.	von Rosen, Maud	Sweden	*Lucky Boy*	6:32	218	215	215	219	221	1068
9.	Hanson, Christilot	Canada	*Armagnac*	6:00	219	229	204	211	218	1061
10.	Swaab, Ninna	Sweden	*Casanova*	6:45	210	201	210	234	212	1067
11.	Mikkelsen, Aksel	Denmark	*Talisman*	6:18	208	210	200	222	220	1060
12.	Johnstone, Hilda Lorna	Great Britain	*El Farruco*	5:55	203	205	190	232	206	1036

OLYMPIC GAMES – MUNICH 1972
Team Results

		Points in GP
1	**Soviet Union 5095 points**	
	Elena Petushkova *Pepel*	1747
	Ivan Kizimov *Ikhor*	1701
	Ivan Kalita *Tarif*	1647
2	**Germany 5083 points**	
	Liselott Linsenhoff *Piaff*	1763
	Joseph Neckermann *Venetia*	1706
	Karin Schlüter *Liostro*	1614
3	**Sweden 4849 points**	
	Ulla Hakanson *Ajax*	1649
	Ninna Swaab *Casanova*	1622
	Maud von Rosen *Lucky Boy*	1578
4	**Denmark 4606 points**	
	Aksel Mikkelsen *Talisman*	1597
	Ulla Petersen *Chigwell*	1534
	Charlotte Ingemann *Souliman*	1475

Points in GP

5   **German Democratic Republic 4552 points**

Gerhard Brockmüller *Marios*	1545
Wolfgang Müller *Semafor*	1521
Horst Köhler *Imanuel*	1486

6   **Canada 4418 points**

Christilot Hanson *Armangac*	1615
Cecil Neal *Bonne Année*	1424
Lorraine Stubbs *Venezuela*	1379

7   **Switzerland 4383 points**

Christine Stückelberger *Granat*	1528
Herman Dür *Sod*	1466
Marita Aeschbacher *Charlamp*	1389

8   **Holland 4309 points**

Annie van Doorne *Pericles*	1480
Friederike Benedictus *Turista*	1420
John Swaab *Maharadscha*	1409

9   **United States of America 4283 points**

Edith Master *Dahlwitz*	1480
John Winnett *Reinald*	1458
Lois Stephens *Fasching*	1345

10   **Great Britain 4268 points**

Hilda Lorna Johnstone *El Farruco*	1576
Jennifer Loriston-Clarke *Kadett*	1450
Margret-Domini Lawrence *San Fernando*	1242

Olympic Games 1976

Montreal, Canada

Participating Countries: 11

Argentina	Germany	Soviet Union
Canada	Great Britain	Switzerland
Denmark	Holland	United States of America
France	Italy	

Participating Riders: 27

Teams: 8 teams with a maximum of 3 riders per team

Number of Teams: 8

Canada	Holland
Denmark	Soviet Union
Germany	Switzerland
Great Britain	United States of America

Individual Riders

Argentina – 1
France – 1
Italy – 1

Competitions

- Grand Prix and Grand Prix Special (Ride-off).

- The 12 best results from the Grand Prix qualify for the Grand Prix Special.

- For the Individual Competition, only the Grand Prix Special counts.

Special Regulations

Article 457 Schooling of Horses

- On no account and under penalty of disqualification, may any horse take part in the Competitions mentioned above, if it has been schooled by anyone other than the competitor concerned, or another competitor belonging to the same team, mounted in the saddle, in or outside the city where the Olympic Games take place. during the whole sojourn preceding the Team Competition and until the end of the Individual Competitions. This means, for instance, that a groom mounted in the saddle may walk the horse on a long rein and that lungeing by someone other than the competitor/competitors is permitted.

Also:
• Each nation may enter 4 competitors (one reserve competitor included) and 6 horses for the Team Competition. However, 3 competitors/horses, all to count, may actually start in the competition.

Number of Judges: 5

Medal Winners

Individual

		Grand Prix	Grand Prix Special
Gold	Christine Stückelberger (Switzerland) *Granat*	1869	1486
Silver	Harry Boldt (Germany) *Woycek*	1863	1435
Bronze	Reiner Klimke (Germany) *Mehmed*	1751	1395

Team

			Points	Grand Prix Placing
Gold	**Germany 5155 points**			
	Harry Boldt *Woycek*		1863	2
	Reiner Klimke *Mehmed*		1751	3
	Gabriella Grillo *Ultimo*		1541	10
Silver	**Switzerland 4684 points**			
	Christine Stückelberger *Granat*		1869	1
	Ulrich Lehman *Widin*		1425	16
	Doris Ramseir *Roch*		1390	21
Bronze	**USA 4647 points**			
	Hilda Gurney *Keen*		1607	4
	Dorothy Morkis *Monaco*		1559	7
	Edith Master *Dahlwitz*		1481	14

Arena: 60m x 20m

Markers: Standard

Judges

	Position GP	Position GPS
Gustaf Nyblaeus (Sweden) President	E	C
A Sommer (Denmark)	C	H
Donald Thackeray (USA)	H	E
Johan Hall (Great Britain)	B	M
Jaap Pot (Holland)	M	B

Tests

• Grand Prix 1975 – maximum score = 500 points per judge.
  Time allowed 10 minutes
• Grand Prix Special 1975 – maximum score = 390 points per judge.
  Time allowed 8 minutes 30 seconds

GRAND PRIX TEST (1975) - OLYMPIC GAMES 1976

		Test	Directive ideas	Marks	Coeff.
1	A X	Enter at collected canter Halt – Immobility – Salute Proceed at collected trot	The entry. The halt and the transition from the halt.	10	
2	C MXK KA	Track to the right Change rein at extended trot Medium trot	The extension and regularity of the steps. The transitions.	10	
3	A FXH	Medium canter Change rein with change of leg at X	The lengthening of the strides. The balance, straightness and calmness; the transition.	10	
4	MXK K	Change rein at extended canter Collected canter and change of leg	The extension, the collection and the change of leg.	10	
5	A FXH H	Collected trot Change rein at extended trot Medium trot	The extension and regularity of the steps. The transitions.	10	
6	HCMBX	Medium trot	The lengthening and regularity of the steps. The balance.	10	
7	X E	Halt – Rein-back 4 steps, advance 4 steps, rein-back 6 steps – immediately proceed at medium trot Track to the left	The rein-back, the advance and the rein-back. The precision and smoothness of these movements.	10	
8	X	The transitions from the medium trot to the halt (included) and from the rein- back to the medium trot		10	
9	XEKA A	Medium trot Collected trot	The lengthening and regularity of the steps. The balance. The transitions.	10	
10	FE	Half-pass	The correctness and the regularity. The carriage and the bend. The balance.	10	
11	EM	Half-pass	The correctness and the regularity. The carriage and the bend. The balance.	10	
12	MCH	Collected walk	The shortening and heightening of the steps. The carriage and the regularity.	10	

		Test	Directive ideas	Marks	Coeff.
13	HSXPF FAK	Change rein at extended walk Medium walk	The extension and regularity of the steps. The transition.	10	2
14	K V Between L and P	Collected walk Turn to the right Half-pirouette to the right	The transition. The regularity of the half-pirouette.	10	
15	Between L and V	Half-pirouette to the left	The regularity of the half-pirouette.	10	
16		The collected walk KV (P) (V) L	The shortening and heightening of the steps. The carriage and regularity.	10	
17	L	Proceed at passage. The transition from the collected walk to the passage.		10	
18	LPBX	Passage	The cadence and regularity.	10	
19	X	Piaffer 10 to 12 steps	The cadence and regularity.	10	
20	X	Proceed at passage. The transitions from the passage to the piaffer and from the piaffer to the passage		10	
21	XESI	Passage	The cadence and regularity.	10	
22	I	Piaffer 10 to 12 steps	The cadence and regularity.	10	
23	I	Proceed at passage. The transitions from the passage to the piaffer and from the piaffer to the passage.		10	
24	IRMG	Passage	The cadence and regularity.	10	
25	G H	Proceed at collected canter left Track to the left	The straightness, calmness and regularity.	10	
26	HK K	Extended canter Collected canter	The extension, the straightness, the transitions.	10	
27	AG G	Down centre line – 5 counter-changes of hand at half-pass to either side of the centre line with change of leg at each change of direction. The first half-pass to the left and the last to the right of 3 strides, the 4 others of 6 strides Finishing on the right leg	The correctness and the regularity of the 6 half-passes and the 5 counter-changes. The carriage and the bend, similar to both sides. The balance.	10	
28	C MXK K	Track to the right Change rein at medium canter with change of leg at X Collected canter	The lengthening of the strides. The balance, straightness and calmness; the transitions.	10	

		Test	Directive ideas	Marks	Coeff.
29	A	Down centre line	The collection.	10	2
	L	Pirouette to the left	The regularity.		
30	X	Change of leg	The change of leg.		2
	I	Pirouette to the right	The collection.	10	
			The regularity.		
31	C	Track to the right	The correctness, straightness,	10	
	MXK	On the diagonal, 9 changes of leg	balance and fluency.		
		every second stride			
		(finishing on the left leg)			
32	FXH	On the diagonal, 15 changes of leg	The correctness, straightness,	10	
		every stride (finishing on the right leg)	balance and fluency.		
33	MF	Medium canter	The lengthening of the strides.		
	F	Collected canter	The balance and straightness.	10	
			The transition.		
34	A	Down centre line	The rein-back.	10	
	L	Halt – Rein-back 4 steps –			
		Immediately proceed at passage.			
35	L	The transitions from the collected canter to the halt		10	
		(included) and from the rein-back to the passage.			
36	L	Passage	The regularity and uniformity of	10	
	X	Circle to the right 8 metres diameter	the two circles and the transition		
		followed by the same circle to the left	from one to the other.		
			The bend of the whole horse.		
			The cadence and regularity.		
37	I	Piaffer 10 to 12 steps .	The cadence and regularity.	10	
38	I	The transitions from the passage to the piaffer		10	
		and from the piaffer to the passage			
39	G	Halt – Immobility – Salute	The halt and the transition.	10	

Leave arena at a walk on a long rein at A.

Total   420

	Marks	Coeff.
Collective marks		
1. Paces (freedom and regularity)	10	2
2. Impulsion (desire to move forward, elasticity of the steps, suppleness of the back and engagement of the hind quarters)	10	2
3. Submission (attention and confidence; harmony, lightness and ease of the movements; acceptance of the bridle and lightness of the forehand)	10	2
4. Rider's position, seat and use of the aids.	10	2
	Total 500	

To be deducted:

For every commenced second exceeding the time allowed : ½ mark

Errors of the course and omissions are penalised:

1st time = 2 marks
2nd time = 4 marks
3rd time = 8 marks
4th time = Elimination

Individual Gold Medallist Christine Stückelberger (SUI) and *Granat*. (Photo: courtesy of Max Ammann)

Individual Silver Medallist Harry Boldt (GER) on *Woycek*. (Photo: courtesy of Max Ammann)

GRAND PRIX SPECIAL TEST (1975) – OLYMPIC GAMES 1976

		Test	Directive ideas	Mark	Coeff.
1	A X	Enter at collected canter. Halt – Immobility – Salute. Proceed at collected trot.	The entry. The halt and the transition from the halt.	10	
2	C HXF F	Track to the left. Change rein at extended trot. Collected trot.	The extension and regularity of the steps. The transitions.	10	
3	VXR	Half-pass.	The correctness and the regularity. The carrriage and the bend. The balance.	10	
4	CHS SEV VKA A	Extended trot. Collected trot. Extended trot. Collected trot.	The extension. The collection. The transitions. The regularity.	10	
5	PXS	Half-pass.	The correctness and the regularity. The carrriage and the bend. The balance.	10	
6	CMR RBP PFA A	Extended trot. Collected trot. Extended trot. Collected trot.	The extension. The collection. The transitions. The balance.	10	
7	KLBH	Extended walk. Collected walk.	The extension and regularity of the steps. The transitions.	10	2
8	HCMG	Collected walk.	The shortening and heightening of the steps. The carriage and the regularity.	10	
9	G	Piaffer 10 to 12 steps.	The cadence and regularity.	10	
10	G	Proceed at passage. The transitions from the passage to the piaffer and from the piaffer to the passage.		10	
11	GHSI RBX	Passage.	The cadence and regularity.	10	
12	X	Piaffer 10 to 12 steps.	The cadence and regularity.	10	
13	X	Proceed at passage. The transitions from the passage to the piaffer and from the piaffer to the passage.		10	

		Test	Directive ideas	Mark	Coeff.
14	XEVL PFA	Passage.	The cadence and regularity.	10	
15	A KXM M	Extended trot. Change rein at extended trot. Collected trot.	The extension and regularity of the steps. The transitions.	10	
16	C SXP P	Collected canter. Half-pass. Change of leg.	The correctness and the regularity. The carriage and the bend. The balance and the change of leg.	10	
17	VXR R	Half-pass. Change of leg.	The correctness and the regularity. The carriage and the bend. The balance and the change of leg.	10	
18	HXF	On the diagonal 9 changes of leg every 2nd stride (finishing on the right leg).	The correctness, straightness, balance and fluency.	10	
19	KXM	On the diagonal 15 changes of leg every stride (finishing on the left leg).	The correctness, straightness, balance and fluency.	10	
20	HK K	Extended canter. Collected canter.	The extension. The straightness. The transitions.	10	
21	A D	Down centre line. Pirouette to the left.	The collection. The regularity.	10	2
22	Between D and G	On the centre line 9 changes of leg every stride (finishing on the right leg).	The correctness, straightness, balance and fluency.	10	
23	G C	Pirouette to the right. Track to the right.	The collection. The regularity.	10	2
24	MF F	Extended canter. Collected canter.	The extension. The straightness. The transitions.	10	
25	A D LG	Down centre line. Collected trot. Passage.	The transition. The cadence and regularity of the passage all the way from L to G.	10	
26	G	Piaffer 10 to 12 steps.	The cadence and regularity.	10	
27	G	The transition from the passage to the piaffer.		10	
28	G	After the piaffer, Halt – Immobility – Salute.	The halt and the transition.	10	

Leave arena at a walk on a long rein at A.

Total 310

	Mark	Coeff.
Collective marks		
1. Paces (freedom and regularity).	10	2
2. Impulsion (desire to move forward, elasticity of the steps, suppleness of the back and engagement of the hindquarters).	10	2
3. Submission (attention and confidence; harmony, lightness and ease of the movements; acceptance of the bridle and lightness of the forehand).	10	2
4. Rider's position, seat and use of the aids.	10	2
	Total 390	

To be deducted:

For every commenced second exceeding the time allowed: ½ mark

Errors of the course and omissions are penalised:

1st time = 2 marks
2nd time = 4 marks
3rd time = 8 marks
4th time = Elimination

Olympic Games 1976

Results – Individual (Grand Prix Special)

	Rider	Nation	Horse	E	H	Judges' Marks C	M	B	Total
1	**Stückelberger, Christine**	**Switzerland**	*Granat*	**298.0**	**297.0**	**285.0**	**306.0**	**300.0**	**1486.0**
2	**Boldt, Harry**	**Germany**	*Woycek*	**302.0**	**286.0**	**263.0**	**293.0**	**291.0**	**1435.0**
3	**Klimke, Reiner**	**Germany**	*Mehmed*	**265.0**	**282.0**	**281.0**	**288.0**	**279.0**	**1395.0**
4	Grillo, Gabriela	Germany	*Ultimo*	247.0	258.0	236.0	256.0	260.0	1257.0
5	Morkis, Dorothy	USA	*Monaco*	244.0	252.0	255.0	246.0	252.0	1249.0
6	Ugriumov, Viktor	Soviet Union	*Said*	239.0	258.0	250.0	246.0	254.0	1247.0
7	Boylen, Chris	Canada	*Gaspano*	240.0	245.0	233.0	250.0	249.0	1217.0
8	Petersen, Ulla	Denmark	*Chigwell*	232.0	236.0	233.0	241.0	250.0	1192.0
9	Rutten, Jo	Holland	*Banjo*	233.0	231.0	241.0	240.0	244.0	1189.0
10	Gurney, Hilda	USA	*Keen*	234.0	240.0	222.0	233.0	238.0	1167.0
11	Stubbs, Lorraine	Canada	*True North*	236.0	233.0	222.0	220.0	242.0	1153.0
12	Jensen, Tonny	Denmark	*Fox*	207.0	225.0	197.0	222.0	225.0	1076.0

OLYMPIC GAMES 1976
Results – Team Competition

Nation/team	Horse	Judges' marks					Total Ind.	Total
		E	H	C	M	B		
1 Germany								**5155.0**
Boldt, Harry	*Woycek*	355.0	366.0	372.0	382.0	388.0	1863.0	
Klimke, Dr Reiner	*Mehmed*	339.0	333.0	351.0	364.0	364.0	1751.0	
Grillo, Gabriela	*Ultimo*	308.0	310.0	301.0	319.0	303.0	1541.0	
2 Switzerland								**4684.0**
Stückelberger, Christine	*Granat*	357.0	366.0	379.0	377.0	390.0	1869.0	
Lehmann, Ulrich	*Widin*	269.0	290.0	291.0	293.0	282.0	1425.0	
Ramsier, Doris	*Roch*	277.0	261.0	281.0	289.0	282.0	1390.0	
3 USA								**4647.0**
Gurney, Hilda	*Keen*	328.0	311.0	330.0	314.0	324.0	1607.0	
Morkis, Dorothy	*Monaco*	307.0	312.0	316.0	326.0	298.0	1559.0	
Master, Edith	*Dahlwitz*	296.0	285.0	293.0	313.0	294.0	1481.0	
4 Soviet Union								**4542.0**
Ugriumov, Viktor	*Said*	296.0	324.0	328.0	315.0	334.0	1597.0	
Kalita, Ivan	*Tarif*	286.0	293.0	320.0	319.0	302.0	1520.0	
Kizimov, Ivan	*Rebus*	278.0	278.0	282.0	304.0	283.0	1425.0	
5 Canada								**4538.0**
Boylen, Chris	*Gaspano*	316.0	316.0	328.0	321.0	309.0	1590.0	
Stubbs, Lorraine	*True North*	302.0	300.0	315.0	319.0	313.0	1549.0	
Stracey, Barbara	*Jungherr II*	283.0	271 .0	275.0	305.0	265.0	1399.0	
6 Denmark								**4448.0**
Petersen, Ulla	*Chigwell*	315.0	289.0	309.0	323.0	316.0	1552.0	
Jensen, Tonny	*Fox*	292.0	297.0	299.0	317.0	316.0	1521.0	
Haagensen, Niels	*Lowenstern*	280.0	262.0	288.0	283.0	262.0	1375.0	
7 Holland								**4380.0**
Rutten, Jo	*Banjo*	301.0	292.0	300.0	324.0	316.0	1533.0	
Van Olphen, Louky	*Aleric*	296.0	268.0	289.0	314.0	282.0	1449.0	
Greave, Marjolyn	*Lucky Boy*	267.0	267.0	282.0	302.0	280.0	1398.0	
8 Great Britain								**4076.0**
Whitmore, Sarah	*Junker*	281.0	264.0	265.0	289.0	276.0	1375.0	
Loriston-Clarke, Jennie	*Kadett*	268.0	265.0	276.0	295.0	271.0	1375.0	
Mason, Diana	*Special Ed*	215.0	254.0	264.0	287.0	270.0	1326.0	
France								
D'Esme, Dominique	*Reims*	283.0	283.0	275.0	277.0	273.0	1391.0	
Argentina								
Pellegrini, Guillermo	*Rosicler*	243.0	255.0	251.0	279.0	266.0	1294.0	
Italy								
Puccini, Fausto	*Palazzo*	253.0	245.0	246.0	251.0	264.0	1258.0	

OLYMPIC GAMES 1980

MOSCOW, SOVIET UNION

Participating Countries: 6

Austria	Poland
Bulgaria	Romania
Finland	Soviet Union

Participating Riders: 14

Teams: 4 teams of three riders

Bulgaria	Poland
Romania	Soviet Union

Individual Riders: 2

Austria – 1   Finland – 1

Competitions

• Grand Prix and, Grand Prix Special

• The 12 best riders from the Grand Prix qualify for the Grand Prix Special.

• For the Individual Competition only the result from the Grand Prix Special counts.

Special Regulations

Article 511 – Certificates of Capability

1. In accordance with the IOC's wish that only competitors and horses really capable of the difficult Olympic competitions should be entered, the National Federations must send to the FEI a declaration of participation three months before the closing date for entries.

2. Declarations must include a record of the results obtained in competitions and any other evidence that the competitors and horses have the necessary experience to take part in a competition of the type and difficulty for which they are entered.

3. The FEI has the right to advise the lOC not to accept the entry of competitors who are not properly qualified.

Article 518 – Participation

1. Each nation may enter 4 competitors (one reserve competitor included) and 6 horses for the Team Competition. However, only 3 competitors/horses, all to count, may actually start in this Competition.

2. A nation which cannot send a team, may enter one or two individual competitors, each with two horses. Each competitor may ride only one horse in the Competition.

3. On no account and under penalty of disqualification, may any horse take part in the competitions mentioned above if it has been schooled by anyone other than the competitor concerned, or another competitor belonging to the same team, mounted in the saddle, in or outside the city where the Olympic Games take place, during the whole sojourn preceding the Team Competition and until the end of the Individual Competition. This means, for instance, that a groom mounted in the saddle may walk the horse on a long rein and that lungeing and work in hand by someone other than the competitor/competitors is permitted.

- Three competitors and horses in the Team Dressage Competition, all to count (Grand Prix).

- The 12 best placed competitors (including those who tie for 12th place) in the Team Dressage Competition go forward to the Grand Prix Special.

Medal Winners

Individual

		GPS Points
Gold	Mrs Elisabeth Theurer (Austria) *Mon Cherie*	1370
Silver	Mr Yuri Kowshow (Soviet Union) *Igrok*	1300
Bronze	Mr Victor Ugryumov (Soviet Union) *Shkval*	1234

Team

		Points GP	Placing in GP
Gold	**Soviet Union 4383 points**		
	Yuri Kovshov *Igrok*	1588	2
	Victor Ugryumov *Shkval*	1541	3
	Vera Miserich *Plot*	1254	6
Silver	**Bulgaria 3580 points**		
	Petar Mandajiev *Stchibor*	1244	7
	Svetuslav Ivanov *Aleko*	1190	8
	Gheorgi Gadjev *Vnimatelen*	1146	9
Bronze	**Romania 3346 points**		
	Anghelache Donescu *Dor*	1255	5
	Dumitru Veliku *Decebal*	1076	10
	Petre Rosca *Derbist*	1015	12

Arena: 60m x 20m

Markers: Standard

Judges

	Position GP	Position GPS
Gustaf Nyblaeus (Sweden) President	M	C
Erich Heinrich (German Democratic Republic)	E	H
Jytte Lemkow (Denmark)	H	E
Jaap Pot (Holland)	C	B
Tilo Koeppel (Columbia)	B	M

Tests – same tests as used in the 1976 Olympic Games (GP 1975 and GPS 1975)

- Grand Prix - maximum score = 500
  Time allowed 10 minutes

- Grand Prix Special – maximum score = 390
  Time allowed 8 minutes 30 seconds

Individual Gold Medallist
Elizabeth Max-Theurer on
Mon Cherie.
(Photo: Werner Ernst)

OLYMPIC GAMES 1980

Results – Individual (Grand Prix Special)

	Rider	Nation	Horse	Judges' marks					
				E	H	C	M	B	Total
1.	Elisabeth Theurer	Austria	*Mon Cherie*	276	272	286	267	269	1370
2.	Yuri Kovshov	Soviet Union	*Igrok*	258	256	267	266	253	1300
3.	Viktor Ugryumov	Soviet Union	*Shkval*	253	259	241	240	241	1234
4.	Vera Misewich	Soviet Union	*Plot*	246	254	233	248	250	1231
5.	Kyra Kyrklund	Finland	*Piccolo*	234	240	211	196	240	1121
6.	Anghelache Donescu	Romania	*Dor*	196	104	185	166	209	960
7.	Gheorghi Gadjev	Bulgaria	*Vnimatelen*	155	178	167	187	194	881
8.	Svestoslav Ivanov	Bulgaria	*Aleko*	171	167	161	170	181	850
9.	Petar Mandajiev	Bulgaria	*Stchibor*	172	181	161	154	178	646
10.	Jozef Zagor	Poland	*Helios*	148	156	151	164	185	804
11.	Petre Rosca	Romania	*Derbist*	136	158	155	133	159	741
12.	Dumitru Veliku	Romania	*Decebal*	131	161	130	137	161	720

OLYMPIC GAMES 1980

Results – Team Competition (Grand Prix)

	Nation/Riders	Horse	Judges' marks					Time	Points	Team points
			E	H	C	M	B			
1.	**Soviet Union**									4383
	Kovshov, Yuri	*Igrok*	313	312	311	333	319	10:00	1588	
	Ugriumov, Viktor	*Shkval*	310	313	301	291	326	9:00	1541	
	Misevich, Vera	*Plot*	239	252	263	231	269	8:52	1254	
2.	**Bulgaria**									3580
	Mandajiev, Petar	*Stchibor*	236	262	244	254	248	8:11	1244	
	Ivanov, Svetuslav	*Aleko*	228	232	239	240	251	8:15	1190	
	Gadjev, Gheorgi	*Vnimatelen*	241	209	223	216	257	9:08	1146	
3.	**Romania**									3346
	Donescu. Anghelache	*Dor*	239	253	258	273	232	8:17	1255	
	Veliku, Dumitru	*Decebal*	225	194	225	208	224	8:57	1076	
	Rosca, Petre	*Derbist*	228	179	224	191	193	8:45	1015	
4.	**Poland**									2945
	Zagor, Josef	*Helios*	205	202	229	207	218	8:33	1061	
	Morciniec, Elke-Karin	*Sum*	183	181	208	167	215	9:08	954	
	Wasowska, Wanda	*Damazy*	173	174	193	184	206	8:23	930	
	Austria									
	Theurer, Elisabeth	*Mon Cherie*	325	321	325	316	336	8:45	1623	
	Finland									
	Kyrklund, Kyra	*Piccolo*	297	303	296	276	286	8:40	1458	

Goodwood Festival 1980

Goodwood, UK

This was a competition between Western countries that boycotted the Olympic games in Moscow in 1980.

Participating Countries: 11

Austria	Denmark	Holland
Australia	France	Switzerland
Belgium	Germany	United States of America
Canada	Great Britain	

Participating Riders: 32

Teams: 8 teams of three riders

Canada	Great Britain
Denmark	Holland
France	Switzerland
Germany	United States of America

Individual Riders: 8

Austria – 2	Germany – 1
Australia – 1	Switzerland – 1
Belgium – 1	United States of America – 1
Canada – 1	

Competitions

• Grand Prix and, Grand Prix Special for the 12 best out of the Grand Prix competition.

• For the individual competition, only the Grand Prix Special will count.

Results

Individual

		Points
1st	Christine Stückelberger (Switzerland) *Granat*	1452
2nd	Uwe Schulten-Baumer (Germany) *Slibowitz*	1373
3rd	Reiner Klimke (Germany) *Ahlerich*	1345

Team

		Points in GP	Placing in GPS
1st	**Germany 4967 points**		
	Uwe Schulten-Baumer *Slibowitz*	1725	2
	Reiner Klimke *Ahlerich*	1633	3
	Uwe Sauer *Hirtentraum*	1609	4

		Points in GP	Placing in GPS
2nd	**Switzerland 4838 points**		
	Christine Stückelberger *Granat*	1749	1
	Ulrich Lehmann *Widin*	1568	7
	Amy C de Bary *Aintree*	1521	10
3rd	**Denmark 4573 points**		
	Finn Larson *Coq d'Or*	1532	12
	Anne Grethe Jensen *Marzog*	1524	11
	Tove Jorr-Jorckston *Lazuly*	1517	14

Arena: 60m x 20m

Markers: Standard

Judges

	Position GP	Position GPS
Johanna Hall (Great Britain)	C	M
Donald Thackeray (USA)	B	
Heinz Schütte (Germany)	M	C
Jaap Pot (Holland)	H	E
Wolfgang Niggli (Switzerland)	E	H
B Willer-Hansen (Denmark)		B

Tests – the same tests as used in the Olympic Games 1976 (GP 1975 and GPS (1975)

- Grand Prix 1975 - maximum score = 500
  Time allowed = 10 minutes

- Grand Prix Special 1975 - maximum score = 390
  Time for information = 8 minutes 30seconds

GOODWOOD FESTIVAL 1980
Results – Grand Prix

	Rider/Nation/Horse	Judges marks					Total
		E	H	C	M	B	
1.	Christine Stückelberger SUI, *Granat*	351	355	349	350	344	1749
2.	Uwe Schulten-Baumer, GER, *Slibowitz*	352	356	343	347	327	1725
3.	Gabriela Grillo GER, *Ultimo*	330	336	332	325	331	1645
4.	Reiner Klimke, GER, *Ahlerich*	313	328	332	328	332	1633
5.	Uwe Sauer, GER, *Hirtentraum*	336	319	326	316	312	1609
6.	Jennie Loriston-Clarke, GBR, *Dutch Courage*	315	318	322	314	324	1593
7.	Ulrich Lehmann, SUI, *Widin*	312	306	310	323	317	1568

	Rider/Nation/Horse	E	H	C	M	B	Total
				Judges marks			
8.	Francis Verbeek-van Rooy, HOL, *Ivar*	322	304	319	304	307	1556
9.	Finn-Saks Larsen, DEN, *Coq d'Or*	295	304	309	323	301	1532
10.	Dominique Flament, FRA, *Vol ma Vent*	297	308	306	310	309	1530
11.	Anne-Grete Jensen, DEN, *Marzog*	307	300	301	304	312	1524
12.	Amy-Catherine de Bary, SUI, *Aintree*	301	291	314	322	293	1521
13.	Annemarie Keyzer, HOL, *Amon*	303	303	312	303	299	1520
14.	Tove Jorck-Jorckston, DEN, *Lazuly*	296	323	314	292	292	1517
15.	Margit Otto-Crepin, FRA, *Caprici*	291	306	311	304	292	1504
16.	Christian Carde, FRA, *Solitaire*	294	310	297	300	286	1487
17.	Gwen Stockebrand, USA, *Bao*	295	288	303	298	294	1478
18.	Anne d'Ieteren, BEL, *Juroto*	277	298	297	294	283	1449
19.	A. Kottas-Heldenberg, AUT, *Moonbeam*	290	287	288	288	295	1448
20.	Rinie van der Schaft, HOL, *Juroen*	279	285	290	291	279	1424
21.	Claire Koch, SUI, *Beau Geste*	276	273	298	284	285	1416
22.	Christilot Boylen, CAN, *Cassius*	277	284	298	280	272	1411
23.	Robert Schifter, AUT, *Marquis*	284	271	300	279	276	1410
24.	Cindy Neale, CAN, *Equus*	282	268	291	274	287	1402
25.	Lendon Gray, USA, Beppo	272	286	286	289	268	1401
26.	Linda Zang, USA, *Fellow Traveller*	265	279	289	283	277	1393
27.	Trisha Gardiner, GBR, *Manifesto*	275	289	285	272	267	1388
28.	John Winnett, USA, *Leopardi*	261	276	282	277	279	1375
29.	Diana Mason, GBR, *Special Edition*	271	275	277	291	259	1373
30.	Bonnie Bonnebo, CAN, *Satchmo*	259	265	272	280	257	1333
31.	Ed Rothkranz, CAN, *My King*	258	246	251	270	248	1273
32.	Judith MacKay, AUS, *Debonair*	248	238	254	255	217	1212

GOODWOOD FESTIVAL 1980

Results – Individual (Grand Prix Special)

Rider	Nation	Horse	C	M	H	B	E	Total
					Judges' marks			
1. **Christine Stückelberger**	Switzerland	*Granat*	287	304	292	288	281	1452
2. **Uwe Schulten-Baumer**	Germany	*Slibowitz*	285	275	275	267	271	1373
3. **Reiner Klimke**	Germany	*Ahlerich*	283	268	269	256	269	1345
4. Uwe Sauer	Germany	*Hirtentraum*	271	265	248	257	273	1314
5. Gabriela Grillo	Germany	*Ultimo*	267	247	268	242	255	1279
6. Jennie Loriston-Clarke	Great Britain	*Dutch Courage*	252	236	252	250	262	1252

Rider	Nation	Horse	Judges' marks					Total
			C	M	H	B	E	
7. Ulrich Lehmann	Switzerland	*Widin*	252	229	255	246	252	1234
8. Frances Verbeek van Rooy	Holland	*Ivar*	252	238	252	234	251	1227
9. Dominique Flament	France	*Vol au Vent*	253	235	245	239	247	1219
10. Amy-Catherine de Bary	Switzerland	*Aintree*	250	230	235	233	246	1194
11. Anne-Grethe Jensen	Denmark	*Marzog*	216	230	241	238	238	1193
12. Finn-Saks Larsen	Denmark	*Coq d'Or*	234	229	232	237	240	1181

Goodwood Festival 1980

Results – Team Competition

Nation/Rider	Horse	Judges' marks					Total	Team total
		C	M	H	B	E		
1. Germany								**4967**
Uwe Schulten-Baumer	*Slibowitz*	352	356	343	347	327	1725	
Uwe Sauer	*Hirtentraum*	336	319	326	316	312	1609	
Reiner Klimke	*Ahlerich*	313	328	332	328	332	1633	
2. Switzerland								**4838**
Christine Stückelberger	*Granat*	351	355	349	350	344	1749	
Ulrich Lehmann	*Widin*	312	306	310	323	317	1568	
Amy-Catherine de Bary	*Aintree*	301	291	314	322	293	1521	
3. Denmark								**4573**
Finn-Saks Larsen	*Coq d'Or*	295	304	309	323	301	1532	
Anne-Grethe Jensen	*Marzog*	307	300	301	304	312	1524	
Tove Jorck-Jorckston	*Lazuly*	296	323	314	292	292	1517	
4. France								**4521**
Dominique Flament	*Vol au Vent*	297	308	306	310	309	1530	
Margit Otto-Crepin	*Caprici*	291	306	311	304	292	1504	
Christian Carde	*Solitaire*	294	310	297	300	286	1487	
5. Holland								**4500**
Frances Verbeek van Rooy	*Ivar*	322	304	319	304	307	1556	
Annemarie Keyzer	*Amon*	303	303	312	303	299	1520	
Rinie van der Schaft	*Juroen*	279	285	290	291	279	1424	
6. Great Britain								**4354**
Jennie Loriston-Clarke	*Dutch Courage*	315	318	322	314	324	1593	
Trisha Gardner	*Manifesto*	275	289	285	272	267	1388	
Diana Mason	*Special Edition*	271	175	177	291	259	1373	

Olympic Games 1984

Los Angeles, USA

Participating Countries: 18

Austria	France	Peru
Australia	Germany	Puerto Rico
Canada	Great Britain	Sweden
Denmark	Holland	Switzerland
Ecuador	Japan	United States of America
Finland	Mexico	Yugoslavia

Participating Riders: 43

Teams: 12 teams of 3 riders

Austria	Germany	Sweden
Canada	Great Britain	Switzerland
Denmark	Holland	United States of America
France	Mexico	Yugoslavia

Individual Riders: 7

Australia – 1	Japan – 2
Ecuador – 1	Peru – 1
Finland – 1	Puerto Rico – 1

Competitions

• Grand Prix and Grand Prix Special for the best 12 combinations in the Grand Prix.

• **Note:** One rider from the French team was eliminated because his horse went lame. Therefore there was no French team in the Team Competition.

Special Regulations

• For each team a maximum of 4 riders and horses may be entered, of whom 3 riders can compete. The fourth rider is only a reserve rider and does not compete.

Medal Winners

Individual

		GP Points	GPS Points
Gold	Reiner Klimke (Germany) *Ahlerich*	1797	1504
Silver	Anne Grete Jensen (Denmark) *Marzog*	1701	1442
Bronze	Otto Hofer (Switzerland) *Limandus*	1609	1364

Team

		Points in GP	Individual Placing in GP
Gold	**Germany 4955 points**		
	Reiner Klimke *Ahlerich*	1797	1
	Uwe Sauer *Montevideo*	1582	7
	Herbert Krug *Muscadeur*	1576	9
Silver	**Switzerland 4673 points**		
	Otto Hofer *Limandus*	1609	3
	Christine Stückelberger *Tansanit*	1606	4
	Amy C de Bary *Aintree*	1458	27
Bronze	**Sweden 4630 points**		
	Ulla Hakanson *Flamingo*	1589	6
	Ingamay Bylund *Aleks*	1582	7
	Louise Nathorst *Inferno*	1459	26

Individual Gold Medallist Reiner Klimke (GER) on *Ahlerich*.
(Photo: courtesy of Max Ammann)

Arena: 60 x 20 m.

Markers: Standard.

Judges

	Position GP	Position GPS
Wolfgang Niggli (Switzerland) President	C	C
Johanna Hall (Great Britain)	B	H
Elena Kondratieva (Soviet Union)	E	M
Donald Thackeray (USA)	H	B
Heinz Schütte (Germany)	M	E

No comparison of scores.

Team Gold Medallists Germany with Team Silver medallists, Switzerland and Bronze medallists, Sweden. (Photo: courtesy of Max Amman)

Tests

- Grand Prix Test (1983) – maximum points per judge = 500 (Time: 8 minutes 40 seconds).
- Grand Prix Special (1983) – maximum points per judge = 410 (Time: 7 minutes 30 seconds).

- **Note: Time penalties not applied; times given are for information only.**

GRAND PRIX TEST (1983) – OLYMPIC GAMES 1984

		Test	Directive ideas	Marks	Coeff
1	A X	Enter in collected canter. Halt — Immobility — Salute. Proceed in collected trot.	The entry. The halt and the transitions from the canter to the halt and from the halt to the trot.	10	
2	C MXK KA	Track to the right. Change rein in medium trot. Medium trot.	The lengthening and regularity of the steps. The transition.	10	
3	A FXH	Collected canter. Change rein in medium canter with change of leg at X.	The lengthening, the regularity of the strides. The balance and straightness. The transition	10	
4	MXK K	Change rein in extended canter. Collected canter and change of leg.	The transition. The extension, the collection and the flying change.	10	
5	A FS SHG	Collected trot. Change rein in extended trot. Collected trot.	The lengthening of the frame, the extension and regularity of the steps. The transitions.	10	
6	G	Halt – rein-back 4 steps, advance 4 steps, rein-back 6 steps – immediately proceed in medium trot.	The halt. The rein-back. The transitions.	10	
7		The transitions from collected trot to the halt and from the rein-back to the medium trot.		10	
8	M RK K	Track to the right. Change rein in extended trot. Collected trot.	The lengthening of the frame. The extension and regularity of the steps. The transitions.	10	
9	FE	Half-pass.	The correctness and regularity. The angle and the bend of the horse. The balance.	10	
10	EM MC	Half-pass. Collected trot.	The correctness and regularity. The angle and the bend of the horse. The balance.	10	

		Test	Directive ideas	Marks	Coeff
11	C H Between G and M	Collected walk. Turn to the left. Half-pirouette to the left.	The transition. The regularity of the half-pirouette.	10	
12	Between G and H	Half-pirouette to the right.	The regularity of the half-pirouette.	10	
13		The collected walk CHG(M)(H)G.	The shortening and heightening of the steps. The carriage and regularity.	10	
14	GMEF	Extended walk.	The extension and regularity of the steps. The lengthening of the frame.	10	2
15	FAK	Collected walk.	The shortening and heightening of the steps. The carriage and the regularity.	10	
16	K	Proceed in passage.	The transition from the collected walk to passage.	10	
17	KVL	Passage.	The cadence and the regularity.	10	
18	L	Piaffe 10 to 12 steps.	The cadence and the regularity.	10	
19	L	Proceed in passage; transitions from passage to piaffe and from piaffe to passage.		10	
20	LPRI	Passage.	The cadence and the regularity.	10	
21	I	Piaffe 10 to 12 steps.	The cadence and the regularity.	10	
22	I	Proceed in passage; transitions from passage to piaffe and from piaffe to passage.		10	
23	ISHC	Passage.	The cadence and the regularity.	10	
24	C	Proceed in collected canter.	The straightness, calmness and regularity.	10	
25	MF F	Medium canter. Collected canter.	The lengthening of the strides. The balance and straightness. The transitions.	10	

		Test	Directive ideas	Marks	Coeff
26	AG	Down centre line – 5 counter changes of hand in half-pass to either side of the centre line with change of leg at each change of direction. The first half-pass to the right and the last to the left of 3 strides, the 4 others of 6 strides,	The correctness and the regularity of the 6 half-passes and the 5 counter-changes. The balance.	10	
	G	Finishing on the left leg			
27	C	Track to the left.	The extension, the collection, the transitions.	10	
	HK	Extended canter			
	K	Collected canter			
28	A	Down centre line.	The collection.	10	2
	L	Pirouette to the left.	The regularity.		
	X	Change of leg.	The change of leg.		
29	I	Pirouette to the right.	The collection.	10	2
	C	Track to the right.	The regularity. The change of leg.		
30	MXK	On the diagonal 9 changes of leg every second stride (finishing on the left leg).	The correctness, straightness, balance and fluency.	10	
31	FXH	On the diagonal 15 changes of leg every stride (finishing on the right leg).	The correctness, straightness, balance and fluency.	10	
32	C	Collected trot.	The lengthening of the frame, the extension and regularity of the steps. The transitions.	10	
	MXK	Change rein in extended trot.			
	K	Collected trot.			
33	A	Down centre line	The halt.	10	
	L	Halt – rein-back 4 steps – immediately proceed in passage.	The rein-back.		
34		The transition from the collected trot to the halt and from the rein-back to passage.		10	

		Test	Directive ideas	Marks	Coeff
35	LX	Passage.	The cadence and the regularity.	10	
	X	Circle right in passage 10m in diameter.	The bend.		
36	X	Piaffe 10 to 12 steps.	The cadence and the regularity.	10	
37	X	Circle left in passage 10 m diameter.	The cadence and the regularity. The bend.	10	
	XI	Passage.			
38		Transitions from passage to piaffe and from piaffe to passage.		10	
39	I	Halt – Immobility – Salute.	The halt and the transition.	10	

Leave arena in a walk on a long rein at A.

Total 420

Collective marks
1. Paces (freedom and regularity) — 10 — 2
2. Impulsion (desire to move forward, elasticity of the steps, suppleness of the back and engagement of the hind quarters) — 10 — 2
3. Submission (attention and confidence; harmony, lightness and ease of the movements; acceptance of the bridle and lightness of the forehand) — 10 — 2
4. Rider's position and seat; correctness and effect of the aids — 10 — 2

Total 500

To be deducted:
Errors of the course and omissions are penalised:
1st time = 2 marks
2nd time = 4 marks
3rd time = 8 marks
4th time = Elimination

GRAND PRIX SPECIAL (1983) – OLYMPIC GAMES 1984

		Test	Directive ideas	Marks	Coeff.
1	A X	Enter in collected canter. Halt – Immobility – Salute. Proceed in collected trot.	The entry. The halt and the transitions to and from the halt.	10	
2	C HXF F	Track to the left. Change rein in extended trot. Collected trot.	The lengthening of the frame, the extension and regularity of the steps. The transitions.	10	
3	VXR RMC	Half-pass. Collected trot.	The correctness and the regularity. The carriage and the bend. The balance.	10	
4	CHS SK KAF	Passage. Extended trot. Passage.	The cadence and regularity of the passage. The extension and regularity.	10	
5	FP PXS SHC	Collected trot. Half-pass. Collected trot.	The correctness and the regularity. The carriage and the bend. The balance.	10	
6	CMR RF FAK	Passage. Extended trot. Passage.	The cadence and regularity of the passage. The extension and regularity.	10	
7		Transitions from passage to extended trot and from extended trot to passage. (Tests 4 and 6)		10	
8	KLBIH	Extended walk. Collected walk.	The extension and regularity of the steps. The transitions.	10	2
9	HCMG	Collected walk.	The shortening and heightening of the steps. The carriage and regularity.	10	
10	G	Piaffe 12 to 15 steps.	The cadence and regularity.	10	
11	G	Proceed in passage. Transitions from collected walk to piaffe and from piaffe to passage.		10	
12	GHSI	Passage.	The cadence and regularity.	10	
13	I	Piaffe 12 to 15 steps.	The cadence and regularity.	10	

		Test	Directive ideas	Marks	Coeff.
14	I	Proceed in passage. Transitions from passage to piaffe and from piaffe to passage.		10	
15	IRBX	Passage.	The cadence and regularity.	10	
16	XEVKAF	Collected canter left.	The correctness and regularity.	10	
17	FLE E	Half-pass in canter. Flying change of leg.	The correctness and regularity. The carriage and the bend. The balance and the change of leg.	10	
18	EIM M MCH	Half-pass in canter. Flying change of leg. Collected canter.	The correctness and regularity. The carriage and the bend. The balance and the change of leg.	10	
19	HXF	On the diagonal 9 changes of leg every second stride (finishing on right leg).	The correcness, straightness, balance and fluency.	10	
20	KXM	On the diagonal 15 changes of leg every stride (finishing on left leg).	The correctness, straightness, balance and fluency.	10	
21	HXF F	Change rein in extended canter. Collected canter and flying change of leg.	The extension. The transition. The flying change of leg.	10	
22	A D	Down centre line. Pirouette right.	The collection. The regularity.	10	2
23	Between D and G	On the centre line 9 flying changes of leg every stride.	The correctness, straightness, balance and fluency.	10	
24	G C	Pirouette left. Track to the left.	The collection. The regularity.	10	2
25	HK K	Medium trot. Collected trot.	The lengthening and regularity of the steps. The transition.	10	
26	A L	Down centre line. Passage.	The cadence and regularity.	10	
27	I	Piaffe 12 to 15 steps.	The cadence and regularity.	10	
28		Transitions from collected trot to passage, from passage to piaffe.		10	

		Test	Directive ideas	Marks	Coeff.
29	IG	Passage.	The cadence and regularity.	10	
30	G	Halt – Immobility – Salute	The halt and the transition.	10	

Leave arena in a walk on a long rein at A.

Total 330

Collective marks

	Marks	Coeff.
1 Paces (freedom and regularity).	10	2
2 Impulsion (desire to move forward, elasticity of the steps, suppleness of the back and engagement of the hind quarters).	10	2
3 Submission (attention and confidence; harmony, lightness and ease of the movements; acceptance of the bridle and lightness of the forehand).	10	2
4 Rider's position and seat; correctness and effect of the aids.	10	2

Total 410

To be deducted:

Errors of the course and omissions are penalised:

1st time = 2 marks
2nd time = 4 marks
3rd time = 8 marks
4th time = Elimination

OLYMPIC GAMES 1984

Results – Individual Competition (Grand Prix Special)

Rider	Nation	Horse	Judges' marks					Total
			E	H	C	M	B	
1. Reiner Klimke	Germany	*Ahlerich*	304	316	288	303	293	1504
2. Anne Grethe Jensen	Denmark	*Marzog*	289	300	279	288	286	1442
3. Otto J Hofer	Switzerland	*Limandus*	281	264	273	272	274	1364
4. Ingamay Bylund	Sweden	*Aleks*	273	264	271	263	261	1332
5. Herbert Krug	Germany	*Muscadeur*	272	262	262	270	257	1323
6. Uwe Sauer	Germany	*Montevideo*	272	249	243	261	254	1279
7. Christopher Bartle	Great Britain	*Wily Trout*	260	257	250	250	262	1279
8. Annemarie Sanders-Keyzer	Holland	*Amon*	250	262	256	249	254	1271
9. Christine Stückelberger	Switzerland	*Tansanit*	252	244	252	257	252	1257
10. Christilot Boylen	Canada	*Anklang*	248	243	244	254	248	1237
11. Elisabeth Max-Theurer	Austria	*Acapulco*	239	247	240	242	246	1214
12. Ulla Hakanson	Sweden	*Flamingo*	226	246	245	236	244	1197

E: Heinz Schütte (Germany)

H: Johanna Hall (Great Britain)

C: Wolfgang Niggli (Switzerland)

M: Elena Kondratieva (Soviet Union)

B: Donald Thackeray (USA)

OLYMPIC GAMES 1984

Results – Team Competition (Grand Prix)

Nation/Riders	Horse	Judges' marks					Total	Team Total
		E	H	C	M	B		
1. Germany								**4955**
Reiner Klimke	*Ahlerich*	360	343	364	361	369	1797	
Uwe Sauer	*Montevideo*	317	321	296	326	322	1582	
Herbert Krug	*Muscadeur*	315	325	304	321	311	1576	
2. Switzerland								**4673**
Otto J Hofer	*Limandus*	317	324	322	320	326	1609	
Christine Stückelberger	*Tansanit*	335	315	319	316	321	1606	
Amy Catherine de Bary	*Aintree*	281	305	286	292	294	1458	

Nation/Riders	Horse	Judges' marks					Total	Team Total
		E	H	C	M	B		
3. Sweden								**4630**
Ulla Hakanson	*Flamingo*	323	316	321	314	315	1589	
Ingamay Bylund	*Aleks*	305	320	313	323	321	1582	
Louise Nathhorst	*Inferno*	296	300	281	291	291	1459	
4. Holland								**4586**
Annermarie Sanders-Keyzer	*Amon*	324	312	313	323	319	1591	
Tineke Bartels de Vrie	*Duco*	299	302	306	317	315	1539	
Jo Rutten	*Ampere*	304	289	290	290	283	1456	
5. Denmark								**4574**
Anne Grethe Jensen	*Marzog*	334	342	340	336	349	1701	
Corben Ulsoe Olsen	*Patricia*	317	281	307	289	302	1496	
Marie-Louise Castenskiold	*Stradivarius*	271	274	290	270	272	1377	
6. USA								**4559**
Hilda Gurney	*Keen*	314	309	309	298	300	1530	
Sandy Pflüger-Clarke	*Marco Polo*	316	305	296	297	302	1516	
Robert Dover	*Romantico*	309	309	299	301	295	1513	
7. Canada								**4503**
Christilot Boylen	*Anklang*	304	308	304	313	311	1540	
Bonny Chesson	*Satchmo*	308	298	305	281	304	1496	
Eva-Maria Pracht	*Little Joe*	315	296	284	284	288	1467	
8. Great Britain								**4463**
Christopher Bartle	*Wily Trout*	320	291	306	309	321	1547	
Jane Bartle-Wilson	*Pinocchio*	305	292	289	307	296	1489	
Jennie Loriston-Clarke	*Prince Consort*	287	294	295	279	272	1427	
9. Austria								**4391**
Elisabeth Max-Theurer	*Acapulco*	319	303	312	310	312	1556	
Peter Ebinger	*Malachit*	284	293	282	285	290	1434	
Christa Winkel	*Richelieu*	287	282	262	286	284	1401	
10. Yugoslavia								**4381**
Alojz Lah	*Maestoso Monteaura*	310	315	302	297	299	1523	
Stojan Moderc	*Maestoso Allegra*	282	272	268	272	268	1362	
Dusan Mavec	*Favory Wera*	299	291	303	301	302	1496	
11. Mexico								**3927**
Cristobal Egerstrom	*Metternich*	292	281	262	253	273	1361	
Margarita Nava	*Pentagon*	256	274	255	256	269	1310	
Manuel Cid	*Civian*	230	280	254	247	245	1256	

Nation/Riders	Horse	Judges' marks					Total	Team Total
		E	H	C	M	B		
12. **Puerto Rico**								
Libby Hernandez	*Rocco*	257	269	241	264	274	1305	
13. **Finland**								
Kyra Kyrklund	*Nor*	312	299	294	301	298	1504	
14. **Japan**								
Osamu Nakamata	*Medina*	245	276	251	253	246	1271	
15. **Ecuador**								
Brigite Morillo	*Ballotage*	253	252	232	247	248	1232	
16. **Australia**								
Margaret Mclver	*C K*	260	254	214	233	241	1202	
17. **Peru**								
Mariain Cunningham	*El Dorado*	258	272	260	267	260	1317	
18. **Japan**								
Nabutada Hiromatsu	*Win-Sol*	257	245	256	240	248	1246	
19. **France**								
Dominique d'Esme	*Fresh Wind*	303	300	306	286	289	1484	
Margit Otto-Crepin	*Caprici*	314	290	297	302	309	1512	
Michel Bertraneu	*Gaillard*	E						

E = Eliminated

OLYMPIC GAMES 1988

SEOUL, SOUTH KOREA

Participating Countries: 18

Australia	Germany	Korea
Canada	Great Britain	Soviet Union
Columbia	Holland	Spain
Denmark	Ireland	Sweden
Finland	Italy	Switzerland
France	Japan	United States of America

Participating Riders: 53

Teams: 11 teams of 4 riders

• The 3 best scores to count for the Team Competition.

Canada	Germany	Sweden
Denmark	Great Britain	Switzerland
Finland	Holland	United States of America
France	Soviet Union	

Individual Riders: 9

Australia – 1
Columbia – 2
Ireland – 1
Japan – 2
Korea – 2
Spain – 1

Competitions

• Grand Prix for the Team Competition and Grand Prix Special for the Individual Competition for the best 12 riders in the Grand Prix.

Special Regulations

• The Team Dressage Competition and the Individual Dressage Competition are held under the rules contained in Chapter Il of the 'Rules for Dressage Events', except where specifically modified below. The tests are those of the Grand Prix and the Grand Prix Special respectively in force at the time of the Olympic Games.

• Article 618 – Participation and Order of Starting

1. Each nation may start 4 competitors and 4 horses for the Team Competition. Each competitor may only ride 1 horse in the Competition. The 3 best placed competitors/horses count for the Team Classification.

2. A nation which cannot send a team, may enter 1 or 2 individual competitors, each with 2 horses. Each competitor may ride only 1 horse in the Competition.

3. The 12 best placed competitors/horses from the Team Competition (including those who tie for the 12th place), may take part in the Individual Competition (Grand Prix Special) but no nation may have more than 3 competitors/horses among them.

4. A draw for the starting order in the Team Competition (Grand Prix) for individual competitors, for teams and for team members within each team will take place according to Art. 614.1., 2., 3. In the individual competition (Grand Prix Special) the starting order will take the reverse order of placings in the Team Competition.

• Article 619 – Schooling of Horses

On no account and under penalty of disqualification, may any horse take part in the Competitions mentioned above, if it has been schooled by anyone other than the competitor concerned, or another competitor belonging to the same team, mounted in the saddle, in or outside the city where the Olympic Games take place, during the whole sojourn preceding the Team Competition and until the end of the Individual Competition. This means, for instance, that a groom mounted in the saddle may walk the horse on a long rein and that lungeing and work in hand by someone other than the competitor/competitors is permitted.

Medal Winners

Individual

		GP Points (placing)	GPS
Gold	Nicole Uphoff (Germany)		
	Rembrandt	1458 (1)	1521
Silver	Margit Otto-Crepin (France)		
	Corlandus	1455 (2)	1462
Bronze	Christine Stückelberger (Switzerland)		
	Gaugin de Lully	1430 (4)	1417

Teams

		GP Points	Individual placing in GP
Gold	**Germany 4302 points**		
	Nicole Uphoff *Rembrandt*	1458	1
	Monica Theodorescu *Ganimedes*	1433	3
	Ann-Kathrin Linsenhoff *Courage*	1411	6
Silver	**Switzerland 4164 points**		
	Christine Stückelberger *Gaugin de Lully*	1430	4
	Otto Hofer *Andiamo*	1392	9
	Daniel Ramseier *Random*	1342	11
Bronze	**Canada 3969 points**		
	Cynthia Ishoi *Dynasty*	1363	10
	Ashley Nicoll *Reipo*	1308	15
	Gina Smith *Malte*	1298	18

ABOVE Individual Gold Medallist Nicole Uphoff (GER) on *Rembrandt*. (Photo: courtesy of Max Ammann.)

Team Gold Medallists Germany. (Left to right) Monica Theodorescu (*Ganimedes*), Reiner Klimke (*Ahlerich*), Nicole Uphoff (*Rembrandt*), Ann-Katherin Linsenhoff (*Courage*). (Photo: courtesy of Max Ammann.)

Arena: 60 x 20 m.

Markers: Standard.

Judges

	Position for GP	Position for GPS
Wolfgang Niggli (Switzerland) President	C	C
Nicolas Williams (New Zealand)	E	E
Heinz Schütte (Germany)	H	H
Elena Kondratieva (Soviet Union)	M	M
Col Donald Thackeray (USA)	B	B

Tests

- Grand Prix 1987 – maximum score per judge = 410. (Time for information only: 7 minutes.)

- Grand Prix Special 1983 – maximum score per judge = 410. (Time for information only: 7 minutes 30 seconds.)

GRAND PRIX TEST (1987) – OLYMPIC GAMES 1988

		Test	Directive ideas	Marks	Coeff.
1	A X	Enter in collected canter. Halt - immobility - salute. Proceed in collected trot.	The entry. The halt and the transitions from the canter to the halt and from the halt to the trot.	10	
2	C MXK KA	Track to the right. Change rein in extended trot. Collected trot.	The lengthening and regularity of the steps. The transitions.	10	
3	A FXH H	Collected canter. Change rein in medium canter with flying change of leg at X. Collected canter.	The lengthening and the regularity of the strides. The flying change of leg. The balance. The transition.	10	
4	C M Between G and H	Collected walk. Turn right. Half-pirouette to the right.	The transition. The regularity of the half-pirouette.	10	
5	Between G and M	Half-pirouette to the left.	The regularity of the half-pirouette.	10	
6		The collected walk CMG (H) (M) G.	The shortening and heightening of the steps. The carriage and regularity.	10	

		Test	Directive ideas	Marks	Coeff.
7	GHS SP PFAKV	Collected trot. Half-pass to the left. Collected trot.	The correctness and regularity. The angle and the bend of the horse. The balance.	10	
8	VR RMCH	Half-pass to the right. Collected trot.	The correctness and regularity. The angle and the bend of the horse. The balance.	10	
9	HXF	Change rein in extended trot.	The extension and regularity of the steps. The transitions.	10	
10	FAK	Passage.	The cadence and the regularity.	10	
11	KXM	Change rein in extended walk.	The extension and regularity of the steps. the lengthening of the frame.	10	2
12	MCH	Collected walk.	The shortening and heightening of the steps. The carriage and regularity.	10	
13	H	Proceed in passage, transition from collected walk to passage.		10	
14	HSI	Passage.	The cadence and the regularity.	10	
15	I	Piaffe 12 to 15 steps.	The cadence and the regularity.	10	
16	I	Proceed in passage, transitions from passage to piaffe and from piaffe to passage.		10	
17	IRBX	Passage.	The cadence and the regularity.	10	
18	X	Piaffe.	The cadence and the regularity.	10	
19	X	Proceed in passage, transitions from passage to piaffe and from piaffe to passage.		10	
20	XEV	Passage.	The cadence and the regularity.	10	
21	V VKA	Proceed in collected canter. Collected canter.	The straightness, calmness and regularity.	10	

		Test	Directive ideas	Marks	Coeff.
22	AG	Down centre line – 5 counter changes of hand in half-pass to either side of the centre line with flying change of leg at each change of direction. The first half-pass to the left and the last to the right of 3 strides, the 4 others of 6 strides finishing on the right leg.	The correctness and the regularity of the 6 half-passes and the 5 counter-changes. The balance.	10	
	G				
23	C	Track to the right.	The extension.	10	
	MXK	Change rein in extended canter.	The collection.		
	K	Collected canter and flying change of leg.	The transitions.		
24	A	Down centre line.	The collection.	10	2
	L	Pirouette to the left.	The regularity.		
	X	Flying change of leg.	The change of leg.		
25	I	Pirouette to the right.	The collection.	10	2
	C	Track to the right.	The regularity.		
26	MXK	On the diagonal 9 flying changes of leg every second stride (finishing on the left leg).	The correctness, straightness, balance and fluency.	10	
27	FXH	On the diagonal 15 changes of leg every stride (finishing on the right leg).	The correctness, straightness, balance and fluency.	10	
	C	Collected trot.			
28	M	Proceed in passage.	The transition.	10	
	MRBXI	Passage.	The cadence and the regularity.		
29	I	Piaffe (12 to 15 steps).	The cadence and the regularity.	10	
30	IG	Passage.	The cadence and the regularity.	10	
31		Transitions from passage to piaffe and from piaffe to passage.		10	
32	G	Halt – immobility – salute	The halt and the transition.	10	

Leave arena in walk at A

	Total		**350**	

	Marks	Coeff.
Collective marks		
1. Paces (freedom and regularity).	10	1
2. Impulsion (desire to move forward, elasticity of the steps, suppleness of the back and engagement of the hind quarters).	10	2
3. Submission (attention and confidence; harmony, lightness and ease of the movements; acceptance of the bridle and lightness of the forehand).	10	2
4. Rider's position and seat; correctness and effect of the aids.	10	1
Total	**410**	

To be deducted:

Errors of the course and omissions are penalised:

1st time = 2 marks
2nd time = 4 marks
3rd time = 8 marks
4th time = Elimination

Grand Prix Special (1987) – Olympic Games 1988

		Test	Directive ideas	Marks	Coeff.
1	A	Enter in collected canter.	The entry.	10	
	X	Halt – Immobility – Salute.	The halt and the transitions to		
		Proceed in collected trot.	and from the halt.		
2	C	Track to the left.	The lengthening of the frame,	10	
	HXF	Change rein in extended trot.	the extension and regularity of		
	F	Collected trot.	the steps. The transitions.		
3	VXR	Half-pass.	The correctness and the regularity.	10	
	RMC	Collected trot.	The carriage and the		
			bend. The balance.		
4	CHS	Passage.	The cadence and regularity of	10	
	SK	Extended trot.	the passage. The extension		
	KAF	Passage.	and regularity.		
5	FP	Collected trot.	The correctness and the regularity.	10	
	PXS	Half-pass.	The carriage and the		
	SHC	Collected trot.	bend. The balance.		
6	CMR	Passage.	The cadence and regularity of	10	
	RF	Extended trot.	the passage. The extension		
	FAK	Passage.	and regularity.		

		Test	Directive ideas	Marks	Coeff.
7		Transitions from passage to extended trot and from extended trot to passage. (Tests 4 and 6)		10	
8	KLBIH	Extended walk. Collected walk.	The extension and regularity of the steps. The transitions.	10	2
9	HCMG	Collected walk.	The shortening and heightening of the steps. The carriage and regularity.	10	
10	G	Piaffe 12 to 15 steps.	The cadence and regularity.	10	
11	G	Proceed in passage. Transitions from collected walk to piaffe and from piaffe to passage.		10	
12	GHSI	Passage.	The cadence and regularity.	10	
13	I	Piaffe 12 to 15 steps.	The cadence and regularity.	10	
14	I	Proceed in passage. Transitions from passage to piaffe and from piaffe to passage.		10	
15	IRBX	Passage.	The cadence and regularity.	10	
16	XEVKAF	Collected canter left.	The correctness and regularity.	10	
17	FLE E	Half-pass in canter. Flying change of leg.	The correctness and regularity. The carriage and the bend. The balance and the change of leg.	10	
18	EIM M MCH	Half-pass in canter. Flying change of leg. Collected canter.	The correctness and regularity. The carriage and the bend. The balance and the change of leg.	10	
19	HXF	On the diagonal 9 changes of leg every second stride (finishing on right leg).	The correcness, straightness, balance and fluency.	10	
20	KXM	On the diagonal 15 changes of leg every stride (finishing on left leg).	The correctness, straightness, balance and fluency.	10	
21	HXF F	Change rein in extended canter. Collected canter and flying change of leg.	The extension. The transition. The flying change of leg.	10	
22	A D	Down centre line. Pirouette right.	The collection. The regularity.	10	2

		Test	Directive ideas	Marks	Coeff.
23	Between D and G	On the centre line 9 flying changes of leg every stride.	The correctness, straightness, balance and fluency.	10	
24	G C	Pirouette left. Track to the left.	The collection. The regularity.	10	2
25	HK K	Medium trot. Collected trot.	The lengthening and regularity of the steps. The transition.	10	
26	A L	Down centre line. Passage.	The cadence and regularity.	10	
27	I	Piaffe 12 to 15 steps.	The cadence and regularity.	10	
28		Transitions from collected trot to passage, from passage to piaffe.		10	
29	IG	Passage.	The cadence and regularity.	10	
30	G	Halt – Immobility – Salute	The halt and the transition.	10	
		Leave arena in a walk on a long rein at A.			

Total 330

Collective marks

1 Paces (freedom and regularity).		10	2
2 Impulsion (desire to move forward, elasticity of the steps, suppleness of the back and engagement of the hind quarters).		10	2
3 Submission (attention and confidence; harmony, lightness and ease of the movements; acceptance of the bridle and lightness of the forehand).		10	2
4 Rider's position and seat; correctness and effect of the aids.		10	2

Total 410

To be deducted:

Errors of the course and omissions are penalised:

1st time = 2 marks
2nd time = 4 marks
3rd time = 8 marks
4th time = Elimination

OLYMPIC GAMES 1988
Results – Grand Prix

Place	Rider	Horse	Nation	E	H	C	M	B	Total
						Judges' Marks (placings)			
1	Nicole Uphoff	*Rembrandt*	GER	284 (5)	283 (5)	286 (6)	307 (1)	298 (1)	1458
2	Margit Otto-Crepin	*Corlandus*	FRA	303 (1)	295 (1)	297 (1)	287 (4)	273 (8)	1455
3	Monica Theodorescu	*Ganimedes*	GER	289 (4)	285 (3)	290 (4)	286 (6)	283 (3)	1433
4	Christine Stückelberger	*Gauguin de Lully*	SUI	271 (11)	280 (7)	297 (1)	296 (2)	286 (2)	1430
5	Kyra Kyrklund	*Matador*	FIN	290 (3)	279 (8)	287 (5)	284 (7)	276 (7)	1416
6	Ann-Kathrin Linsenhoff	*Courage*	GER	276 (7)	293 (2)	276 (11)	293 (3)	273 (8)	1411
7	Reiner Klimke	*Ahlerich*	GER	275 (9)	284 (4)	285 (7)	281 (8)	277 (5)	1402
8	Nina Menkova	*Dixon*	URS	279 (6)	283 (5)	281 (8)	287 (4)	265 (15)	1395
9	Otto Hofer	*Andiamo*	SUI	293 (2)	274 (9)	293 (3)	263 (14)	269 (11)	1392
10	Cynthia Ishoy	*Dynasta*	CAN	276 (7)	265 (14)	279 (9)	264 (12)	279 (4)	1363
11	Daniel Ramseier	*Random*	SUI	270 (12)	266 (13)	277 (10)	271 (9)	258 (23)	1342
12	Robert Dover	*Federleicht*	USA	263 (15)	258 (20)	270 (12)	259 (19)	277 (5)	1327
13	Jung-Kyun Suh	*Pascal*	KOR	269 (13)	258 (20)	266 (17)	264 (12)	267 (14)	1324
14	Ellen Bontje	*Petit Prince*	HOL	266 (14)	268 (11)	261 (17)	255 (24)	262 (18)	1312
15	Ashley Nicoll	*Reipo*	CAN	272 (10)	255 (24)	265 (14)	248 (35)	268 (12)	1308
15	Jessica Ransehousen	*Orpheus*	USA	263 (15)	269 (10)	258 (19)	265 (11)	253 (32)	1308
17	Annemarie Sanders-Keyzer	*Amon*	HOL	257 (25)	263 (16)	255 (21)	260 (17)	268 (12)	1303
18	Gina Smith	*Malte*	CAN	262 (17)	267 (12)	254 (23)	255 (24)	260 (20)	1298
19	Nils Haagensen	*Cantat*	DEN	256 (27)	265 (14)	259 (18)	254 (28)	259 (22)	1293
19	Jennie Loriston-Clarke	*Dutch Gold*	GBR	262 (17)	255 (24)	263 (16)	261 (16)	252 (35)	1293
21	Tineke Bartels	*Olympic*	HOL	259 (20)	259 (18)	247 (30)	260 (17)	263 (17)	1288
22	Daria Fantoni	*Sonny Boy*	ITA	261 (19)	254 (28)	254 (23)	251 (31)	264 (16)	1284
23	Tricia Gardiner	*Wily Imp*	GBR	258 (22)	256 (23)	250 (27)	256 (23)	254 (28)	1274
24	Olga Klimko	*Buket*	URS	235 (45)	263 (16)	264 (15)	270 (10)	240 (43)	1272
25	Ulla Hakansson	*Cesam*	SWE	248 (33)	249 (30)	258 (19)	255 (24)	261 (19)	1271
26	Morten Thomsen	*Diplomat*	DEN	257 (25)	259 (18)	251 (26)	255 (24)	247 (38)	1269
27	Anne-Grethe Törnblad	*Ravel*	DEN	259 (20)	246 (32)	250 (27)	251 (31)	257 (25)	1263
28	Yuri Kovchov	*Barin*	URS	248 (33)	255 (24)	247 (30)	237 (44)	272 (10)	1259
29	Eva-Maria Pracht	*Emirage*	CAN	249 (31)	257 (22)	250 (27)	246 (37)	253 (32)	1255
30	Louise Nathorst	*Cirac*	SWE	249 (31)	244 (37)	246 (34)	252 (29)	260 (20)	1251
31	Anatoli Tankov	*Izharsk*	URS	251 (29)	240 (40)	245 (36)	257 (20)	256 (26)	1249
31	Lars Anderson	*Herkules*	SWE	245 (36)	245 (34)	243 (37)	263 (14)	253 (32)	1249
33	Belinda Baudin	*Christopher*	USA	240 (41)	255 (24)	255 (21)	244 (41)	254 (28)	1248
34	Erica Taylor	*Crown Law*	AUS	258 (22)	245 (34)	235 (42)	249 (34)	258 (23)	1245
35	Tutu Sohlberg	*Pakistan*	FIN	242 (38)	253 (29)	247 (30)	245 (38)	255 (27)	1242
36	Anky van Grunsven	*Prisco*	HOL	258 (22)	255 (24)	232 (45)	247 (36)	247 (38)	1239
37	Diana Mason	*Prince Consort*	GBR	231 (49)	243 (38)	253 (25)	252 (29)	251 (36)	1230
38	Hector Rodriguez	*El Sahib*	COL	250 (30)	234 (43)	246 (34)	245 (38)	254 (28)	1229
39	Jennifer Eriksson	*My Way*	FIN	237 (44)	246 (32)	231 (46)	257 (20)	254 (28)	1225
39	Samuel Schatzmann	*Rochus*	SUI	239 (43)	245 (34)	247 (30)	251 (31)	243 (41)	1225

Place	Rider	Horse	Nation	Judges' Marks (placings)					Total
				E	H	C	M	B	
41	Dominique d'Esme	*Hopal Fleuri HN*	FRA	254 (28)	242 (39)	229 (48)	257 (20)	237 (47)	1219
42	Anne Koch	*Le Fiere*	DEN	243 (37)	247 (31)	238 (40)	240 (43)	249 (37)	1217
43	Lendon Gray	*Later On*	USA	241 (40)	239 (41)	242 (39)	245 (38)	245 (40)	1212
44	Juan Matute	*Rex the Blacky*	ESP	242 (38)	236 (42)	243 (37)	241 (42)	243 (41)	1205
45	Barbara Hammond	*Krist*	GBR	234 (47)	228 (47)	236 (41)	236 (45)	240 (43)	1174
46	Kikuko Inoue	*Teldor*	JPN	247 (35)	216 (50)	231 (46)	235 (46)	240 (43)	1169
47	Eva Lindsten	*Cello*	SWE	240 (41)	232 (44)	233 (44)	235 (46)	227 (51)	1167
48	Maarit Raiskio	*Nor*	FIN	235 (45)	230 (45)	235 (42)	229 (49)	232 (48)	1161
49	Philippe Limousin	*Iris de Ia Fosse*	FRA	234 (47)	229 (46)	222 (49)	235 (46)	238 (46)	1158
50	Chang-Moo Shin	*Lugana*	KOR	224 (50)	207 (52)	216 (51)	226 (50)	228 (50)	1101
51	James Walsh	*Robby*	IRL	223 (51)	214 (51)	204 (52)	224 (51)	231 (49)	1096
52	Naoko Sakurai	*Ravello*	JPN	211 (52)	217 (49)	220 (50)	210 (52)	223 (52)	1081
53	Maria-Paula Bemal	*Armagnac*	COL	199 (53)	191 (53)	201 (53)	172 (53)	215 (53)	978

Olympic Games 1988 – Seoul

Results – Individual (Grand Prix Special)

	Rider	Horse	Nation	Judges' marks					Total
				E	H	C	M	B	
1	**Nicole Uphoff**	***Rembrandt***	**GER**	**290** (2)	**293** (1)	**307** (1)	**318** (1)	**313** (1)	**1521**
2	**Margit Otto-Crepin**	***Corlandus***	**FRA**	**296** (1)	**279** (3)	**304** (2)	**294** (2)	**289** (2)	**1462**
3	**Christine Stückelberger**	***Gaugin de Lully***	**SUI**	**284** (3)	**292** (2)	**296** (3)	**270** (10)	**275** (5)	**1417**
4	Cynthia Ischoy	*Dynasty*	CAN	275 (6)	276 (5)	284 (5)	287 (4)	279 (3)	1401
5	Kyra Kirkland	*Matador*	FIN	283 (4)	275 (6)	293 (4)	273 (7)	269 (8)	1393
6	Monica Theodorescu	*Ganimedes*	GER	277 (5)	270 (8)	282 (7)	281 (5)	275 (5)	1385
7	Otto Hofer	*Andiamo*	GER	270 (9)	279 (3)	279 (9)	288 (3)	267 (10)	1383
8	Ann-Kathrin Linsenhoff	*Courage*	GER	275 (6)	269 (9)	282 (7)	271 (8)	277 (4)	1374
9	Nina Mendkova	*Dixon*	URS	275 (6)	263 (13)	278 (10)	271 (8)	267 (10)	1354
10	Jung-Kyun Soh	*Pascal*	KOR	269 (10)	267 (10)	283 (6)	268 (11)	262 (14)	1349
11	Daniel Ramseier	*Random*	SUI	267 (11)	266 (11)	274 (11)	266 (12)	257 (16)	1330
12	Gina Smith	*Malte*	CAN	261 (14)	259 (18)	264 (12)	275 (6)	267 (10)	1326
13	Robert Dover	*Federleicht*	USA	267 (11)	271 (7)	263 (13)	265 (13)	254 (17)	1320
14	Jennie Loriston-Clarke	*Dutch Gold*	GBR	264 (13)	263 (13)	257 (15)	249 (18)	271 (7)	1304
15	Ellen Bontje	*Petit Prince*	HOL	260 (15)	258 (19)	257 (15)	261 (14)	261 (15)	1297
16	Ashley Nicoll	*Reipo*	CAN	245 (19)	263 (13)	262 (14)	258 (16)	268 (9)	1296
17	Jessica Ransehausen	*Orpheus*	USA	254 (16)	260 (17)	256 (17)	249 (18)	263 (13)	1282
18	Nils Haagensen	*Cantat*	DEN	254 (16)	261 (16)	253 (18)	259 (15)	253 (18)	1280
19	Anne-Marie Sanders Keyzer	*Amon*	HOL	250 (18)	265 (12)	250 (19)	257 (17)	245 (19)	1267

OLYMPIC GAMES 1988
Results – Team Competition

| | | | | Judges' Marks | | | | |
	Rider	Horse	E	H	C	M	B	Total
1.	**Germany**							**4302**
	Reiner Klimke	*Ahlerich*	275	284	286	281	277	1402
	Ann-Kathrin Linsenhoff	*Courage*	276	293	276	293	273	1411
	Monica Theodorescu	*Ganimedes*	289	285	290	286	283	1433
	Nicole Uphoff	*Rembrandt*	284	283	286	307	298	1458
2.	**Switzerland**							**4164**
	Otto Hofer	*Andiamo*	293	274	293	263	269	1392
	Christine Stückelberger	*Gauguin de Lully*	271	280	297	296	286	1430
	Daniel Ramseier	*Random*	270	266	277	271	258	1342
	Samuel Schatzmann	*Rochus*	239	245	247	251	243	1225
3.	**Canada**							**3969**
	Cynthia Ishoy	*Dynasty*	276	265	279	264	279	1363
	Eva-Maria Pracht	*Emirage*	249	257	250	246	253	1255
	Gina Smith	*Malte*	262	267	254	255	260	1298
	Ashley Nicoll	*Reipo*	272	255	265	248	268	1308
4.	**Soviet Union**							**3926**
	Yuri Kovchov	*Barin*	248	255	247	237	272	1259
	Olga Klimko	*Buket*	235	263	264	270	240	1272
	Nina Menkova	*Dixon*	279	283	281	287	265	1395
	Anatoli Tankov	*Izharsk*	251	240	245	257	256	1249
5.	**Holland**							**3903**
	Annemarie Sanders-Keyzer	*Amon*	257	263	255	260	268	1303
	Tineke Bartels	*Olympic*	259	259	247	260	263	1288
	Ellen Bontje	*Petit Prince*	266	268	261	255	262	1312
	Anky van Grunsven	*Prisco*	258	255	232	247	247	1239
6.	**United States of America**							**3883**
	Belinda Baudin	*Christopher*	240	255	255	244	254	1248
	Robert Dover	*Federleicht*	263	258	270	259	277	1327
	Lendon Gray	*Later On*	241	239	242	245	245	1212
	Jessica Ransehousen	*Orpheus*	263	269	258	265	253	1308
6.	**Finland**							**3883**
	Kyra Kyrklund	*Matador*	290	279	287	284	276	1416
	Jennifer Eriksson	*My Way*	237	245	231	257	254	1225
	Maarit Raiskio	*Nor*	235	230	235	229	232	1161
	Tutu Sohlberg	*Pakistan*	242	253	247	245	255	1242

	Rider	Horse	Judges' Marks					Total
			E	H	C	M	B	
8.	**France**							**3832**
	Margit Otto-Crepin	*Corlandus*	303	295	297	287	273	1455
	Dominique d'Esme	*Hopal Fleury HN*	254	242	229	257	237	1219
	Philippe Limousin	*Iris de Ia Fosse*	234	229	222	235	238	1158
9.	**Denmark**							**3825**
	Nils Haagensen	*Cantat*	256	265	259	254	259	1293
	Morten Thomsen	*Diplomat*	257	259	251	255	247	1269
	Anne Koch	*Le Fiere*	243	247	238	240	249	1217
	Anne-Grethe Jensen	*Ravel*	259	246	250	251	257	1263
10.	**Great Britain**							**3797**
	Jennie Loriston-Clarke	*Dutch Gold*	262	255	263	261	252	1293
	Barbara Hammond	*Krist*	234	228	236	236	240	1174
	Diana Mason	*Prince Consort*	231	243	253	252	251	1230
	Tricia Gardiner	*Wily Imp*	258	256	250	256	254	1274
11.	**Sweden**							**3771**
	Eva Lindsten	*Cello*	240	232	233	235	227	1167
	Ulla Hakansson	*Cesam*	248	249	258	255	261	1271
	Louise Nathorst	*Cirac*	249	244	246	252	260	1251
	Lars Anderson	*Herkules*	245	245	243	263	253	1249

OLYMPIC GAMES 1992

BARCELONA, SPAIN

Participating Countries: 18

Australia	France	Japan
Austria	Germany	Confederation of Independent States
Bermuda	Great Britain	Spain
Canada	Holland	Sweden
Denmark	Ireland	Switzerland
Finland	Italy	United States of America

Participating Riders: 48

Teams: 11 teams of a maximum of 4 riders
• The best 3 results to count for the Team Competition.

Teams of 4 riders:

Denmark	Holland
France	Italy
Germany	Sweden
Great Britain	United States of America

Teams of 3 riders:
Canada
Confederation of Independent States
Switzerland

Individual Riders: 7

Australia – 1	Ireland – 1
Austria – 1	Japan – 1
Bermuda – 1	Spain – 1
Finland – 1	

Competitions

• Grand Prix and Grand Prix Special for the Individual Competition, for the 16 best combinations out of the Grand Prix, but with a maximum of 3 riders per country.

• The results from the Grand Prix are used for the Team Competition.

Special Regulations

• Limited number of horses: maximum 53.

• Qualification of horse and rider combination required in the year before the Games up until date of entry. In Europe: 2 Grand Prix results of 300 points from an Official International Judge who is not from the rider's own country.

- **Article 617 – Olympic Sojourn**

The 'Olympic Sojourn' for all three disciplines is the period between the 11th July, 1992 and the day the last competition of the relevant disciplines is scheduled, and corresponds to the date of enforcement of the Rules and Regulations.

The event stables will be officially open for horses from 11th July, 1992 until 15th August, 1992.

- **Article 618 – Rules**

The team Dressage Competition and the Individual Dressage Competition are held under the rules contained in Chapter II of the 'Rules for Dressage Events', except where specifically modified below. The tests are those of the Grand Prix and the Grand Prix Special respectively in force at the time of the Olympic Games.

- **Article 619 – Participation and Order of Starting**

1. Each nation may start 4 competitors and 4 horses for the Team Competition. Each competitor may only ride 1 horse in the Competition. The 3 best placed competitors' horses count for the Team Classification.

2. A nation that cannot send a team, may enter 1 or 2 individual competitors, each with 2 horses. Each competitor may ride only 1 horse in the Competition.

3. The number of competitors/horses to take part in the Individual Dressage Competition (Grand Prix Special) is limited to and compulsory for, the best one third (however, minimum 12 and maximum 18, including those who tie for the 18th place) of the total number of competitors in the initial Grand Prix. However, no nation may have more than 3 competitors in the competition.

4. A draw for the starting order in the Team Competition (Grand Prix) for individual competitors, for teams and for team members within each team, will take place according to Art 614.1., 2., 3. The organisers have the following options for the order of starting in the Grand Prix Special:

   a. The reverse order of the placing in the Grand Prix.

   b. The riders placed 13th to… (max. 18) in the Grand Prix will start first followed by the group of riders placed 7th to 12th and then by the group placed 1st to 6th. The order of starting within these groups is determined by draw.

   The order of starting applied for a particular event must be stated in the schedule.

- **Article 620 – Schooling of Horses**

On no account and under penalty of disqualification, may any horse take part in the Competitions mentioned above, if it has been schooled by anyone other than the competitor concerned, or another competitor belonging to the same team, mounted in the saddle, in or outside the city where the Olympic Games take place, during the whole sojourn preceding the Team Competition and until the end of the lndividual Competition.

Medal Winners

Individual

		GPS	Placing in GP
Gold	Nicole Uphoff (Germany) *Rembrandt*	1625	1
Silver	Isabell Werth (Germany) *Gigolo*	1551	2
Bronze	Klaus Balkenhol (Germany) *Goldstern*	1515	3

Teams

		GPS	Placing in GP
Gold	**Germany 5224 points**		
	Nicole Uphoff *Rembrandt*	1768	1
	Isabell Werth *Gigolo*	1762	2
	Klaus Balkenhol *Goldstern*	1694	3
Silver	**Holland 4742 points**		
	Anky van Grunsven *Olympic Bonfire*	1631	5
	Ellen Bontje *Olympic Larius*	1577	8
	Tineke Bartels *Olympic Courage*	1534	15
Bronze	**USA 4645 points**		
	Mrs Carol Lavell *Gifted*	1629	6
	Mrs Charlotte Brehdal *Monsieur*	1507	22
	Robert Dover *Lectron*	1507	22

Individual Gold medallist Nicole Uphoff (GER) on *Rembrandt*. (Photo: courtesy of Max Ammann.)

Arena: 20 x 60 m.

Markers: standard.

Judges

	Judging position for:	
	Grand Prix	Grand Prix Special
Wolfgang Niggli (Switzerland) President	C	C
Eric Lette (Sweden)	H	H
Nicolas Williams (New Zealand)	M	M
Eizo Osaka (Japan)	E	E
Uwe Mechlem (Germany)	B	B

Tests

- Grand Prix (1991): maximum score = 470 points per judge. (Time for information only: 7 minutes.)

- Grand Prix Special (1983) – same test as used in 1984 and 1988 Olympic Games: maximum score = 410 points per judge. (Time for information only 7 minutes 30 seconds.)

OLYMPIC GAMES 1992
Grand Prix Test (1991)

		Test	Directive ideas	Marks	Coeff.
1	A X	Enter in collected canter. Halt – Immobility – Salute. Proceed in collected trot.	The entry. The halt and the transitions from canter to the halt and from the halt to the trot.	10	
2	C MXK KA	Track right. Change rein in extended trot. Collected trot.	The lengthening and regularity of the steps. The transitions.	10	
3	A FXH H	Collected canter. Change rein in medium canter with a flying change of leg at X. Collected canter.	The lengthening and regularity of the strides. The flying change of leg. The balance. The transition.	10	
4	C	Collected walk.	The transition.	10	
5	M Between G and H	Turn right. Half-pirouette to the right.	The regularity of the half-pirouette.	10	
6	Between G and M	Half-pirouette to the left.	The regularity of the half-pirouette.	10	
7		The collected walk CMG (H) (M) (G).	The shortening and the heightening of the steps. The carriage and the regularity.	10	

		Test	Directive ideas	Marks	Coeff.
8	GHS SP PFAKV	Collected trot. Half-pass to the left. Collected trot.	The correctness and regularity. The angle and bend of the horse. The balance.	10	
9	VR RMCH	Half-pass to the right. Collected trot.	The correctness and regularity. The angle and bend of the horse. The balance.	10	
10	HXF	Change rein in extended trot.	The extension and regularity of the steps. The transitions.	10	
11	FAK	Passage.	The cadence and the regularity.	10	
12	KVXRM	Change rein in extended walk.	The extension and regularity of the steps. The lengthening of the frame.	10	2
13	MCH	Collected walk.	The shortening and the heightening of the steps. The carriage and the regularity.	10	
14	H	Proceed in passage, transition from collected walk to passage.		10	
15	HSI	Passage.	The cadence and the regularity.	10	
16	I	Piaffe 12 to 15 steps.	The cadence and the regularity.	10	
17	I	Proceed in passage, transitions to piaffe and piaffe to passage. from passage		10	
18	IRBX	Passage.	The cadence and the regularity.	10	
19	X	Piaffe 12 to 15 steps.	The cadence and the regularity.	10	
20	X	Proceed in passage, transitions from passage to piaffe and piaffe to passage.		10	
21	XEV	Passage.	The cadence and the regularity.	10	
22	V VKA	Proceed in collected canter. Collected canter.	The straightness, calmness and regularity.	10	
23	AG	Down centre line – 5 counter changes of hand in half-pass to either side of the centre line with flying changes of leg at each change of direction. The first half-pass to the	The correctness and regularity of the 6 half- passes and the 5 counter changes. The balance.	10	

		Test	Directive ideas	Marks	Coeff.
		left and the last to the right of 3 strides, the 4 others of 6 strides, finishing on the right leg.			
24	C MXK K	Track to the right. Change rein in extended canter. Collected canter and flying change.	The extension, the collection. The transitions.	10	
25	A L X	Down centre line. Pirouette to the left. Flying change.	The collection. The regularity. The change of leg.	10	2
26	I G C	Pirouette to the right. Flying change. Track to the left.	The collection and the balance. The regularity. The change of leg.	10	2
27	HXF	On the diagonal 9 flying changes every second stride (finishing on the right leg).	The correctness, straightness, balance and fluency.	10	
28	KXM	On the diagonal 15 flying changes every stride (finishing on the left leg).	The correctness, straightness, balance and fluency.	10	
29	HXF F	Change rein in extended canter. Collected canter and flying change of leg.	The extension, the collection, the transitions.	10	
30	A L	On centre line. Halt, rein-back 6 steps. Proceed in passage.	The halt. The balance. The correctness and regularity.	10	
31		Transitions from collected canter to halt and from rein-back to passage.		10	
32	LX	Passage.	The cadence and the regularity.	10	
33	X	Piaffe (12 to 15 steps).	The cadence and the regularity.	10	
34		Transitions from passage to piaffe and from piaffe to passage.		10	
35	XG	Passage.	The cadence and the regularity.	10	
36	G	Halt – Immobility – Salute.	The halt and the transition.	10	
		Leave arena in walk at A		10	
				Total 390	

	Marks	Coeff.
Collective marks		
1. Paces (freedom and regularity).	10	2
2. Impulsion (desire to move forward; elasticity of the steps; suppleness of the back and engagement of the hindquarters).	10	2
3 Submission (attention and confidence; harmony; lightness and ease of the movements; acceptance of the bridle and lightness of the forehand).	10	2
4. Rider's position and seat; correctness and effect of the aids.	10	2
	Total 470	

To be deducted:

Errors of the course and omissions are penalised:

1st time	=	2 points
2nd time	=	4 points
3rd time	=	8 points
4th time	=	Elimination

Olympic Games 1992

Results – Grand Prix Test

Place	Rider	Horse	Nation	Judges' Marks (Placing)					Total
				B	H	C	M	B	
1	Nicole Uphoff	*Rembrandt*	GER	348 (1)	357 (1)	357 (1)	348 (2)	358 (1)	1768
2	Isabell Werth	*Gigolo*	GER	346 (2)	354 (2)	344 (2)	362 (1)	356 (2)	1762
3	Klaus Balkenhol	*Goldstern*	GER	341 (3)	351 (3)	337 (3)	327 (5)	338 (3)	1694
4	Monica Theodorescu	*Grunox*	GER	337 (4)	334 (4)	333 (5)	336 (3)	336 (4)	1676
5	Anky van Grunsven	*Olympic Bonfire*	HOL	322 (6)	327 (7)	334 (4)	329 (4)	319 (6)	1631
6	Carol Lavell	*Gifted*	USA	326 (5)	332 (5)	326 (6)	320 (6)	325 (5)	1629
7	Elisabeth Max-Theurer	*Liechtenstein*	AUT	309 (12)	323 (11)	318 (8)	320 (6)	315 (7)	1585
8	Ellen Bontje	*Olympic Larius*	HOL	303 (23)	329 (6)	318 (8)	314 (9)	313 (9)	1577
9	Kyra Kyrklund	*Edinburg*	FIN	306 (15)	325 (8)	317 (10)	318 (8)	305 (14)	1571
9	Pia Laus	*Adrett*	ITA	310 (10)	324 (10)	317 (10)	308 (12)	312 (11)	1571
11	Otto Hofer	*Renzo*	SUI	312 (8)	312 (15)	307 (16)	302 (15)	315 (7)	1548
12	Christilot Hanson-Boylen	*Biraldo 2*	CAN	304 (20)	325 (8)	306 (20)	296 (21)	312 (11)	1543
13	Anne van Olst	*Chevalier*	DEN	309 (12)	317 (12)	307 (16)	305 (13)	304 (17)	1542
14	Anne-Grete Törnblad	*Ravel*	DEN	306 (15)	312 (15)	320 (7)	302 (15)	300 (23)	1540
15	Tineke Bartels	*Olympic Courage*	HOL	313 (7)	306 (23)	309 (13)	309 (11)	297 (27)	1534
16	Anna Merveldt	*Rapallo 16*	IRL	306 (15)	299 (26)	309 (13)	298 (19)	315 (7)	1527
17	Carl Hester	*Giorgione*	GBR	310 (10)	317 (12)	294 (36)	298 (19)	304 (17)	1523

				Judges' Marks (Placing)					
Place	Rider	Horse	Nation	B	H	C	M	B	Total
18	Tinne Wilhelmson	*Caprice*	SWE	304 (20)	311 (17)	306 (20)	294 (22)	307 (13)	1522
19	Margit Otto-Crepin	*Maritim*	FRA	303 (23)	308 (19)	315 (12)	290 (29)	305 (14)	1521
20	Ann Behrenfors	*Leroy*	SWE	307 (14)	310 (18)	307 (16)	286 (34)	304 (17)	1514
21	Emile Faurie	*Virtu*	GBR	303 (23)	299 (26)	304 (24)	311 (10)	296 (28)	1513
22	Charlotte Bredahl	*Monsieur*	USA	300 (27)	308 (19)	305 (23)	301 (17)	293 (31)	1507
22	Robert Dover	*Lectron*	USA	311 (9)	287 (42)	304 (24)	304 (14)	301 (22)	1507
24	Annica Westerberg	*Taktik*	SWE	297 (31)	303 (24)	303 (26)	294 (22)	304 (17)	1501
25	Ruth Hunkeler	*Afghadi*	SUI	299 (29)	303 (24)	306 (20)	294 (22)	296 (28)	1498
25	Catherine Durand	*Orphee RBO*	FRA	301 (26)	292 (34)	300 (30)	300 (18)	305 (14)	1498
27	Michael Poulin	*Graf George*	USA	305 (19)	299 (26)	308 (15)	281 (39)	302 (21)	1495
28	Christine Doan	*Dondolo*	AUS	299 (29)	307 (21)	291 (41)	294 (22)	300 (23)	1491
29	Laura Fry	*Quarryman*	GBR	304 (20)	295 (30)	303 (26)	293 (26)	291 (33)	1486
29	Suzanne Dunkley	*Highness*	BER	296 (33)	299 (26)	307 (16)	286 (34)	298 (26)	1486
31	Giani Paolo Margi	*Destino Di Acci*	ITA	293 (38)	307 (21)	297 (32)	285 (36)	299 (25)	1481
32	Doris Ramseier	*Renatus*	SUI	286 (45)	313 (14)	299 (31)	289 (30)	291 (33)	1478
33	Carol Parsons	*Vashkar*	GBR	297 (31)	292 (34)	295 (34)	291 (28)	293 (31)	1468
34	Cynthia Ishoy	*Dakar*	CAN	294 (36)	295 (30)	295 (34)	288 (32)	294 (30)	1466
35	Eva-Karin Oscarsson	*Lille Claus*	SWE	300 (27)	290 (36)	303 (26)	287 (33)	280 (43)	1460
36	Lene Hoberg	*Bayard*	DEN	295 (35)	290 (36)	302 (29)	277 (44)	287 (37)	1451
37	Serge Cornut	*Olifant Charrie*	FRA	287 (43)	295 (30)	293 (37)	279 (41)	290 (35)	1444
38	Inna Zhurakovskaia	*Podgon*	CIS	296 (33)	294 (33)	293 (37)	278 (42)	282 (41)	1443
39	Dari Fantoni	*Sonny Boy*	ITA	288 (41)	289 (41)	296 (33)	283 (38)	283 (40)	1439
40	Annemarie Sanders	*Olympic Montreux*	HOL	290 (40)	290 (36)	283 (43)	289 (30)	284 (39)	1436
41	Yoshinaga Sakurai	*Matador*	JPN	306 (15)	282 (44)	277 (46)	292 (27)	278 (45)	1435
42	Dominique D'Esme	*Rapport II*	FRA	291 (39)	287 (42)	279 (44)	281 (39)	289 (36)	1427
43	Juan Matute	*N'Est Pas*	ESP	288 (41)	282 (44)	292 (39)	278 (42)	286 (38)	1426
44	Olga Klimko	*Shipovnik*	CIS	294 (36)	281 (46)	292 (39)	273 (46)	280 (43)	1420
45	Laura Conz	*Lahti*	ITA	287 (43)	290 (36)	284 (42)	276 (45)	282 (41)	1419
46	Bent Jensen	*Ariston*	DEN	285 (46)	290 (36)	275 (45)	284 (37)	277 (46)	1411
47	Irina Zouikova	*Barin*	CIS	273 (47)	273 (47)	269 (47)	262 (47)	263 (48)	1340
48	Martina Pracht	*Emirage*	CAN	267 (48)	264 (48)	264 (48)	251 (48)	267 (47)	1313

OLYMPIC GAMES 1992

Results – Individual competition (Grand Prix Special)

Place	Rider	Horse	Nation	Judges' Marks (Placing)					Total
				B	H	C	M	B	
1	Nicole Uphoff	*Rembrandt*	GER	338 (1)	328 (1)	320 (1)	313 (1)	327 (1)	1626
2	Isabell Werth	*Gigolo*	GER	319 (2)	311 (2)	307 (2)	307 (2)	307 (3)	1551
3	Klaus Balkenhol	*Goldstern*	GER	298 (3)	308 (3)	298 (3)	301 (3)	310 (2)	1515
4	Anky van Grunsven	*Olympic Bonfire*	HOL	280 (5)	297 (4)	291 (4)	288 (4)	291 (4)	1447
5	Kyra Kyrklund	*Edinburg*	FIN	291 (4)	295 (5)	286 (5)	275 (8)	281 (6)	1428
6	Carol Lavell	*Gifted*	USA	280 (5)	275 (11)	285 (6)	283 (5)	285 (5)	1408
7	Pia Laus	*Adrett*	ITA	280 (5)	279 (7)	276 (8)	273 (9)	281 (6)	1389
8	Elisabeth Max-Theurer	*Liechtenstein*	AUT	271 (9)	281 (6)	283 (7)	282 (6)	263 (14)	1380
9	Ellen Bontje	*Olympic Larius*	HOL	263 (12)	276 (10)	276 (8)	271 (10)	275 (11)	1361
10	Anne van Olst	*Chevalier*	DEN	273 (8)	274 (12)	265 (11)	270 (11)	276 (10)	1358
11	Anna Merveldt	*Rapallo 16*	IRL	255 (15)	278 (8)	269 (10)	281 (7)	272 (12)	1355
12	Christilot Hanson-Boylen	*Biraldo 2*	CAN	261 (13)	278 (8)	263 (13)	267 (13)	278 (9)	1347
13	Anne-Grete Törnblad	*Ravel*	DEN	268 (11)	271 (13)	264 (12)	265 (14)	266 (13)	1334
14	Otto Hofer	*Renzo*	SUI	269 (10)	263 (14)	248 (16)	268 (12)	280 (8)	1328
15	Tineke Bartels	*Olympic Courage*	HOL	258 (14)	261 (15)	260 (14)	261 (15)	262 (15)	1302
16	Carl Hester	*Giorgione*	GBR	243 (16)	253 (16)	254 (15)	258 (16)	246 (16)	1254

OLYMPIC GAMES 1992

Results – Team Competition (Grand Prix)

Rider/nation	Horse	Judges' Marks					Totals
		B	H	C	M	E	
1 Germany							**5224**
Nicole Uphoff	*Rembrandt*	348	357	357	348	358	1768*
Monica Theodorescu	*Grunox*	337	334	333	336	336	1676
Isabell Werth	*Gigolo*	346	354	344	362	356	1762*
Klaus Balkenhol	*Goldstern*	341	351	337	327	338	1694*
2 Holland							**4742**
Anky van Grunsven	*Olympic Bonfire*	322	327	334	329	319	1631*
Annemarie Sanders	*Olympic Montreux*	290	290	283	289	284	1436
Tineke Bartels	*Olympic Courage*	313	306	309	309	297	1534*
Ellen Bontje	*Olympic Larius*	303	329	318	314	313	1577*
3 USA							**4643**
Charlotte Bredahl	*Monsieur*	300	308	305	301	293	1507*
Michael Poulin	*Graf George*	305	299	308	281	302	1495
Robert Dover	*Lectron*	311	287	304	304	301	1507*
Carol Lavell	*Gifted*	326	332	326	320	325	1629*

Rider/nation	Horse	Judges' Marks					Totals
		B	H	C	M	E	
4 Sweden							**4537**
Annica Westerberg	*Taktik*	297	303	303	294	304	1501*
Ann Behrenfors	*Leroy*	307	310	307	286	304	1514*
Eva-Karin Oscarsson	*Lille Claus*	300	290	303	287	280	1460
Tinne Wilhelmson	*Caprice*	304	311	306	294	307	1522*
5 Denmark							**4533**
Bent Jensen	*Ariston*	285	290	275	284	277	1411
Anne-Grete Törnblad	*Ravel*	306	312	320	302	300	1540*
Lene Hoberg	*Bayard*	295	290	302	277	287	1451*
Anne van Olst	*Chevalier*	309	317	307	305	304	1542*
6 Switzerland							**4524**
Ruth Hunkeler	*Afghani*	299	303	306	294	296	1498*
Doris Ramseier	*Renatus*	286	313	299	289	291	1478*
Otto Hofer	*Renzo*	312	312	307	302	315	1548*
7 Great Britain							**4522**
Emile Faurie	*Virtu*	303	299	304	311	296	1513*
Carl Hester	*Giorgione*	310	317	294	298	304	1523*
Laura Fry	*Quarryman*	304	295	303	293	291	1486*
Carol Parsons	*Vashkar*	297	292	295	291	293	1468
8 Italy							**4491**
Laura Conz	*Lahti*	287	290	284	276	282	1419
Giani Paolo Margi	*Destino Di Acci*	293	307	297	285	299	1481*
Dari Fantoni	*Sonny Boy*	288	289	296	283	283	1439*
Pia Laus	*Adrett*	310	324	317	308	312	1571*
9 France							**4463**
Serge Cornut	*Olifant Charrie*	287	295	293	279	290	1444*
Dominique D'Esme	*Rapport II*	291	287	279	281	289	1427
Margit Otto-Crepin	*Maritim*	303	308	315	290	305	1521*
Catherine Durant	*Orphee RBO*	301	292	300	300	305	1498*
10 Canada							**4322**
Christilot Hanson-Boylen	*Biraldo 2*	304	325	306	296	312	1543*
Martina Pracht	*Emirage*	267	264	264	251	267	1313*
Cynthia Ishoy	*Dakar*	294	295	295	288	294	1466*
11 CIS							**4203**
Irma Zouikova	*Barin*	273	273	269	262	263	1340*
Olga Klimko	*Shipovnik*	294	281	292	273	280	1420*
Inna Zhurakovskaia	*Podgon*	296	294	293	278	282	1443*

* Marks used to calculate Team Competition results

Olympic Games 1996

Atlanta, USA

Participating Countries: 18

Australia	Finland	Mexico
Austria	France	Netherlands
Belgium	Germany	Spain
Bermuda	Great Britain	Sweden
Canada	Ireland	Switzerland
Denmark	Italy	United States of America

Participating Riders: 49

Teams: 10 teams with a maximum of 4 riders

- The 3 best scores to count for the Team Competition.

Canada	Italy	Switzerland
France	Netherlands	United States of America
Germany	Spain	
Great Britain	Sweden	

Individual Riders: 9

Australia – 1	Denmark – 2
Austria – 1	Finland – 1
Belgium – 1	Ireland – 1
Bermuda – 1	Mexico – 1

Competitions

A. Grand Prix – Team Competition

The FEI Grand Prix de Dressage in which all competitors must participate, is the Team Dressage and the first Individual Qualifying Competition.

B. Grand Prix Special and Grand Prix-level Freestyle Test – Individual Competitions

B 1. Grand Prix Special

The Grand Prix Special is limited to and compulsory for the 24 best rider/horse combinations in the initial Grand Prix, including those who tie for 24th place. If all 4 riders of a team qualify, they may all participate.

B 2. Grand Prix-level Freestyle Test

The Grand Prix-level Freestyle Test is limited to and compulsory for the overall best 12 out of competitions A and B1 by adding the percentages of these competitions as points. In case of a tie for 12th place, the higher score in the Grand Prix Special will decide for the placing.

- In case of certified illness of rider and/or horse, the next rider/horse combination in the respective classification will move up to fill the number of combinations allowed.

- The Team Dressage Competition and the Individual Dressage Competitions are held under the rules contained in Chapter II, except where stated differently under this Chapter.

Special Regulations

Article 454 – Participation

1. Teams

An NF having obtained eligibility and qualification according to Olympic Games Eligibility and Qualification procedure may enter a team composed of minimum 3 maximum 4 rider/horse combinations with the 3 best results to count for the team classification.

2. Individuals Instead of Teams

NFs having obtained eligibility and qualification according to Olympic Games Eligibility and Qualification procedure to enter 1 or 2 individuals, may enter such individuals with 1 horse each.

3. Reserve Horses

No reserve horses are allowed.

Article 619 – Eligibility Procedure for Dressage

Total Quota: 50 riders and 50 horses.

1. Teams

Eleven nations will be eligible to take part with a team of 3 riders and 3 horses or 4 riders and 4 horses as follows:

A.	(1)	The holder of the 1992 Olympic Team Title: GER.
B.	(1)	The host Nation: USA.
C.	(8)	8 best placed teams of WEG 1994, excluding GER and USA.
D.	(1)	The best placed Team from 1995 Open European Championship which has not become eligible under 1.C. above.
E.	(+)	If there are not enough teams eligible from A, B and D above, the remaining teams will be elected from the 1994 WEG classification in the order of their placing.

Total (11)

2. Individuals

A minimum of 6 nations not represented by a team, with 1 individual rider and 1 horse each will be eligible to take part as follows:

| A. | (1) | Holder of the 1992 Individual Olympic title : Nicole Uphoff (GER) (automatically eligible if not included as a member of the GER Team). |
| B. | (1) | The best placed individual of the WEG 1994 in the Team and Individual |

Qualifying Competition (Grand Prix), including GER, but excluding 2.A above.

C. (1) The best placed individual in the Team and Individual Qualifying Competition (Grand Prix) from the 1995 Open European Championship of a Nation not yet eligible through WEG 1994.

D. (3) 1 each from nations belonging to Samsung Regions I–III (*see Annex C.3*), participating in the higher level 1995 FEI Samsung International Dressage Competition. (For eligibility procedure, see Art. 620.2 below relating to the Assessing Delegate.)

E. (+) If there are not enough individuals eligible from 2.A, C and D above, the remaining Individuals will be elected from the 1994 WEG classification in the order of their placing.

Total (6 minimum)

3. Completion of Quota

Teams:

3.1 The completion of the team quota as a result of eligible teams not entering, will only take place if there are no eligible individuals under 2.B and E above and 3.2 below.

3.2 In the event that a Nation eligible for the Team Competition is only able to send 3 rider/horse combinations, an individual from another Nation will become eligible in addition to 2.B and E above.

Individuals:

3.3 In the event that a Nation eligible for the Team Competition is unable to participate with a team, it may send 1 or 2 rider/horse combinations for the Individual Competition. The total number of participating teams will be reduced (except in case 3.1 above) and the number of Nations with individuals increased (2.B and E).

3.4 In the event that a Nation eligible for the Individual Competition is unable to participate, its place will be taken by the next highest placed Nation in the Individual WEG classification or the Open 1995 European Championship, if no nation can take the place from the WEG.

3.5 Any vacancy still remaining after the application of the above will be filled by allowing NFs with 1 individual only, to enter an extra individual in the order of their placing at the WEG 1994.

Article 620 – Qualification Procedure for Dressage

1. Qualification is established as follows:

300 points (= 60 %), attributed in a Grand Prix by any of the FEI Official International Dressage Judges of a nationality other than that of the rider, must be reached in a Grand Prix at 2 CDIs/CDI-Ws and upwards from 1st January of the year preceding the Olympic Games until deadline for receipt of Certificates of Capability. For riders of non-European and non-North American countries this number of points must be achieved at 1 CDI/CDI-W, respectively 1 Grand Prix presented. However, if any of these riders wish to qualify in Europe or North America, where 2 CDI/CDI-Ws are required these riders must also perform at 2 CDIs/CDI-Ws.

Proof of such results must accompany applications for Certificates of Capability.

2. Assessing Delegate

Nations participating in higher level Samsung International Dressage Competitions which do not gain eligibility under paragraph Article 619.2 B or E above, but wish to send competitors to the Olympic Games, have the additional possibility to request by 1st May 1995 to the FEI that an FEI Assessing Delegate (Samsung Official International Judge) judge the rider concerned in a Grand Prix under competition conditions on the occasion of a 1995 Samsung Competition. In each case, the number of points for qualification of 282 (60%)* must be reached as per point 2 above. The country of the highest placed rider/horse combination per Samsung Region, out of those who had requested assessment would be eligible and the rider/horse combination would become qualified at the same time.

The report of the Assessing/Qualifying Delegate is sent to the Secretary General who, in turn, sends a copy to the Chairman of the Dressage Committee. The NFs of the qualified rider/horse combinations will be informed by the FEI immediately after the eligibility/qualification is given.

*The total marks available in the Grand Prix test that was in effect up until January 1995 was 470. Thus 60% = 282.

Medal Winners

Individual

		GP	GPS	Kür	Total
Gold	Isabell Werth (Germany) *Nobilis Gigolo*	76.60 (1)	75.49 (2)	83.00 (1)	235.09
Silver	Anky van Grunsven (Netherlands) *Cameleon Bonfire*	75.72 (2)	77.72 (1)	79.58 (2)	233.02
Bronze	Sven Rothenberger (Netherlands) *Weyden*	74.16 (4)	74.00 (4)	76.78 (4)	224.94

Teams

		Points	Placing in GP
Gold	**Germany 5553 points**		
	Isabell Werth *Nobilis Gigolo FRH*	1915	1
	Monica Theodorescu *Grunox*	1845	5
	Klaus Balkenhol *Goldstern*	1793	6
Silver	**The Netherlands 5437 points**		
	Anky van Grunsven *Cameleon Bonfire*	1893	2
	Sven Rothenberger *Weyden*	1854	4
	Tineke Bartels-de Vries *Olympic Barbria*	1690	14
Bronze	**USA 5309 points**		
	Michelle Gibson *Peron*	1880	3
	Günther Siedel *Graf George*	1734	11
	Steffen Peters *Udon*	1695	13

Arena Size: 20 x 60 m.

Markers: Standard.

Judges:

	Judging Position		
	GP	GPS	Kür
Mr Eric Lette (Sweden) President	C	C	C
Mr Uwe Mechlem (Germany)	H	B	M
Mrs Linda Zang (USA)	E	M	B
Mr Bernard Maurel (France)	B	H	E
Mr Jan Peters (Netherlands)	M	E	H

Team Gold Medallists Germany. (Left to right) Klaus Balkenhol (*Goldstern*), Isabell Werth (*Gigolo*), Monica Theodorescu (*Grunox*) and Martin Schaudt (*Durgo*). (Photo: courtesy of Max Ammann.)

Tests and Scoring:

• Grand Prix(1995) – maximum score = 500 points per judge (100%).

• Grand Prix Special (1995) – maximum score = 430 points per judge (100%).

• Freestyle to Music (Kür) (1995) – maximum score = 200 (Technical) + 200 (Artistic) = 400 per judge (100%).

• For the final Individual Competition result, the percentages of all 3 competitions were calculated to 2 decimal places and added together.

Individual Gold Medallist
Isabell Werth (GER) on
Gigolo. (Photo: courtesy
of Max Ammann.)

GRAND PRIX (1995) – OLYMPIC GAMES 1996

		Test	Directive ideas	Marks	Coeff.
1	A X	Enter in collected canter. Halt – Immobility – Salute. Proceed in collected trot.	The entry. The halt and the transitions from the canter to the halt and from the halt to the trot.	10	
2	C MXK KA	Track to the right. Change rein in extended trot. Collected trot.	The lengthening and regularity of the steps. The transitions.	10	
3	A FXH H	Collected canter. Change rein in medium canter with flying change of leg at X. Collected canter.	The lengthening and the regularity of the strides. The flying change of leg. The balance. The transition.	10	
4	C	Transition to collected walk.	The transition.	10	
5	M Between G and H	Turn right. Half-pirouette to the right.	The regularity of the half-pirouette.	10	
6	Between G and M	Half-pirouette to the left.	The regularity of the half-pirouette.	10	
7		The collected walk CMG (H) (M) G.	The shortening and heightening of the steps. The carriage and regularity.	10	
8	GHS SP PF F	Collected trot. Half-pass to the left. Collected trot. Turn right.	The correctness and regularity. The angle and the bend of the horse. The balance.	10	
9	D K	Halt – rein-back 4 steps – forward 4 steps – rein-back 6 steps and immediately proceed in collected trot. Track to the right.	The halt. The balance. The correctness and regularity.	10	
10	VR RMCH	half-pass to the right. Collected trot.	The correctness and regularity. The angle and the balance of the horse. The balance.	10	
11	HXF	Change rein in medium trot.	The lengthening and regularity of the steps. The transitions.	10	

		Test	Directive ideas	Marks	Coeff.
12	FAK	Passage	The cadence and the regularity.	10	
13	KVXRM	Change rein in extended walk.	The extension and regularity of the steps. The lengthening of the frame.	10	2
14	MCH	Collected walk.	The shortening and heightening of the steps. The carriage and regularity.	10	
15	H	Proceed in passage, transition from collected walk to passage.	Submission and willingness. The collection.	10	
16	HIS	Passage.	The cadence and the regularity.	10	
17	I	Piaffe l2 to 15 steps.	The cadence and the regularity.	10	
18	I	Proceed in passage, transitions from passage to piaffe and from piaffe to passage.	Submission and willingness.	10	
19	IRBX	Passage.	The cadence and the regularity.	10	
20	X	Piaffe 12 to 15 steps.	The cadence and the regularity.	10	
21	X	Proceed in passage, transitions from passage to piaffe and from piaffe to passage.	Submission and willingness.	10	
22	XEV	Passage.	The cadence and the regularity.	10	
23	V VKA	Proceed in collected canter. Collected canter.	The straightness, calmness and regularity.	10	
24	A	On centre line – 4 counter changes of hand in half-pass to the either side of the centre line with flying change of leg at each change of direction. The first half-pass to left and the last to the left of 3 strides, the 3 others of 6 strides.	The correctness and the regularity of the 5 half-passes and the 4 counter changes. The balance.	10	2
	G		Flying change of leg.		

		Test	Directive ideas	Marks	Coeff.
25	C MXK K	Track to the right. Change rein in extended canter. Collected canter and flying change of leg.	The extension. The collection. The transitions.	10	
26	A L	Down the centre line. Pirouette to the left.	The collection. The regularity.	10	2
27	X	Flying change of leg.	The change of leg.	10	
28	I	Pirouette to the right.	The collection and the balance.		2
29	G C	Flying change of leg. Track to the left.	The regularity. The change of leg.	10	
30	HXF	On the diagonal 9 flying changes of leg every second stride.	The correctness, straightness, balance and fluency.	10	
31	KXM	On the diagonal 15 flying changes of leg every stride.	The correctness, straightness, balance and fluency.	10	
32	C HXF F A	Collected trot. Extended trot. Collected trot. Down the centre line.	The extension. The collection.	10	
33		Transitions from collected canter to collected trot and from collected trot to extended trot and back to collected trot	Submission and willingness.	10	
34	DX	Passage.	The cadence and the regularity.	10	
35	X	Piaffe l2 to 15 steps.	The cadence and the regularity.	10	
36	X	Proceed in passage. Transitions from passage to piaffe and from piaffe to passage.	Submission and willingness.	10	
37	XG	Passage.	The cadence and the regularity.	10	
38	G	Halt – Immobility – Salute.	The transition and the halt.	10	
		Leave arena in walk at A.			

Total 420

			Marks	Coeff.

Collective marks

	Marks	Coeff.
1. Paces (freedom and regularity).	10	2
2. Impulsion (desire to move forward, elasticity of the steps, suppleness of the back and engagement of the hindquarters).	10	2
3. Submission (attention and confidence; harmony, lightness and ease of the movements; acceptance of the bridle and lightness of the forehand).	10	2
4. Rider's position and seat; correctness and effect of the aids.	10	2

Total 500

To be deducted:

Errors of the course and omissions are penalised:

1st time	=	2 marks
2nd time	=	4 marks
3rd time	=	8 marks
4th time	=	Elimination

GRAND PRIX SPECIAL (1995) – OLYMPIC GAMES 1996

Test		Directive ideas	Marks	Coeff.
1	A	Enter in collected canter.	The entry.	10
	X	Halt – Immobility – Salute. Proceed in collected trot.	The halt and the transitions to and from the halt.	
2	C	Track to the left.	The lengthening of the frame, the extension and the regularity of the steps. The transitions.	10
	HXF	Change rein in extended trot.		
	F	Collected trot		
3	VXR	Half-pass.	The correctness and regularity. The carriage and the bend. The balance.	10
	RMC	Collected trot.		
4	CHS	Passage.	The cadence and regularity of the passage. The extension and regularity.	10
	SK	Extended trot.		
	KAF	Passage.		
5		Transitions from passage to extended trot and from extended trot to passage.	Submission and willingness.	10
6	FP	Collected trot.	The correctness and regularity. The carriage and the bend.	10
	PXS	Half-pass.		
	SHC	Collected trot.		

		Test	Directive ideas	Marks	Coeff.
7	CMR RF FAK	Passage. Extended trot. Passage.	The cadence and regularity of the passage. The extension and regularity.	10	
8		Transitions from passage to extended trot and from extended trot to passage.	Submission and willingness.	10	
9	KLBIH H	Extended walk. Collected walk.	The extension and regularity of the steps. The transitions.	10	2
10	HCMG	Collected walk.	The shortening and heightening of the steps. The carriage and regularity.	10	
11	G	Piaffe l2 to 15 steps.	The cadence and the regularity.	10	
12	G	Proceed in passage, transition from collected walk to piaffe and from piaffe to passage.	Submission and willingness.	10	
13	GHSI	Passage.	The cadence and the regularity.	10	
14	I	Piaffe l2 to 15 steps.	The cadence and the regularity.	10	
15	I	Proceed in passage, transitions from passage to piaffe and from piaffe to passage.	Submission and willingness.	10	
16	IRBX	Passage.	The cadence and the regularity.	10	
17	XEVKAF	Collected canter left.	The correctness and regularity.	10	
18	FLE E	Half-pass in canter. Flying change of leg.	The correctness and regularity. The carriage and the bend. The balance and the change of leg.	10	
19	EIM M MCH	Half-pass in canter. Flying change of leg. Collected canter.	The correctness and regularity. The carriage and the bend. The balance and the change of leg.	10	
20	HXF	On the diagonal 9 flying changes of leg every second stride.	The correctness, straightness, balance and fluency.	10	
21	KXM	On the diagonal 15 flying changes of leg every stride.	The correctness, straightness, balance and fluency.	10	

		Test	Directive ideas	Marks	Coeff.
22	HXF F	Change rein in extended canter. Collected canter and flying change of leg.	The extension. The transition. The flying change of leg.	10	
23	A D	Down the centre line. Pirouette to the right.	The collection. The regularity. Slightly before or after 'D' is acceptable.	10	2
24	Between D and G	On the centre line, 9 flying changes of leg every stride. and fluency.	The correctness, straightness, balance	10	
25	G	Pirouette to the left.	The collection. The regularity. Slightly before or after 'G' is acceptable.	10	2
26	HS SK K	Collected trot. Extended trot. Collected trot.	The lengthening of the frame, the extension and the regularity of the steps. The transitions.	10	
27		Transitions from collected canter to collected trot and collected trot to extended trot and back to collected trot.	Submission and willingness.	10	
28	A LX XEX	Down centre line. Passage. Volte to the left 10m diameter in passage.	The regularity and cadence. The bend.	10	
29	X	Piaffe 12 to 15 steps.	The cadence and the regularity.	10	
30		Transitions from passage to piaffe and piaffe to passage.	Submission and willingness.	10	
31	XBX XI	Volte to the right 10m diameter in passage. Passage.	The regularity and cadence. The bend.	10	
32	I	Halt – Immobility – Salute.	The transition and the halt.	10	
		Leave arena at walk on a long rein at A.			

Total 350

	Marks	Coeff.
Collective marks		
1. Paces (freedom and regularity)	10	2
2. Impulsion (desire to move forward, elasticity of the steps, suppleness of the back and engagement of the hind quarters).	10	2
3. Submission (attention and confidence; harmony, lightness and ease of the movements; acceptance of the bridle and lightness of the forehand).	10	2
4. Rider's position and seat; correctness and effect of the aids.	10	2

Total 430

To be deducted:

Errors of the course and omissions are penalised:

1st time   =   2 marks
2nd time   =   4 marks
3rd time   =   8 marks
4th time   =   Elimination

Freestyle Test (Kür) Grand Prix Level (1995) – Olympic Games 1996

Time allowed:
Performance to be finished between 5 minutes 30 seconds and 6 minutes

	Technical marks	Marks	Points	Coeff.	Final marks
1	Collected walk (minimum 20m)	10			
2	Extended walk	10			
3	Collected trot including Half-pass to the right	10			
4	Collected trot including Half-pass to the left	10			
5	Extended trot	10			
6	Collected canter including Half-pass to the right	10			
7	Collected canter including Half-pass to the left	10			
8	Extended canter	10			
9	Flying changes of leg every second stride (minimum 5 times consecutively)	10			

	Technical marks	Marks	Points	Coeff.	Final marks
10	Flying changes of leg every stride (minimum 5 times consecutively)	10			
11	Canter pirouette to the right	10		2	
12	Canter pirouette to the left	10		2	
13	Passage (minimum 20m)	10		2	
14	Piaffe (minimum 10 steps)	10		2	
15	Transitions from passage to piaffe and from piaffe to passage	10		2	
	Total for technical executions	**200**			

	Artistic marks*	Marks	Points	Coeff.	Final marks
16	Rhythm, energy and elasticity	10		3	
17	Harmony between rider and horse	10		3	
18	Choreography. Use of arena. Inventiveness	10		4	
19	Degree of difficulty. Well calculated risks.	10		4	
20	Choice of music and interpretation of the music	10		6	
	Total for artistic presentation	**200**			

* half points may be given

To be deducted:
Time penalty: more than 6 minutes or less than 5 minutes 30 seconds, deduct 2 points from the total of artistic presentation

Total for technical execution divided by 20	10
Total for artistic presentation divided by 20	10
Final score	**20**

In case two competitors have the same final score, the one with the higher marks for artistic impression is leading.

OLYMPIC GAMES 1996
Results – Grand Prix Test

	Rider	Nation	Horse	Judges' marks (placings)					Total
				E	H	C	M	B	
1.	Isabell Werth	GER	*Nobilis Gigolo FRH*	386 (2)	390 (1)	387 (1)	378 (1)	374 (1)	1915
2.	Anky van Grunsven	NED	*Cameleon Bonfire*	382 (3)	382 (2)	383 (2)	378 (1)	368 (2)	1893
3.	Michelle Gibson	USA	*Peron*	393 (1)	378 (3)	377 (3)	370 (4)	362 (4)	1880
4.	Sven Rothenberger	NED	*Weyden*	380 (4)	367 (5)	373 (5)	377 (3)	357 (6)	1854
5.	Monica Theodorescu	GER	*Grunox*	365 (5)	370 (4)	376 (4)	368 (5)	366 (3)	1845
6.	Klaus Balkenhol	GER	*Goldstern*	358 (7)	363 (7)	366 (6)	359 (6)	347 (9)	1793
7.	Margit Otto-Crepin	FRA	*Lucky Lord*	351 (10)	365 (6)	355 (8)	353 (10)	359 (5)	1783
8.	Martin Schaudt	GER	*ESGE-Durgo*	365 (5)	347 (10)	360 (7)	355 (8)	354 (7)	1781
9.	Nicole Uphoff-Becker	GER	*Rembrandt Borbet*	344 (13)	355 (8)	348 (10)	359 (6)	345 (10)	1751
10.	Ignacio Rambla Algarin	ESP	*Evento*	347 (12)	344 (12)	355 (8)	349 (11)	349 (8)	1744
11.	Günter Seidel	USA	*Graf George*	355 (8)	354 (9)	341 (13)	355 (8)	329 (17)	1734
12.	Lars Petersen	DEN	*Uffe Korshojgaard*	355 (8)	346 (11)	341 (13)	334 (16)	329 (17)	1705
13.	Steffen Peters	USA	*Udon*	351 (10)	342 (14)	342 (12)	332 (18)	328 (19)	1695
14.	Tineke Bartels-de Vries	NED	*Olympic Barbria*	330 (17)	340 (16)	335 (20)	346 (12)	339 (12)	1690
15.	Gonnelien Rothenberger	NED	*Olympic Dondolo*	339 (14)	340 (16)	332 (21)	341 (13)	321 (28)	1673
15.	Annette Solmell	SWE	*Strauss*	330 (17)	335 (22)	346 (11)	336 (15)	326 (21)	1673
17.	Richard Davison	GBR	*Askari*	335 (16)	341 (15)	330 (23)	332 (18)	330 (16)	1668
18.	Ulla Hakansson	SWE	*Bobby*	338 (15)	336 (19)	337 (17)	329 (24)	326 (21)	1666
19.	Christine Stückelberger	SUI	*Aquamarin*	328 (21)	330 (25)	337 (17)	325 (29)	342 (11)	1662
20.	Arlette Holsters	BEL	*Faible*	327 (23)	340 (16)	337 (17)	328 (26)	326 (21)	1658
21.	Louise Nathhorst	SWE	*Walk on Top*	328 (21)	344 (12)	320 (31)	328 (26)	337 (13)	1657
22.	Dominique Brieussel	FRA	*Akazie*	324 (25)	335 (22)	328 (24)	328 (26)	335 (14)	1650
23.	Robert Dover	USA	*Metallic*	315 (33)	336 (19)	326 (26)	339 (14)	333 (15)	1649
24.	Mary Hanna	AUS	*Mosaic*	326 (24)	336 (19)	322 (30)	334 (16)	326 (21)	1644
25.	Finn Hansen	DEN	*Bergerac*	329 (20)	330 (25)	331 (22)	330 (22)	316 (30)	1636
26.	Heike Holstein	IRL	*Ballaseyr Devereaux*	330 (17)	324 (32)	323 (29)	332 (18)	322 (27)	1631
27.	Hans Staub	SUI	*Dukaat*	324 (25)	321 (35)	338 (16)	322 (32)	323 (26)	1628
28.	Kyra Kyrklund	FIN	*Amiral*	324 (25)	322 (33)	340 (15)	330 (22)	304 (36)	1620
29.	Leonie Bramall	CAN	*Gilbona*	320 (31)	322 (33)	328 (24)	332 (18)	311 (34)	1613
30.	Dominique D'Esme	FRA	*Arnoldo*	313 (35)	325 (29)	326 (26)	320 (35)	328 (19)	1612
31.	Caroline Hatlapa	AUT	*Merlin*	314 (34)	327 (28)	320 (31)	324 (30)	324 (25)	1609
32.	Beatriz Ferrer Salat	ESP	*Brillant*	323 (28)	318 (37)	326 (26)	323 (31)	314 (32)	1604
33.	Eva Senn	SUI	*Renzo*	321 (29)	325 (29)	320 (31)	322 (32)	315 (31)	1603
34.	Pia Laus	ITA	*Liebenberg*	321 (29)	325 (29)	320 (31)	329 (24)	305 (35)	1600
35.	Paolo Giani Margi	ITA	*Destino di Acciarella*	304 (40)	334 (24)	320 (31)	320 (35)	317 (29)	I595
36.	Joanna Jackson	GBR	*Mester Mouse*	320 (31)	319 (36)	316 (37)	321 (34)	301 (38)	1577
37.	Tinne Wilhelmsson	SWE	*Caprice*	312 (37)	329 (27)	318 (36)	308 (38)	275 (46)	1542
38.	Rafael Soto	ESP	*Invasor*	311 (38)	309 (39)	296 (43)	299 (43)	312 (33)	1527
39.	Joachim Orth	MEX	*Bellini*	303 (41)	302 (42)	312 (38)	314 (37)	287 (42)	1518
40.	Marie-Hélène Syre	FRA	*MarIon*	305 (39)	307 (40)	295 (44)	308 (38)	301 (38)	1516
40.	Vicky Thompson	GBR	*Enfant*	301 (42)	310 (38)	300 (40)	301 (41)	304 (36)	1516
42.	Suzanne Dunkley	BER	*Elliot*	297 (43)	299 (45)	299 (41)	307 (40)	300 (40)	1502
43.	Daria Fantoni	ITA	*Sonny Boy*	313 (35)	295 (47)	297 (42)	301 (41)	290 (41)	1496

Rider	Nation	Horse	E	H	C	M	B	Total
44. Jane Bredin	GBR	*Cupido*	286 (47)	304 (41)	306 (39)	288 (45)	284 (45)	1468
45. Evi Strasser	CAN	*Lavinia*	294 (45)	301 (43)	290 (45)	291 (44)	286 (43)	1462
46. Gina Smith	CAN	*Faust*	295 (44)	297 (46)	288 (47)	280 (47)	274 (47)	1434
47. Fausto Puccini	ITA	*Fiffikus*	272 (49)	289 (48)	290 (45)	282 (46)	285 (44)	1418
48. Juan Matute	ESP	*Hermes*	292 (46)	300 (44)	286 (48)	280 (47)	258 (49)	1416
49. B v Grebel Schiendorfer	SUI	*Ramar*	273 (48)	262 (49)	257 (49)	263 (49)	269 (48)	1324
Thomas Dvorak	CAN	*World Cup*	withdrawn					

OLYMPIC GAMES 1996
Results – Grand Prix Special Test

Rider	Nation	Horse	E	H	C	M	B	Total
1. Anky van Grunsven	NED	*Cameleon Bonfire*	346 (1)	325 (1)	330 (1)	330 (1)	340 (1)	1671
2. Isabell Werth	GER	*Nobilis Gigolo FRH*	323 (2)	315 (2)	323 (5)	324 (3)	338 (2)	1623
3. Michelle Gibson	USA	*Peron*	320 (5)	308 (8)	324 (4)	320 (4)	325 (5)	1597
4. Sven Rothenberger	NED	*Weyden*	318 (6)	310 (6)	321 (6)	327 (2)	315 (9)	1591
5. Monica Theodorescu	GER	*Grunox*	322 (3)	311 (4)	314 (8)	315 (7)	327 (4)	1589
6. Klaus Balkenhol	GER	*Goldstern*	315 (8)	311 (4)	325 (2)	315 (7)	321 (7)	1587
7. Louise Nathhorst	SWE	*Walk on Top*	312 (10)	300 (11)	325 (2)	316 (5)	328 (3)	1581
8. Nicole Uphoff-Becker	GER	*Rembrandt Borbet*	318 (6)	312 (3)	315 (7)	300 (11)	325 (5)	1570
9. Margit Otto-Crepin	FRA	*Lucky Lord*	322 (3)	309 (7)	310 (10)	316 (5)	311 (11)	1568
10. Günter Seidel	USA	*Graf George*	315 (8)	301 (9)	307 (11)	308 (9)	313 (10)	1544
11. Martin Schaudt	GER	*ESGE-Durgo*	296 (17)	301 (9)	312 (9)	301 (10)	316 (8)	1526
12. Ignacio Rambla Algarin	ESP	*Evento*	303 (11)	299 (12)	304 (13)	298 (12)	305 (12)	1509
13. Lars Petersen	DEN	*Uffe Korshojgaard*	297 (16)	297 (13)	300 (14)	292 (14)	292 (15)	1478
14. Gonnelien Rothenberger	NED	*Olympic Dondolo*	300 (14)	290 (15)	307 (11)	283 (19)	291 (16)	1471
15. Tineke Bartels-de Vries	NED	*Olympic Barbria*	300 (14)	291 (14)	293 (17)	294 (13)	290 (19)	1468
16. Ariette Holsters	BEL	*Faible*	290 (18)	288 (17)	298 (15)	290 (15)	299 (13)	1465
17. Christine Stückelberger	SUI	*Aquamarin*	301 (12)	290 (15)	292 (19)	284 (18)	297 (14)	1464
18. Steffen Peters	USA	*Udon*	301 (12)	286 (18)	291 (20)	285 (17)	291 (16)	1454
19. Ulla Hakansson	SWE	*Bobby*	281 (22)	282 (20)	290 (21)	289 (16)	288 (20)	1430
20. Annette Solmell	SWE	*Strauss*	281 (22)	286 (18)	293 (17)	281 (20)	288 (20)	1429
21. Finn Hansen	DEN	*Bergerac*	282 (21)	280 (21)	295 (16)	275 (21)	279 (23)	1411
22. Richard Davison	GBR	*Askari*	287 (19)	274 (23)	278 (23)	267 (24)	291 (16)	1397
23. Mary Hanna	AUS	*Mosaic*	283 (20)	271 (24)	276 (24)	271 (22)	282 (22)	1383
24. Dominique Brieussel	ERA	*Akazie*	278 (24)	276 (22)	283 (22)	270 (23)	272 (24)	1379
25. Robert Dover	USA	*Metallic*	264 (25)	248 (25)	250 (25)	252 (25)	250 (25)	1264

OLYMPIC GAMES 1996

Results – Grand Prix Freestyle to Music (Kür)

Rider	Nation	Horse	Judges' marks (placings)					Total
			E	H	C	M	B	
1. Isabell Werth	GER	*Nobilis Gigolo FRH*	16.63 (1)	16.60 (2)	16.80 (1)	16.73 (1)	16.25 (1)	83.00
2. Anky van Grunsven	NED	*Cameleon Bonfire*	15.68 (2)	16.68 (1)	15.82 (2)	15.78 (3)	15.63 (2)	79.58
3. Monica Theodorescu	GER	*Grunox*	15.07 (5)	15.35 (4)	15.25 (4)	15.75 (4)	15.43 (3)	76.85
4. Sven Rothenberger	NED	*Weyden*	14.73 (7)	15.57 (3)	15.48 (3)	15.80 (2)	15.20 (5)	76.78
5. Klaus Balkenhol	GER	*Goldstern*	15.30 (4)	15.10 (5)	15.03 (6)	15.43 (6)	15.43 (4)	76.28
6. Margit Otto-Crepin	FRA	*Lucky Lord*	15.40 (3)	14.70 (6)	15.18 (5)	15.40 (7)	14.88 (7)	75.55
7. Günter Seidel	USA	*Graf George*	14.48 (8)	14.63 (7)	14.68 (9)	15.20 (9)	14.88 (7)	73.85
8. Michelle Gibson	USA	*Peron*	14.80 (6)	14.38 (9)	14.05 (11)	15.23 (8)	14.90 (6)	73.35
9. Louise Nathhorst	SWE	*Walk on Top*	13.65 (10)	14.53 (8)	14.70 (8)	15.55 (5)	14.30 (11)	72.73
10. Ignacio Rambla Algarin	ESP	*Evento*	13.90 (9)	14.30 (10)	14.73 (7)	14.82 (10)	14.43 (10)	72.18
11. Lars Petersen	DEN	*Uffe Korshojgaard*	13.55 (12)	14.30 (10)	14.53 (10)	14.57 (12)	13.93 (12)	70.88
12. Martin Schaudt	GER	*ESGE-Durgo*	13.60 (11)	13.75 (13)	13.85 (13)	14.78 (11)	14.55 (09)	70.53
13. Tineke Bartels-de Vries	NED	*Olympic Barbria*	13.40 (13)	14.23 (12)	14.00 (12)	14.30 (13)	13.73 (13)	69.66

OLYMPIC GAMES 1996

Results – Individual Competition

Rider	Nation	Horse	Percentage scores (placing)			Total
			Grand Prix	Grand Prix Special	Grand Prix Kür	
1. Isabell Werth	**GER**	***Nobilis Gigolo FRH***	**76.60 (1)**	**75.49 (2)**	**83.00 (1)**	**235.09**
2. Anky van Grunsven	**NED**	***Cameleon Bonfire***	**75.72 (2)**	**77.72 (1)**	**79.58 (2)**	**233.02**
3. Sven Rothenberger	**NED**	***Weyden***	**74.16 (4)**	**74.00 (4)**	**76.78 (4)**	**224.94**
4. Monica Theodorescu	GER	*Grunox*	73.80 (5)	73.91 (5)	76.85 (3)	224.56
5. Michelle Gibson	USA	*Peron*	75.20 (3)	74.28 (3)	73.35 (8)	222.83
6. Klaus Balkenhol	GER	*Goldstern*	71.72 (6)	73.81 (6)	76.28 (5)	221.81
7. Margit Otto-Crepin	FRA	*Lucky Lord*	71.32 (7)	72.93 (8)	75.55 (6)	219.89
8. Guenter Seidel	USA	*Graf George*	69.36 (10)	71.81 (9)	73.85 (7)	215.02
9. Martin Schaudt	GER	*ESGE-Durgo*	71.24 (8)	70.98 (10)	70.53 (12)	212.75
10. Louise Nathhorst	SWE	*Walk on Top*	66.28 (13)	73.53 (7)	72.73 (9)	212.54
11. Ignacio Rambla Algarin	ESP	*Evento*	69.76 (09)	70.19 (11)	72.18 (10)	212.13
12. Lars Petersen	DEN	*Uffe Korshojgaard*	68.20 (11)	68.74 (12)	70.88 (11)	207.82
13. Tineke Bartels-de Vries	NED	*Olympic Barbria*	67.60 (12)	68.28 (13)	69.66 (13)	205.54

OLYMPIC GAMES 1996
Results – Team Competition (Grand Prix Test)

Nation/Rider	Horse	Judges' marks					Total
		E	H	C	M	B	
1. Germany							**5553**
Isabell Werth	*Nobilis Gigolo FRH*	386	390	387	378	374	1915*
Klaus Balkenhol	*Goldstern*	358	363	366	359	347	1793*
Monica Theodorescu	*Grunox*	365	370	376	368	366	1845*
Martin Schaudt	*ESGE-Durgo*	365	347	360	355	354	1781
2. Netherlands							**5437**
Tineke Bartels-de Vries	*Olympic Barbria*	330	340	335	346	339	1690*
Sven Rothenberger	*Weyden*	380	367	373	377	357	1854*
Anky van Grunsven	*Cameleon Bonfire*	382	382	383	378	368	1893*
Gonnelien Rothenberger	*Olympic Dondolo*	339	340	332	341	321	1673
3. USA							**5309**
Robert Dover	*Metallic*	315	336	326	339	333	1649
Michelle Gibson	*Peron*	393	378	377	370	362	1880*
Steffen Peters	*Udon*	351	342	342	332	328	1695*
Günter Seidel	*Graf George*	355	354	341	355	329	1734*
4. France							**5045**
Dominique D'Esme	*Arnoldo*	313	325	326	320	328	1612*
Margit Otto-Crepin	*Lucky Lord*	351	365	355	353	359	1783*
Dominique Brieussel	*Akazie*	324	335	328	328	335	1650*
Marie-Hélène Syre	*Marlon*	305	307	295	308	301	1516
5. Sweden							**4996**
Tinne Wilhelmsson	*Caprice*	312	329	318	308	275	1542
Annette Solmell	*Strauss*	330	335	346	336	326	1673*
Ulla Hakansson	*Bobby*	338	336	337	329	326	1666*
Louise Nathhorst	*Walk on Top*	328	344	320	328	337	1657*
6. Switzerland							**4893**
Eva Senn	*Renzo*	321	325	320	322	315	1603*
Hans Staub	*Dukaat*	324	321	338	322	323	1628*
Christine Stückelberger	*Aquamarin*	328	330	337	325	342	1662*
B Grebel Schiendorfer	*Ramar*	273	262	257	263	269	1324
7. Spain							**4875**
Rafael Soto	*Invasor*	311	309	296	299	312	1527*
Beatriz Ferrer Salat	*Brillant*	323	318	326	323	314	1604*
Juan Matute	*Hermes*	292	300	286	280	258	1416
Ignacio Rambla Algarin	*Evento*	347	344	355	349	349	1744*

Nation/Rider	Horse	Judges' marks					Total
		E	H	C	M	B	
8. Great Britain							**4761**
Joanna Jackson	*Mester Mouse*	320	319	316	321	301	1577 *
Jane Bredin	*Cupido*	286	304	306	288	284	1468
Vicky Thompson	*Enfant*	301	310	300	301	304	1516 *
Richard Davison	*Askari*	335	341	330	332	330	1668 *
9. Italy							**4691**
Paolo Giani Margi	*Destino di Acciarella*	304	334	320	320	317	1595 *
Fausto Puccini	*Fiffikus*	272	289	290	282	285	1418
Daria Fantoni	*Sonny Boy*	313	295	297	301	290	1496 *
Pia Laus	*Liebenberg*	321	325	320	329	305	1600 *
10. Canada							**4509**
Thomas Dvorak	*World Cup*		withdrawn				——
Evi Strasser	*Lavinia*	294	301	290	291	286	1462 *
Leonie Bramall	*Gilbona*	320	322	328	332	311	1613 *
Gina Smith	*Faust*	295	297	288	280	274	1434 *

* Denotes scores used to calculate Team Competitiion

OLYMPIC GAMES 2000

SYDNEY, AUSTRALIA

Participating countries: 18

Australia	Great Britain	Portugal
Austria	Ireland	Russia
Brazil	Italy	Spain
Denmark	Mexico	Sweden
Finland	Netherlands	Switzerland
Germany	New Zealand	United States of America

Participating riders: 48

Teams: 9 teams of a maximum of 4 riders

• The 3 best scores to count for the Team Competition.

Australia	Spain
Denmark	Sweden
Germany	Switzerland
Great Britain	United States of America
Netherlands	

Individual Riders: 12

Austria – 2	Mexico – 1
Brazil – 1	New Zealand – 1
Finland – 2	Portugal – 1
Ireland – 1	Russia – 2
Italy – 1	

Competitions

• **Grand Prix – Team Competition and 1st Individual Qualifier**

The FEI Grand Prix de Dressage in which all competitors must participate, is the Team Competition and the first Individual Qualifying Competition.

• **Grand Prix Special – 2nd Individual Qualifier**

The Grand Prix Special is the second Individual Qualifying Competition which is limited to and compulsory for the 25 best rider/horse combinations in the initial Grand Prix, including those who tie for 25th place. If all 4 riders from a team qualify, they may all participate.

• **Grand Prix Level Freestyle Test – Individual Competition**

The Grand Prix Level Freestyle test is the final Individual Competition which is limited to and compulsory for the overall best 15 out of the Grand Prix and Grand Prix Special by adding the percentages of these competitions as points. A maximum of 3 riders per country may participate (IOC Charter, Art 604, Point 1). In the case of a tie for 15th place, the higher score in the Grand Prix Special will decide for the placing.

- In case of certified illness of rider and/or horse, the next rider/horse combination, in respective classification, will move up to fill the number of combinations allowed.

Article 623.2 – Participation

1. Teams

An NF having obtained eligibility and qualification according to Olympic Games Eligibility and Qualification procedure may enter a team composed of a minimum of 3, maximum of 4 rider/horse combinations and a reserve horse with the 3 best results to count for the team classification.

2. Individuals Instead of Teams

NFs having obtained eligibility and qualification according to Olympic Games Eligibility and Qualification procedure to enter 1 or 2 individuals, may enter such individuals with 1 horse each.

Article 624 Qualification Procedure – Dressage

Total Quota = 50 riders and 50 horses (+10 reserve horses).

1. Teams

Ten (10) nations are qualified to take part with a team consisting of 4 riders and 4 horses or 3 riders and 3 horses, as follows:

A	The host nation(Aus).	1
B	The 8 best placed teams from the WEG 1998 excluding AUS.	8
C	The best placed team from 1999 'Open' European Championship Excluding teams qualified as above.	1

Total 10

1.1 Reserve horse
Each nation qualified with a team is allowed to take 1 reserve horse which must have been duly entered with one of the team members. If the case of certified substitution arises, this reserve horse may be ridden by any of the team members.

1.2 Completion of quota – Teams
If a nation qualified with a team is unable to participate, the number of teams will not be completed. The nation may participate with 1 or 2 individual competitors in order of the next highest NF (Individual ranking) on the FEI Dressage Rider Ranking List.

2. Individuals

Ten (10) spaces will be reserved for NFs not represented by a team, each competitor with 1 horse and with a maximum of 2 riders per nation being qualified to take part.

A   Three (3) spaces will be reserved for NFs belonging to the
    FEI World Dressage Challenge Regions I – III (the best rider/horse
    combination per region), participating in the higher level 1999 FEI
    World Dressage Challenge and not having reached qualification
    for an individual at 1998 WEG or 1999 European 'Open' Championship.   (3)

B   Except for riders qualified under A above, selection of NFs takes
    place as follows:

    1. The NF of the 3 best placed individuals of 1998 WEG in the
       Team and 1st Individual Qualifying Competition (Grand Prix).   (3)

    2. The NF of the 2 best placed individuals in the Team and the
       1st Individual Qualifying Competition (Grand Prix) from 1999
       European 'Open' Championship of a nation not qualified
       through 1998 WEG.   (2)

    3. The NF of the 2 best placed riders from the FEI approved
       World Ranking List for Dressage Riders.   (2)
                                                                         ————————
                                                                        Total 10

2.1 Completion of Quota – Individuals

In case an NF qualified under A and B above is unable to participate or in the case that there is no qualified NF under A above, the next highest placed NF will be taken from the FEI approved World Ranking List for Dressage Riders (Rider List).

The number of individuals to be taken from the Dressage Rankings may be increased as a result of a country sending a team of 3 instead of a team of 4 riders.

3. Riders Ranking List

The point system to be used for establishing the Riders Ranking List for Dressage: see Annex E-2.

The standing as of 1st March 2000 will count.

Article 625 Minimum Requirements for Riders and Horses

All horses and riders who take part in the 2000 Olympic Games Dressage Competitions must fulfil the minimum requirements as follows:

1. Period for obtaining minimum requirements

Riders and horses may obtain the minimum requirements at events which take place from 1st January 1999, the year preceding the Olympic Games, until the deadline of the nominated entries 3rd July 2000.

2. Minimum requirements

Riders and horses must have obtained the following results as a combination:

300 points (60%)*, attributed in a Grand Prix by any of the FEI Official International Dressage Judges of a nationality other than that of the rider must be reached in a Grand Prix at 2 CDI***/CDI-Ws and upwards.

For riders of non-European and non-North American countries, this number of points must be achieved at 1 CDI***/CDI-W only. However, if any of these riders wish to qualify in

Europe or North America, where 2 CDI***/CDI-Ws are required these riders must also perform at 2 CDI***/CDI-Ws.

* Note: 246 points (60%) attributed in a Short Grand Prix.

3. Assessing Delegate

Nations participating in the higher level FEI World Dressage Challenge (see Olympic Games Qualification Groups, Annex D* of this document) wishing to send competitors to the Olympic Games, have the possibility to request the FEI by 1st May 1999 that an FEI Assessing Delegate (Official International Judge) judge the rider concerned in a Grand Prix under competition conditions on the occasion of the 1999 FEI World Dressage Challenge. In each case, the number of points for minimum requirements of 300 (60%) points must be reached.

The report of the Assessing Delegate is sent to the FEI Secretary General who, in turn, sends a copy to the Chairman of the Dressage Committee. The FEI will confirm immediately to the relevant NFs if the rider/horse combination has reached the minimum requirement.

* Note: Further countries may be added to relevant groups if they join the Challenge in 1999 and request assessment before 1st May 1999.

Article 606 – Eligibility of Competitors and Horses

1. Competitors

1.1 To be eligible for participation in the equestrian events of the Olympic Games, competitors and horses must comply with all current FEI Regulations as well as Rule 45 of the Olympic Charter and its Bye-Law (see Annex A).

1.2 From and including year in which they reach their 18th birthday, competitors are eligible to take part in the Three Day Event and in the Jumping Competitions. In Dressage they are allowed to take part from and including the year in which they reach their 16th birthday.

1.3 1996 Olympic Title Holders: No past Olympic title holder (Team or Individual) will be automatically eligible for the 2000 Olympic Games.

2. Horses

2.1 Age
Horses of any origin and a minimum of 7 years of age (the age being counted from 1st January of the year of birth) are eligible to compete.

2.2 Ownership
2.2.1 Horses entered in the equestrian events at the Olympic Games must have been registered with the FEI as property of the owners of the same nationality as the competitor by 31st December of the year preceding the Olympic Games.

2.2.2 Horses with multinational ownership must be registered with the FEI by the 31st December (as per the above paragraph) under the name of the NF for which the horse will compete during the Olympic Games.

2.2.3 National Federations are responsible to ensure that horses which do not meet owner-ship requirements as laid down by the FEI, are not entered for the Olympic Games' equestrian events.

Medal Winners

Individual

		GP	GPS	Kür	Total
Gold	Anky van Grunsven (Netherlands) *Bonfire*	75.00(2)	78.13(1)	86.05(1)	239.18
Silver	Isabell Werth (Germany) *Gigolo*	76.32(1)	75.67(2)	82.20(2)	234.19
Bronze	Ulla Saltzgeber (Germany) *Rusty*	73.16(7)	76.74(4)	80.67(3)	230.57

Teams

		Points	Placing in GP
Gold	**Germany 5632 points**		
	Isabell Werth *Gigolo*	1908	1
	Nadine Capellmann *Farbenfroh*	1867	4
	Alexandra Simons de Ridder *Chacomo*	1857	5
	Ulla Salzgeber *Rusty*	1829	7
Silver	**Netherlands 5579 points**		
	Anky van Grunsven *Bonfire*	1875	2
	Coby van Balen *Ferro*	1873	3
	Arjen Teeuwissen *Goliath*	1831	6
	Ellen Bontje *Silvano*	1786	9
Bronze	**USA 5166 points**		
	Christine Traurig *Etienne*	1746	10
	Susan Blinks *Flim Flam*	1725	12
	Günter Siedel *Voltaire*	1695	15
	Robert Dover *Ranier*	1678	17

Arena Size: 20 x 60 m.

Markers: Standard.

Judges

	Judging Position		
	GP	GPS	Kür
Eric Lette (Sweden) President	C	C	C
Jan Peeters (Netherlands)	H	M	B
Axel Steiner (USA)	M	B	E
Mary Seefried (Australia)	B	E	H
Volker Moritz (Germany)	E	H	M

Tests and Scoring

- Grand Prix (1995) – maximum score = 500 points per judge (100%).

- Grand Prix Special (1999) – maximum score = 430 points per judge (100%).

- Freestyle to Music (Kür) – Grand Prix Level (1996, Rev 1999) – maximum score = 200 + 200 = 400 per judge (100%).

- For the final Individual Competition result, the percentages of all 3 competitions were calculated to 2 decimal places and added together.

Individual Medallists (left to right) Isabel Werth (Silver) (GER) (*Gigolo*), Anky van Grunsven (Gold) (NED) (*Bonfire*), Ulla Salzgeber (Bronze) (GER) (*Rusty*) (Photo: HorseSource/Peter Llewellyn.)

Team Gold Medallists Germany. (Left to right) Ulla Salzgeber on *Rusty*, Alexandra Simmons de Ridder on *Chacomo*, Nadine Capellmann on *Farbenfroh* and Isabell Werth on *Gigolo*. (Photo: HorseSource/Peter Llewellyn.)

GRAND PRIX (1999) – OLYMPIC GAMES 2000

		Test	Directive ideas	Marks	Points	Coeff.	Total
1.	A X	Enter in collected canter Halt – immobility – salute Proceed in collected trot	The entry. The halt and the transitions to and from the halt.	10			
2.	C HXF F	Track to the left Change rein in extended trot Collected trot	The lengthening of the frame, the extension and regularity of the steps. The transitions.	10			
3.	VXR RMC	Half-pass Collected trot	The correctness and the regularity. The carriage and the bend. The balance.	10			
4.	CHS SK KAF	Passage Extended trot Passage	The cadence and regularity of the passage. The extension and regularity.	10			
5.		Transitions from passage to extended trot and from extended trot to passage	Submission and willingness.	10			
6.	FP PXS SHC	Collected trot Half-pass Collected trot	The correctness and the regularity. The carriage and the bend.	10			
7.	CMR RF FAK	Passage Extended trot Passage	The cadence and regularity of the passage. The extension and regularity.	10			
8.		Transitions from passage to extended trot and from extended trot to passage	Submission and willingness.	10			
9.	KLBIH H	Extended walk Collected walk	The extension and regularity of the steps. The transitions.	10		2	
10.	HCMG	Collected walk	The shortening and heightening of the steps. The carriage and regularity.	10			

		Test	Directive ideas	Marks	Points	Coeff.	Total
11.	G	Piaffe 12 to 15 steps	The cadence and regularity.	10			
12.	G	Proceed in passage. Transitions from collected walk to piaffe and from piaffe to passage	Submission and willingness.	10			
13.	GHSI	Passage	The cadence and regularity.	10			
14.	I	Piaffe 12 to 15 steps	The cadence and regularity.	10			
15.	I	Proceed in passage Transitions from passage to piaffe and from piaffe to passage	Submission and willingness.	10			
16.	IRBX	Passage	The correctness and regularity.	10			
17.	XEVKAF	Collected canter left	The correctness and regularity.	10			
18.	FLE E	Half-pass in canter Flying change of leg	The correctness and regularity. The carriage and the bend. The balance and the change of leg.	10			
19.	EIM M MCH	Half-pass in canter Flying change of leg Collected canter	The correctness and regularity. The carriage and the bend. The balance and the change of leg.	10			
20.	HXF	On the diagonal 9 flying changes of leg every second stride (finishing on right leg)	The correctness, straightness, balance and fluency.	10			
21.	KXM	On the diagonal 15 flying changes of leg every stride	The correctness, straightness, balance and fluency.	10			

		Test	Directive ideas	Marks	Points	Coeff.	Total
22.	HXF	Change rein in extended canter	The extension. The transition.				
	F	Collected canter and flying change of leg	The flying change of leg.	10			
23.	A	Down centre line	The collection. The regularity.	10		2	
	D	Pirouette right	Slightly before or after D is acceptable.				
24.	Between D & G	On the centre line 9 flying changes of leg every stride	The correctness, straightness, balance and fluency.	10			
25.	G	Pirouette left	Slightly before or after G is acceptable.				
	C	Track to the left	The collection. The regularity.	10		2	
26.	HS	Collected trot	The lengthening of the frame.				
	SK	Extended trot	The extension and regularity of the steps.	10			
	K	Collected trot	The transitions.				
27.		Transitions from collected canter to collected trot and collected trot to extended trot and back to collected trot	Submission and willingness.	10			
28.	A	Down centre line	The regularity and cadence.				
	DX	Passage	The bend.	10			
29.	X	Piaffe 12 to 15 steps	The cadence and regularity.	10			
30.		Transitions from passage to piaffe and from piaffe to passage	Submission and willingness.	10			
31.	XG	Passage	The regularity and cadence. The bend.	10			
32.	G	Halt – immobility – salute	The transition and the halt.	10			
Leave arena at A in walk on a long rein							
		Total		**350**			

	Marks	Points	Coeff.	Total
Collective marks				
1. Paces (freedom and regularity)	10		2	
2. Impulsion (desire to move forward, elasticity of the steps, suppleness of the back and engagement of the hind quarters)	10		2	
3. Submission (attention and confidence; harmony, lightness and ease of the movements; acceptance of the bridle and lightness of the forehand)	10		2	
4. Rider's position and seat; correctness and effect of the aids	10		2	

Total   430

To be deducted:

Errors of the course and omissions are penalised:

1st Time = 2 marks
2nd Time = 4 marks
3rd Time = 8 marks
4th Time = Elimination

OLYMPIC GAMES 2000
Freestyle Test (Kür) Grand Prix level (1999)

	Technical marks	Marks	Points	Coeff.	Final marks
1.	Collected walk (minimum 20m)	10			
2.	Extended walk (minimum 20m)	10			
3.	Collected trot including half-pass right	10			
4.	Collected trot including half-pass left	10			
5.	Extended trot	10			
6.	Collected canter including half-pass right	10			
7.	Collected canter including half-pass left	10			
8.	Extended canter	10			
9.	Flying changes every second stride (minimum 5 times consecutively)	10			
10.	Flying changes every stride (minimum 9 times consecutively)	10			
11.	Canter pirouette right	10		2	
12.	Canter pirouette left	10		2	
13.	Passage (minimum 20m)	10		2	
14.	Piaffe (minimum 10 steps)	10		2	
15.	Transitions from passage to piaffe and from piaffe to passage	10		2	
	Total for technical executions	**200**			

	Artistic marks*	Marks	Points	Coeff.	Final marks
16.	Rhythm, energy and elasticity	10		3	
17.	Harmony between horse and rider	10		3	
18.	Choreography. Use of arena. Inventiveness	10		4	

	Artistic marks*	Marks	Points	Coeff.	Final marks
19.	Degree of difficulty. Well calculated risks	10		4	
20.	Choice of music and interpretation of the music	10		6	
	Total for artistic presentation	**200**			

To be deducted:

Time penalty: more than 6 minutes or less than 5 minutes 30 seconds, deduct 2 points from the total of the artistic presentation.

Total for technical execution divided by 20		10
Total for artistic presentation divided by 20		10
	Final score	**20**

World Cup:
In case two competitors have the same final score, the one with the higher marks for artistic impression is leading.

CDI***:
In case two competitors have the same final score, the one with the higher technical mark is leading.

Olympic Games Sydney 2000
Results – Grand Prix

	Country	Rider	Horse	Points/rank E	H	C	M	B	Total	% Score
1	GER	Isabell Werth	*Gigolo*	386 (1)	375 (3)	383 (1)	383 (2)	381 (1)	1908	76.32 Q
2	NED	Anky van Grunsven	*Bonfire*	367 (4)	382 (2)	377 (4)	371 (3)	378 (2)	1875	75.00 Q
3	NED	Coby van Baalen	*Ferro*	371 (2)	384 (1)	383 (1)	369 (4)	366 (7)	1873	74.92 Q
4	GER	Nadine Capellmann	*Farbenfroh*	361 (5)	362 (8)	377 (4)	393 (1)	374 (3)	1867	74.68 Q
5	GER	Alexandra Simons de Ridder	*Chacomo*	368 (3)	373 (4)	377 (4)	369 (4)	370 (5)	1857	74.28 Q
6	NED	Arjen Teeuwissen	*Goliath*	353 (7)	372 (5)	370 (7)	369 (4)	367 (6)	1831	73.24 Q
7	GER	Ulla Salzgeber	*Rusty*	350 (8)	362 (8)	378 (3)	366 (7)	373 (4)	1829	73.16 Q
8	DEN	Lone Jorgensen	*Kennedy*	349 (9)	368 (7)	366 (6)	353 (9)	360 (8)	1796	71.84 Q
9	NED	Ellen Bontje	*Silvano*	356 (6)	370 (6)	351(11)	357 (8)	352(10)	1786	71.44 Q
10	USA	Christine Traurig	*Etienne*	345(10)	344(15)	353(10)	353 (9)	351(11)	1746	69.84 Q
11	DEN	Jon Pedersen	*Esprit de Vald*	345(10)	345(13)	357 (9)	342(13)	339(16)	1728	69.12 Q
12	USA	Susan Blinks	*Flim Flam*	341(13)	347(11)	344(15)	350(11)	343(14)	1725	69.00 Q
13	ESP	Beatriz Ferrer-Salat	*Beauvalais*	338(15)	345(13)	347(13)	327(23)	353(9)	1710	68.40 Q
14	AUS	Kristy Oatley-Nist	*Wall Street*	335(17)	338(16)	337(19)	346(12)	348(13)	1704	68.16 Q
15	USA	Günter Siedel	*Foltaire*	343(12)	351(10)	338(17)	328(21)	335(19)	1695	67.80 Q
16	ITA	Pia Laus	*Renoir*	326(22)	346(12)	350(12)	333(17)	337(17)	1692	67.68 Q
17	USA	Robert Dover	*Ranier*	337(16)	331(26)	347(13)	331(19)	332(22)	1678	67.12 Q
18	GBR	Emile Faurie	*Rascher Hopes*	331(18)	338(16)	332(21)	324(27)	349(12)	1674	66.96 Q
19	SUI	Daniel Ramseier	*Rali Baba*	340(14)	336(21)	332(21)	327(23)	329(25)	1664	66.56 Q
20	ESP	Rafael Soto	*Invasor*	331(18)	337(18)	328(29)	342(13)	325(31)	1663	66.52 Q
21	NZL	Kalista Field	*Waikare*	323(25)	330(27)	342(16)	336(16)	330(24)	1661	66.44 Q
22	SWE	Tinne Vilhelmson	*Cezar*	327(21)	337(18)	324(34)	323(30)	335(19)	1646	65.84 Q
23	RUS	Elena Sidneva	*Podkhod*	329(20)	333(22)	327(31)	321(31)	334(21)	1644	65.76 Q
24	AUT	Peter Gmoser	*Candidat*	326(22)	332(23)	335(20)	318(34)	327(27)	1638	65.52 Q
24	ESP	Juan Antonio Jiminez	*Guizo*	319(29)	332(23)	329(27)	337(15)	321(35)	1638	65.52 Q
26	SUI	Christine Stückelberger	*Aquamarin*	324(24)	337(18)	325(33)	324(27)	327(27)	1637	65.48 Q
27	POR	Daniel Pinto	*Weldon Surprise*	317(32)	329(28)	329(27)	330(20)	327(27)	1632	65.28
28	SWE	Pether Markne	*Amiral*	321(26)	319(37)	338(17)	327(23)	325(31)	1630	65.20
29	DEN	Anne van Olst	*Any How*	320(27)	332(23)	324(34)	324(27)	325(31)	1625	65.00
30	SUI	Francoise Cantamessa	*Sir S*	311(38)	327(30)	332(21)	317(36)	336(18)	1623	64.92
31	GBR	Carl Hester	*Argentille Gullit*	312(37)	327(30)	323(39)	328(21)	332(22)	1622	64.88
32	SUI	Patricia Bottani	*Diamond*	316(34)	325(32)	332(21)	313(41)	329(25)	1615	64.60
33	AUS	Rachel Downs	*Aphrodite*	318(31)	321(35)	323(39)	311(42)	340(15)	1613	64.52
34	AUS	Mary Hanna	*Limbo*	317(32)	322(35)	326(32)	319(33)	324(34)	1608	64.32
35	AUS	Ricky MacMillan	*Crisp*	319(29)	324(33)	324(34)	317(36)	318(39)	1602	64.08
35	GBR	Richard Davidson	*Askari*	320(27)	324(33)	324(34)	315(39)	319(37)	1602	64.08

Rank	Country	Rider	Horse	E	H	C	M	B	Total	% Score
37	FIN	Elisabet Ehrnrooth	*Harald*	308(39)	328(29)	324(34)	320(32)	321(35)	1601	64.04
38	AUT	Stefan Peter	*Bon Voyage*	314(35)	318(39)	330(25)	318(34)	315(40)	1595	63.80
39	RUS	Svetlana Kniazeva	*Russian Dance*	313(36)	308(44)	328(29)	315(39)	314(42)	1578	63.12
40	SWE	Jan Brink	*Briar*	299(43)	313(42)	310(44)	332(18)	319(37)	1573	62.92
41	GBR	Kirsty Mepham	*Dikiloo*	292(45)	316(40)	322(41)	325(26)	315(40)	1570	62.80
42	IRL	Heike Holstein	*Royale*	307(41)	319(37)	330(25)	299(44)	314(42)	1569	62.76
43	ESP	Luis Lucio	*Aljarafe*	308(39)	310(43)	304(45)	304(43)	327(27)	1553	62.12
44	MEX	Antonio Rivera	*Aczydos*	299(43)	305(45)	318(43)	317(36)	302(44)	1541	61.64
45	DEN	Morten Thomsen	*Gay*	302(42)	314(41)	319(42)	299(44)	302(44)	1536	61.44
46	FIN	Heidi Svanborg	*Bazalt*	292(45)	286(46)	272(46)	291(46)	296(46)	1437	57.48
47	BRA	Jorge Rocha	*Quixote Lancia*	255(47)	271(47)	269(47)	278(47)	277(47)	1350	54.00
	SWE	Ulla Hakansson	*Bobby*	withdrawn						

Q = qualified for Grand Prix Special

OLYMPIC GAMES SYDNEY 2000

Results – Grand Prix Special

	Country	Rider	Horse	GP %Score	Rank	E	H	C	M	B	Total	%Score	%GP+ %GPS
1	NED	Anky van Grunsven	*Bonfire*	75.00	2	346 (1)	331 (2)	327 (2)	340 (1)	336 (2)	1680	78.13	153.13 Q
2	GER	Isabell Werth	*Gigolo*	76.32	1	323 (5)	338 (1)	317 (6)	331 (2)	318 (5)	1627	75.67	151.99 Q
3	GER	Nadine Capellmann	*Farbenfroh*	74.68	4	326 (4)	322 (4)	332 (1)	327 (4)	340 (1)	1647	76.60	151.28 Q
4	GER	Alexandra Simons de Ridder	*Chacomo*	74.28	5	333 (3)	315 (6)	324 (4)	325 (5)	329 (3)	1626	75.62	149.90 Q
4	GER	Ulla Salzgeber	*Rusty*	73.16	7	346 (1)	325 (3)	327 (2)	329 (3)	323 (4)	1650	76.74	149.90 Q
6	DEN	Lone Jorgensen	*Kennedy*	71.84	8	322 (6)	321 (5)	321 (5)	324 (6)	318 (5)	1606	74.69	146.53 Q
7	NED	Coby van Baalen	*Ferro*	74.92	3	316 (9)	310 (8)	312 (8)	307 (8)	289(19)	1534	71.34	146.26 Q
8	NED	Ellen Bontje	*Silvano*	71.44	9	317 (8)	313 (7)	309(10)	312 (7)	310 (8)	1561	72.60	144.04 Q
9	NED	Arjen Teeuwissen	*Goliath*	73.24	6	307(12)	289(18)	301(13)	307 (8)	311 (7)	1515	70.46	143.70 Q
10	USA	Christine Traurig	*Etienne*	69.84	10	321 (7)	305(11)	296(14)	300(15)	303(10)	1525	70.93	140.77 Q
11	USA	Susan Blinks	*Flim Flam*	69.00	12	311(10)	307(10)	303(12)	307 (8)	303(10)	1531	71.20	140.20 Q
12	ESP	Beatriz Ferrer-Salat	*Beauvalais*	68.40	13	300(15)	309 (9)	307(11)	303(14)	297(14)	1516	70.51	138.91 Q
13	AUS	Kristy Oatley-Nist	*Wall Street*	68.16	14	307(12)	297(15)	311 (9)	306(11)	289(19)	1510	70.23	138.39 Q
14	ESP	Rafael Soto	*Invasor*	66.52	20	306(14)	304(12)	292(16)	304(13)	307 (9)	1513	70.37	136.89 Q

	Country	Rider	Horse	GP %Score	Rank	E	H	C	M	B	Total	%Score	%GP+ %GPS	
15	SUI	Daniel Ramseier	*Rali Baba*	66.56	19	292(17)	299(14)	316 (7)	306(11)	293(16)	1506	70.04	136.60	Q
16	DEN	Jon Pedersen	*Esprit de Vald*	69.12	11	289(19)	281(21)	294(15)	287(20)	298(12)	1449	67.39	136.51	Q
17	ITA	Pia Laus	*Renoir*	67.68	16	292(17)	300(13)	288(18)	299(16)	292(18)	1471	68.41	136.09	Q
18	NZL	Kalista Field	*Waikare*	66.44	21	300(15)	292(17)	282(23)	291(18)	298(12)	1463	68.04	134.48	
19	ESP	Juan Antonio Jiminez	*Guizo*	65.52	24	309(11)	294(16)	289(17)	293(17)	297(14)	1482	68.93	134.45	
20	GBR	Emile Faurie	*Rascher Hopes*	66.96	18	281(21)	280(22)	286(20)	287(20)	276(23)	1410	65.58	132.54	
21	AUT	Peter Gmoser	*Candidat*	65.52	24	286(20)	282(20)	287(19)	286(22)	289(19)	1430	66.51	132.03	
22	SUI	Christine Stückelberger	*Aquamarin*	65.48	26	279(22)	287(19)	285(21)	289(19)	286(22)	1426	66.32	131.80	
23	USA	Robert Dover	*Ranier*	67.12	17	264(24)	271(24)	278(24)	268(24)	293(16)	1374	63.90	131.02	
24	RUS	Elena Sidneva	*Podkhod*	65.76	23	273(23)	275(23)	284(22)	279(23)	258(24)	1369	63.67	129.43	
25	SWE	Tinne Vilhelmson	*Cezar*	65.84	22	254(25)	249(25)	247(25)	245(25)	256(25)	1251	58.18	124.02	

Q = qualified for grand Prix special

OLYMPIC GAMES SYDNEY 2000

Results – Grand Prix Freestyle and Final Placings

Rank	Country/Rider		Horse	%GP+%GPS	Rank	Technical/Artistic Marks E	H	C	M	B	Total	% Score	Overall Total
1	NED	Anky van Grunsven	*Bonfire*	153.13	1	7.85/9.00	7.90/9.15	8.05/9.00	8.20/9.02	8.25/9.62	40.25/45.79	86.05	239.18
2	GER	Isabell Werth	*Gigolo*	151.99	2	7.45/8.60	7.25/8.65	8.05/8.77	7.75/8.92	7.85/8.90	38.35/43.84	82.20	234.19
3	GER	Ulla Salzgeber	*Rusty*	149.90	4	7.35/8.25	7.50/8.92	7.45/8.47	7.60/8.60	7.80/8.72	37.70/42.96	80.67	230.57
4	GER	Nadine Capellmann	*Farbenfroh*	151.28	3	7.15/7.90	7.15/8.02	7.00/7.55	7.15/7.90	7.20/7.57	35.65/38.94	74.60	225.88
5	NED	Coby van Baalen	*Ferro*	146.26	7	7.00/7.57	7.35/8.07	7.45/7.87	7.20/7.67	7.25/7.65	36.25/38.83	75.10	221.36
6	NED	Ellen Bontje	*Silvano*	144.04	8	6.75/7.55	6.95/8.00	7.00/7.82	6.85/7.85	6.95/7.82	34.50/39.04	73.55	217.59
7	DEN	Lone Jorgensen	*Kennedy*	146.53	6	6.45/7.77	6.55/7.25	6.75/7.77	6.70/7.27	6.60/7.25	33.05/37.31	70.37	216.90
8	USA	Susan Blinks	*Flim Flam*	140.20	11	6.90/7.87	7.30/8.15	6.90/7.72	6.85/7.90	6.95/7.90	34.90/39.54	74.45	214.65
9	AUS	Kristy Oatley-Nist	*Wall Street*	138.39	13	6.50/7.00	7.20/7.75	7.05/7.62	6.80/7.50	7.10/7.87	34.65/37.74	72.40	210.79
10	ESP	Beatriz Ferrer-Salat	*Beauvalais*	138.91	12	6.60/7.22	6.80/7.50	6.90/7.65	7.05/7.67	6.70/7.32	34.05/37.36	71.42	210.33
11	USA	Christine Traurig	*Etienne*	140.77	10	6.30/7.40	6.30/7.32	6.30/7.35	5.90/6.82	6.45/7.42	31.25/36.31	67.57	208.34
12	ESP	Rafael Soto	*Invasor*	136.89	14	6.85/7.32	7.05/7.62	6.60/7.07	7.05/7.52	6.80/7.42	34.35/36.95	71.32	208.21
13	SUI	Daniel Ramseier	*Rali Baba*	136.60	15	6.55/7.07	6.55/7.47	6.60/7.15	6.65/7.27	6.60/7.07	32.95/36.03	69.00	205.60
14	ITA	Pia Laus	*Renoir*	136.09	17	6.40/7.15	6.50/7.05	6.70/7.55	6.75/7.17	6.75/7.32	33.10/36.24	69.35	205.44
15	DEN	Jon Pedersen	*Esprit de Vald*	136.51	16	6.40/6.82	6.40/6.82	6.70/7.47	6.45/7.02	6.50/7.07	32.45/35.20	67.67	204.18

Olympic Games Sydney 2000
Results – Teams

Nation/Rider	Horse	Points					Total
		E	H	C	M	B	
1. Germany							**5632**
Isabell Werth	*Gigolo*	386	375	383	383	381	1908 *
Nadine Capellmann	*Farbenfroh*	361	362	377	393	374	1867 *
Alexandra Simons de Ridder	*Chacomo*	368	373	377	369	370	1857 *
Ulla Salzgeber	*Rusty*	350	362	378	366	373	1829
2. Netherlands							**5579**
Anky van Grunsven	*Bonfire*	367	382	377	371	378	1875 *
Coby van Baalen	*Ferro*	371	384	383	369	366	1873 *
Arjen Teeuwissen	*Goliath*	353	372	370	369	367	1831 *
Ellen Bontje	*Silvano*	356	370	351	357	352	1786
3. USA							**5166**
Christine Traurig	*Etienne*	345	344	353	353	351	1746 *
Susan Blinks	*Flim Flam*	341	347	344	350	343	1725 *
Gunter Siedel	*Foltaire*	343	351	338	328	335	1695 *
Robert Dover	*Ranier*	337	331	347	331	332	1678
4. Denmark							**5149**
Lone Jorgensen	*Kennedy*	349	368	366	353	360	1796 *
Jon Pedersen	*Esprit de Vald*	345	345	357	342	339	1728 *
Anne van Olst	*Any How*	320	332	324	324	325	1625 *
Morten Thomsen	*Gay*	302	314	319	299	302	1536
5. Spain							**5011**
Beatriz Ferrer-Salat	*Beauvalais*	338	345	347	327	353	1710 *
Rafael Soto	*Invasor*	331	337	328	342	325	1663 *
Juan Antonio Jiminez	*Guizo*	319	332	329	337	321	1638 *
Luis Lucio	*Aljarafe*	308	310	304	304	327	1553
6. Australia							**4925**
Kristy Oatley-Nist	*Wall Street*	335	338	337	346	348	1704 *
Rachel Downs	*Aphrodite*	318	321	323	311	340	1613 *
Mary Hanna	*Limbo*	317	322	326	319	324	1608 *
Ricky MacMillan	*Crisp*	319	324	324	317	318	1602

Nation/Rider	Horse	Points					Total
		E	H	C	M	B	
7. Switzerland							**4924**
Daniel Ramseier	*Rali Baba*	340	336	332	327	329	1664 *
Christine Stückelberger	*Aquamarin*	324	337	325	324	327	1637 *
Francoise Cantamessa	*Sir S*	311	327	332	317	336	1623 *
Patricia Bottani	*Diamond*	316	325	332	313	329	1615
8. Great Britain							**4898**
Emile Faurie	*Rascher Hopes*	331	338	332	324	349	1674 *
Carl Hester	*Argentille Gullit*	312	327	323	328	332	1622 *
Richard Davidson	*Askari*	320	324	324	315	319	1602 *
Kirsty Mepham	*Dikiloo*	292	316	322	325	315	1570
9. Sweden							**4849**
Ulla Hakanson	*Bobby*	Withdrawn					
Tinne Vilhelmson	*Cezar*	327	337	324	323	335	1646 *
Pether Markine	*Amiral*	321	319	338	327	325	1630 *
Jan Brink	*Briar*	299	313	310	332	319	1573 *

* Denotes scores used to calculate Team Competition result.